Promoting children's wellbeing: policy and practice

Working together for children

This innovative series brings together an interdisciplinary team of authors to provide an accessible collection of ideas, debates, discussions and reflections on childhood, practice and services for children. The books have been designed and written as illustrative teaching texts, giving voice to children's and practitioners' own accounts as well as providing research, policy analysis and examples of good practice. These books are aimed at students, practitioners, academics and educators across the wide range of disciplines associated with working with children.

There are three books in the *Working together for children* series:

- *Connecting with children: developing working relationships*, edited by Pam Foley and Stephen Leverett

- *Promoting children's wellbeing: policy and practice*, edited by Janet Collins and Pam Foley

- *Changing children's services: working and learning together*, edited by Pam Foley and Andy Rixon

Promoting children's wellbeing:

policy and practice

Edited by Janet Collins and Pam Foley

The Open University

Published by

The Policy Press
University of Bristol
Fourth Floor, Beacon House
Queen's Road, Clifton
Bristol BS8 1QU
United Kingdom
http://www.policypress.org.uk

in association with

The Open University
Walton Hall, Milton Keynes
MK7 6AA
United Kingdom

First published 2008

Edited and designed by The Open University.

Typeset in India by Alden Prepress Services, Chennai.

Printed and bound in the United Kingdom by Bell & Bain Ltd, Glasgow

This book forms part of an Open University course KE312 *Working together for children*. Details of this and other Open University courses can be obtained from the Student Registration and Enquiry Service, The Open University, PO Box 197, Milton Keynes MK7 6BJ, United Kingdom: tel. +44 (0)845 300 60 90, email general-enquiries@open.ac.uk

http://www.open.ac.uk

British Library Cataloguing in Publication Data

A catalogue record for this book is available from the British Library.

Library of Congress Cataloging-in-Publication Data

A catalog record for this book has been requested.

ISBN 9781847420596

1.1

Contributors

James Blewett is a Lecturer in Social Work at the Department of Health and Social Care, Royal Holloway, University of London.

Janet Collins is a Senior Lecturer in Primary Education at The Open University's Faculty of Education and Language Studies. Her practice background is in teaching and learning in primary schools.

Victoria Cooper is a Staff Tutor in the Faculty of Education and Language Studies at The Open University.

Pam Foley is a Senior Lecturer in Children and Families at The Open University's Faculty of Health and Social Care. Her practice background is in women's and children's health.

Mark Gladwin is a Play Officer (participation) with Bradford Metropolitan District Council's Early Years and Childcare service.

Michael Isles runs his own training company focusing on social welfare law, mental health and quality assurance for vocational training. He also works for The Open University on K269 'Social care, social work and the law (England and Wales)'.

Sue Johnston-Wilder is an Associate Professor of Mathematics Education at Warwick University's Institute of Education.

Doug Springate is a former teacher, teacher trainer and Primary Ofsted Inspector since 1995. His main areas of interest are the sociology of education and comparative education. He is now retired.

Other contributors

This series of three books forms part of the Open University course *Working together for children* and has grown out of debates and discussions within the course team working at the University. We would like to thank the following for their critical reading and invaluable feedback: Judith Argles, Brigitte Beck-Woerner, Sheila Campbell, Maurice Crozier, Hasel Daniels, Trevor Evans, Louise Garrett, Gill Goodliff, Glo Potter, Lin Miller, Kate New, Janet Seden and our developmental testers. We would also like to thank our focus group, our Editors Carol Price, Alison Cadle and Kate Hunter, our Course Team Assistant Val O'Connor, and our External Assessor, Denise Hevey, who has provided insightful and timely comments at every turn.

We should especially like to acknowledge the contribution of our Course Manager, Tabatha Torrance, who has guided, assisted and supported the course team throughout.

Contents

Introduction

Pam Foley

Is the UK a good place to be a child right now? Just how many of the policies, practices, agencies, institutions and services ostensibly working to promote children's wellbeing actually improve the quality of their lives? Adults are legally and practically responsible for children's wellbeing and their wellbeing is understood to be crucial to the social and economic infrastructure of healthy and wealthy nations. So how can policies and practices improve children's lives?

Promoting the wellbeing of all children requires sustained commitment from many different kinds of people, their governments and their institutions, among whom there will be widely contrasting views about roles and responsibilities towards children and families. Social issues, including the wellbeing of children, have replaced economic issues at the top of the political agenda. Among the core reasons that will make any government and its agencies prepared to make changes to the ways in which they work with children is a belief that supporting the health and education of children, addressing child poverty and providing a protective environment for children will significantly contribute to the nation's wellbeing. There is, however, less of a consensus on the changes needed to the wider economy, society and culture to promote children's wellbeing in the here and now.

Policies that address the lives of children in the UK prominently feature family responsibilities and privacy, and the care and control of children and young people. These policies need to traverse a fine line between upholding parental responsibility and pursuing certain goals; for example, a policy that would introduce universal free childcare is held back by a commitment to maintaining parental responsibility to provide for their children and urged forward by an anti-poverty strategy that stresses employment.

Most governments would like simple, clear-cut answers to questions about what constitutes a good childhood and the extent of the state's responsibilities to contribute to children's wellbeing. Services are developed according to the answers posed to these kinds of questions. So, to analyse policy and practice trajectories is to ask why certain issues are focused on and why certain methods, as opposed to others, are selected. A focus on early intervention, for example, is justified in terms of addressing social and educational disparities as early as possible, preventing or ameliorating problems in families with young children, and safeguarding children. But this leads governments into complex and contested areas. Questions arise, for example, about whether early intervention services can or should be specifically targeted to reach those children and families deemed 'hard to reach'. Policies and practices involve not only issues of resources, management and outcome measurement, but also political issues, themselves threaded through with particular values and ethics.

While children's agencies and institutions work to improve the lives of children, they undoubtedly also reflect social and economic developments. Yet discussions about children, and the agencies and services that are provided for them, too often end up in narrow reviews of the success or otherwise of the socialisation and education of children. Governments, in particular, seek to measure the success or otherwise of interventions using objectifiable standards. Things are done to or for children, by adults in families or on behalf of the state, with particular outcomes in mind. But what if we were to look as closely at processes as at outcomes? Perhaps it is as important to look at the effects of how we do things as at the things we do. This would mean asking what kinds of characteristics, what kinds of people, do these processes contribute towards developing? If we decide to question and change processes as well as outcomes, what kinds of effects could be achieved? What is possible that is not happening?

Within Western European liberal democracies, the state now has an established and recognised interest in working to ensure that children grow into the kinds of citizens who can be trusted to function within certain social, economic and political structures and authorities. The state, therefore, continues to exercise considerable control over family actions. For UK governments there has also been a social justice agenda which has given rise to a series of strategies and a large number of policies aimed at children and families. Most prominent has been the attempt to improve life chances through education and a focus on children's early years as the foundation for future growth and development. Such overarching strategies mean, of course, that any improvements will be measurable only in the long term. Long-term outcomes versus short-term politics is just one of the dimensions of children's services that make their evaluation so difficult.

Changes around and within families present a complex and ever-changing area in which to work. Current family policy debates tend to centre on three closely related areas. First, the extent to which children and their families can and should look to the state for financial assistance through universal or targeted benefits and tax credits. Second, the extent to which broad and specific social policies can and should be directed at families in order to influence the kinds of families they are and the kinds of children (and adults) they produce. While there are strong financial arguments for targeting the neediest, there are other issues such as the level of intrusiveness associated with state support and how support is available for some families rather than others. Governments have to negotiate a line between interventions in some families and leaving others alone.

In political and popular discourse, the family, largely independent of the state, is still seen as the glue that holds a society together. Modern western societies strive to bring about a level of cooperation between the majority of families and the state in relation to economic and social outcomes for children. Liberal political theory rests on a consensual division of responsibilities between families and the state. Around the children and the family is played out a classic paradox of liberal humanism – offering choice and free will, but hoping and sometimes directing people towards the 'right' choices. But while the family is a prime instrument of government, it remains essential that it be experienced as a private institution beyond the intervention of state agents (Parton, 2006).

Third, while the balance of individual, family, government and global responsibility to manage perceived risks remains a contested and important area for children and parents, the particular uncertainties and anxieties of this era have particular significance for our feelings and actions with regard to children (Parton, 2006). Such anxieties include the impact of the internet and technology generally and the possibility of a generation of children growing up to be less healthy than their parents' generation. Modern parents may be experiencing unusual levels of anxiety about children which is reflected in, for example, allowing their own children considerably less spatial freedom than they experienced in their own childhood, with a consequential negative effect on children's wellbeing today.

Children in the UK now experience their childhood in a global context, and the processes of a postmodern society, particularly around the impact of globalisation and individualisation, can generate high levels of anxiety and uncertainty about the future (Beck, 1992). Perceptions of risk, for example, are on a global scale, and yet increasingly people are being encouraged to take individual responsibility for their economic, environmental and personal circumstances (Beck, 1992; Power, 2004). The relative certainties of long-term employment and collective welfare provision experienced by the post Second World War generations may appear less desirable today. But people, as individuals, have to make sense of new issues such as climate change, the internet revolution and the global movements of people and capital.

Focusing on the lives of modern children can be a disquieting experience. It can involve confronting the question of how protected and safe childhoods can exist apart from the economic and social context of children's lives and the wide disparities between children of the better and worse off. The absence of data in some key areas makes it impossible to assess fully the scale of improvement or deterioration in children's wellbeing, not least the absence of a universal definition of children's wellbeing; this could reflect some of the ambiguities within understandings of childhood itself. The extent to which the views of children are now sought, or not, on what contributes to their wellbeing is, however, revealing. At a conference to discuss the English government's *Every Child Matters'* five outcomes for children (DfES, 2003) children, working with the Children's Rights Office, produced their own prioritised list: staying safe, being healthy, enjoying life and learning, helping others and having enough money (Morgan, 2005). The challenge to government, and indeed to practitioners, is to ensure that children's views and aspirations underpin the development of policy and practice at local and national levels. The issues raised by children as being most important to them and what makes for a good life were family, friends, enough to eat and drink, fun, love, respect and being happy; all of these should figure largely in any government's 'to do' list (Morgan, 2005).

UNICEF's (2007) report *An Overview of Child Wellbeing in Rich Countries* identifies six dimensions of child wellbeing: material wellbeing, health and safety, educational wellbeing, family and peer relationships, behaviours and risks and subjective wellbeing. Drawing on forty separate indicators relevant to children's lives and children's rights, the report makes it clear that its purpose is to 'encourage monitoring to permit comparison and to stimulate the discussion and development of policies to improve children's lives' (UNICEF, 2007, p. 2). It describes itself as informed by the *United Nations Convention on the Rights of the Child* (United Nations, 1989), including the participation rights of the child, and so incorporates a dimension solely based on children's own sense of wellbeing. International measurements and comparisons such as these should give an indication of a country's strengths and weaknesses and of what is achievable; children's wellbeing in rich countries is, in reality, policy-susceptible. It would appear that the UK has rather more weaknesses than strengths; the UK, at the time of writing, was in the bottom third of the rankings for five of the six dimensions of children's wellbeing in the UNICEF report.

Children's lives are grounded in the diverse cultural, economic and social conditions in which they live. The picture of child wellbeing in the UK continues to be mixed, with the list of improving indicators more or less equal to the list of deteriorating/no change indicators (Bradshaw and Mayhew, 2005). Living standards and educational attainment are improving, but limitations to children's use of space, their exclusion from schools and aspects of their health are moving in the wrong direction (Bradshaw and Mayhew, 2005). 'Childhood' is a distinct social category that intersects with other social categories, such as class, gender and ethnicity, and brings with it specific rights, opportunities and, sometimes, barriers. Questions about evolving competence, rights, voice and participation have surfaced, contributing to understandings of what it means to be a child and what it means to be a child in contemporary Western European societies. These introduce a more complex and varied set of causes and consequences for policies and practices for children.

Policies have to be reshaped to reflect shifting notions of childhood, the ambiguities inherent in childhood and childhood as an important period of life in its own right. The UK state, through its devolved levels of government and its different agencies, will continue to assume a level of responsibility for children based on particular understandings of children, their capabilities and their requirements. Consequently there are wide national variations in how services are delivered, organised, funded and staffed. A critical approach, with an emphasis on evolving competence, rights and agency, means children's services, and the work and relationships that take place in them, can be examined and can evolve. And shifting focus from outcomes to processes means looking more consistently at the ways in which practitioners work with children.

This series of books focuses on the 0–12 age group, but we have omitted children's ages, unless they are particularly relevant, to avoid reproducing the 'age and stage' thinking that has often obscured children's individual capacities and capabilities. In fact, we hope to encourage people with an interest in childhood to look outwards and consider how this important period in children's lives connects with the rest of the life course. We have drawn together writers and practitioners from a variety of disciplines to contribute to this book, and this is reflected in the diversity of language and terminology; both 'disabled children' and 'children with disabilities' are used, for example. We have not standardised language when it reflects a considered and valid viewpoint.

The first two chapters focus on children's emotional, psychological and social wellbeing. Aiming to highlight children's voices, they draw on original work with a focus group of children. Chapter 1, 'Children and identity', explores children's perceptions of identity in general and their own identities in particular. An understanding of the processes by which identities are formed, negotiated and developed over time is important for anyone wanting to develop practice that promotes children's wellbeing. Drawing on research in sociology and psychology, the chapter discusses and applies a model of identity in which both the agency of the individual and influences of the wider society are examined and the relationship between them explored. Chapter 2, 'Children negotiating identities', builds on the idea that children's wellbeing depends, in part, on positive experiences with regard to identity. It explores the development of self-esteem and of resilience. Emphasising a social constructivist perspective, the chapter addresses the issue of labels and the processes of labelling with regard to children's identities. These chapters encourage practice informed by an understanding of children's wellbeing located within a social group, with particular reference to a sense of belonging.

Chapter 3, 'Health matters', addresses some of the key issues of children's health, encompassing emotional and mental, or psychological, health as well as physical health. The chapter begins with a discussion of why child health and welfare policies remain, nationally and internationally, at the top of government agendas. Having introduced the various paradigms that influence health policies and health promotion, the chapter goes on to examine how health and healthcare are both private and public issues and, at one and the same time, the domains of individuals and of governments. The chapter concludes with a discussion of healthy behaviour and health education in schools as prime sites to promote children's health and wellbeing.

Chapter 4, 'Play matters', explores the common threads within the leading theories around play and asks what characterises and influences the play of children. Here, the focus is on the value of play to children and what kinds of working practices can support the contribution of play to children's quality of life. It is widely understood that play is crucial to children's healthy development and quality of life, but is this reflected in children's services today? This chapter challenges practitioners to consider and perhaps support the contribution of inclusive play to the wellbeing of children. It also introduces an international perspective on the way play is considered and supported.

Children's lives can be strongly influenced by adults' anxieties for and about them. Chapter 5, 'Anxieties and risks', considers what is meant by risk in today's society and what we mean by a 'risk society'. It explores the implications for services offered to children and for practitioners who work with children of how contemporary society perceives and manages risk. Some risk-taking is important to children's healthy development. We ask how perceptions of and anxieties about risk affect children's day-to-day lives, their healthy development, the perceptions of their needs and aspirations, and the promotion of their life skills.

In Chapter 6, 'Staying safe', we look at the development of policy concerning safeguarding children, asking what a protective environment means for children, and those working with children, today. The chapter offers practice principles for people working in both universal and specialist services in order to make considered judgements using the broad concept of 'staying safe'. It asks how those who work with children should respond to the adverse environments of some childhoods. The chapter also examines the importance of feeling safe, and includes a discussion of how to develop skills among children that can help them keep themselves safe.

Finally, Chapter 7, 'Children, families and the law', provides an overview of the evolving legislation that underpins the provision of support and services for the wellbeing of children. It discusses some of the primary sources of law, guidance and regulation, and examines the changing relationship between the state, the family and children. The chapter goes on to outline the history of children's rights and to explore the significance of rights and their potential contribution to promoting children's wellbeing.

References

Beck, U. (1992) *Risk Society: Towards a New Modernity*, London, Sage Publications.

Bradshaw, J. and Mayhew, E. (eds) (2005) *The Well-being of Children in the UK*, London, Save the Children.

Department for Education and Skills (DfES) (2003) *Every Child Matters*, London, The Stationery Office.

Morgan, R. (2005) *Your Rights, Your Say: Younger Children's Views on 'Every Child Matters'* available online at <http://www.everychildmatters.gov.uk/resources-and-practice/search/RS00004>, accessed 22 August 2007.

Parton, N. (2006) *Safeguarding Childhood: Early Intervention and Surveillance in a Late Modern Society*, Basingstoke, Palgrave Macmillan.

Power, M. (2004) *The Risk Management of Everything: Rethinking the Politics of Uncertainty*, London, Demos.

UNICEF (2007) *Child Poverty in Perspective: An Overview of Child Wellbeing in Rich Countries*, Innocenti Report Card 7, Florence, UNICEF Innocenti Research Centre.

United Nations (1989) *United Nations Convention on the Rights of the Child (UNCRC)*, Geneva, United Nations.

Chapter 1

Children and identity

Victoria Cooper and Janet Collins

Introduction

> I am Louis. I am eleven. I live with my family. I have speech
> problems and sometimes I cannot hear everything that is said
> to me. I have always felt different to my friends. Sometimes
> people look at me as if I am different. My friends don't. They
> know me now. I know I look different. Sometimes I find it hard to
> get my words out right. It takes me such a long time. My friends
> understand me now. Not everyone understands me. I have a
> learning difficulty.
>
> (Louis, aged eleven)

Louis was part of a focus group, made through contact with three local
primary schools, with whom we had the privilege of working during our
writing. The group was made up of eighteen children (eight boys aged
between five and eleven and ten girls aged between four and eleven); five
expectant mothers; one family (one male and one female parent and two
boys aged four and six); and three other adults (two females aged
thirty-nine and forty-six years and one male aged forty-two). Four children
disclosed that they had 'special needs', including one statement for
dyslexia, one for cerebral palsy and two for Attention Deficit Hyperactivity
Disorder (ADHD), and two children made reference to their Indian and
bi-cultural heritage respectively.

The voices of these children and others are central to this chapter and
extracts from the focus group are used throughout (with details changed to
ensure confidentiality), so that our exploration of identity is presented
through the voices of children rather than our own. As a means to examine
children and their identities, we asked them the question 'Who are you?'.
Louis' answer (above) offers us some insight into aspects of his identity
and how he feels about himself. He gives his name and age and then,
after mentioning his family, speaks about how others may perceive
him as 'different', using the label 'learning difficulty' to explain his
speech problems.

As well as exploring how children describe who they are, this chapter draws on a range of parent/adult focus group extracts to highlight how, rather than being fixed from birth (with some social factors at play even before birth), identity is fluid, complex and malleable. The children's descriptions and adults' reflections draw our attention to the changeable nature of identity throughout life.

The emphasis on change in both this chapter and Chapter 2 points to the possibilities for children to move beyond limiting labels, reach their potential and actively construct and reconstruct their identities. Research highlights the clear link between feelings of wellbeing and self-worth, success and mental health. If people working with children are to understand and support them, they need insight not just into who they are, but also into who they could be or wish to be. Chapters 1 and 2 highlight the need for practitioners to understand how identity develops. Identity formation is a central focus of this chapter; Chapter 2 focuses more specifically on strategies by which practitioners can help support children to negotiate and develop their identities.

Socio-constructionist perspective: a model in which both the individual agent and wider society are examined and the relationship between them is explored.

The 'learning difficulty' label Louis uses in the opening extract may be useful to practitioners in multi-agency professional settings, but such labels are potentially limiting. In this chapter we argue that an understanding of childhood and identity can be gained through an approach that draws on research in sociology and psychology, with particular emphasis on a **socio-constructionist** perspective. In particular, we focus on the process of labelling. While we examine the impact of outside influences on identity development, the importance of the individual agent as a constructor of their life experiences lies at the heart of our discussion.

We begin the chapter with a critical consideration of the concept of identity.

Core questions

- Why is identity important?
- What theoretical perspectives are there to help explain children's identity development?
- Does identity develop over time and when does this process begin?
- What role do children play in actively constructing their own identities?
- What are the effects of using labels to describe children?

1 What do we mean by identity?

> Identity as a concept is fully as elusive as is everyone's sense of his own personal identity.
>
> (Strauss, 1959, cited in Weigert et al., 1986, p. 30)

This quote from Strauss draws our attention to the difficulty of locating and exploring *identity* as a concept. In the light of this difficulty, how can we capture, explain and understand something that is so personal, and why is this important in our work with children?

A growing body of research indicates how identity formation is an important indicator of feelings of wellbeing and self-worth (Canino et al., 2004; Rapee et al., 2006). Our individual perception of, and how we value, ourselves is linked to our behaviour and social performance. This process becomes important to all who work with children because identity formation and feelings of wellbeing are strongly linked to life experiences and success (Kernis, 1995). Poor self-esteem is associated with anxiety development among young children (Canino et al., 2004; Rapee et al., 2006), identity conflict (Kendall and Kessler, 2002) and, in extreme cases, psychiatric distress and disorder (Burns and Rapee, 2006).

Government initiatives such as *Every Child Matters: Change for Children* (DfES, 2004) attempt to address the issue of identity and self-esteem, stressing the importance of supporting *all* children's social and emotional development. Such support needs to be based on an understanding of identity formation, which involves a consideration of definitions of 'identity' and of the complexity of the term.

Thinking point 1.1   What is your identity? How would you describe yourself and how would this definition change according to context?

Descriptions of ourselves tend to vary according to the circumstances in which we find ourselves and our knowledge and experience of those around us. They depend on context and can change over time. There may, however, be aspects of ourselves that we see as more enduring and lasting. Such inconsistencies make identity hard to define. As Strauss says, identity is an elusive concept.

We set about exploring identity from a child's perspective by asking a group of ten-to-eleven year olds 'What is identity?'. The following descriptors were offered:

It's about who you are.

It's what makes us different.

Our attitudes and behaviour.

How you think.

We can be different at school and different at home.

Your feelings about yourself.

We do change as we get older. I am more confident.

Children readily demonstrated a clear understanding of the concept of identity. While the descriptions are different, they each offer some insight into the complexity of identity and the enormity of answering what, on the surface, might appear to be a very simple question. There is no single answer because conceptualisations of identity represent how we as individuals describe ourselves in place and time. The children focused on the uniqueness of a person's identity and differences in behaviour and thought. The emphasis on difference presents further complexity as it places the individual within a social arena where comparisons can be made. The quotes also highlight how aspects of identity can change, not only in response to a space or setting, but also as we develop over time.

This emphasis on change is important. Many authors have explored how identity formation is constantly evolving (Kelleher and Leavey, 2004;

Identity is created at different times and in different places

Layder, 2004) and may follow a developmental sequence (Bennett and Sani, 2004). This is not to suggest that we are continually revising our identity according to how we present ourselves, but implies that changes can and do occur through the interaction of social circumstances, life events and an individual's reactions to them. Examining how a person changes over a period of time and attending to their inner feelings and thought patterns presents a challenge. So, how can we understand a person's identity?

Let us now go back to the case of Louis. If we were to set about understanding and supporting Louis, we might wish to address a few basic questions. Why does he feel as he does? Why do other people perceive him as different and why is that difference assumed to be significant? Such questions are important for people working with children and are central to the definition of identity.

Identity is a complex term with varying connotations, and the origins and development of an individual's identity have long been the focus of debate. The concept is synonymous with notions of self, me, I, self-image and self-awareness (see Fuhrer, 2004; Harter, 1999; Sani and Bennett, 2004), but for the purposes of this discussion we focus primarily on the terms 'identity' and 'self'.

We began this chapter with Louis' answer to the question 'Who are you?'. The following extracts show how other children in the focus group defined themselves.

> I am Amy. I am a girl. I am me. I like playgroup. My friend is Chantelle. She plays duck, duck goose. I have long hair. Chantelle is pretty.
>
> (Amy, aged four years, two months)

> I am Berty. I am a boy. I like Pokemon. I play with Joseph, Edward and Aiden. I like running. I like jumping. I like climbing. My brother makes dens. I do karate. I am good at maths. I live in my house. I live in Stroud.
>
> (Berty, aged five years, seven months)

> I am Layla. I am a girl. I have a pink room. I squabble with my brother. I play with him as well. I am a human. My teacher is called Miss Sullivan. She teaches us and me as well. I help my Mum cook. Berty is my little brother. I live with him. I love him. We live happy in this house. Josie is my best friend. I play with her a lot.
>
> (Layla, aged six years, eight months)

> I am Jasmin. I am a girl. I am seven. I am the tallest in my class. I love dogs. I like dancing. I don't like cats much. I have two sisters and my Mum. Julia is nineteen. Much older than me and so is Talia. My Dad lives with his girlfriend and they have a new baby girl. She's my sister. She's brown like me. Mum says I have lovely brown skin. She doesn't. My Dad does. Both my sisters have

blondie hair. I feel different to my sisters. My Mum has black hair like me, but she is really, really white. I am half-and-half. I like being half-and-half. Sometimes it makes my Mum cross. She says that people are unkind because I'm half-and-half.

(Jasmin, aged seven years)

I am Silvia. I am eight-and-a-half. I like Mrs Jones my teacher. Martha is my best friend. We play stuck in the mud at playtime. I have another teacher, Miss Steele. She helps me get changed for PE and at games. She doesn't help at playtime. My friends help me then. I have special needs and that's why Miss Steele helps me.

(Silvia, aged eight years, five months)

I am William Fern. I am ten. My birthday is in May. My best friend is Joe. He is good fun. I go to St Patrick's School. I have two sisters. They can be a pain sometimes. I am not very tall. I am good at cricket. My house is really big. I live in the country. This can be a pain as we go everywhere in the car.

(William, aged nine years, six months)

I am Oscar Bovey. I am aged eleven. I was born on 3 November 1995. I like drawing castles that are very detailed and playing Warhammer. My best friend is Ed. I live in Chippenham. I live at Daisyhouse, Lake Road, Chippenham. I go to Lakeways Primary School. My favourite subject is art. I am five feet tall. I have size four feet. I have six people in my family. My Mum, my Dad, Rob and my brother and my sister. I have long blond hair and bright blue eyes.

(Oscar, aged eleven years)

Thinking point 1.2   What are the salient points in the children's comments? What are the common themes?

Each child dwells on factual aspects of who they are, of self. Most state their gender and age and many introduce their significant others and their position within the family. They each go on to discuss their likes and dislikes. Place is often important in giving a child a sense of belonging. (The concept of belonging is discussed in section 2 of this chapter.) Common themes in how we may describe our identity to others include:

- name (which itself may reveal much about gender, class and ethnicity)
- age, gender and physical appearance
- likes and dislikes
- place/home
- significant others/family relationships
- social roles.

There was a marked difference in how the children relayed the information. The younger children were happy to describe themselves and for it to be noted verbatim. By comparison, the older children wanted to see how their words looked written down and appreciated the opportunity to change what they said until it looked and sounded 'right' to them.

Harter (1999) examined a range of studies in which children were asked to describe themselves. She noticed a developmental sequence in which young children tend to focus on their behaviour and objective facts which could be identified by others. As children get older, they shift to describing themselves in qualitative terms, using more in-depth descriptions. Older children and adults tend to define themselves in relation to their feelings and emotions, using quite complex language. It is difficult to ascertain whether young children can think of themselves in accordance with how they feel or whether they are cognitively equipped to apply the language of emotions.

The significance of our social world and how we imagine others may see us is an important consideration here. For early pioneering symbolic interactionists within the field of psychology, such as Charles Horton Cooley and George Mead, the importance of social context and symbolic interaction is central.

Cooley (1902) is famous for the idea that society and the individual are not separate phenomena but different aspects of the same thing. He suggested that we develop a sense of self from the reactions and behaviours of those around us, terming this the 'looking glass self'. Cooley described this as a reciprocal process in which how we see ourselves is very much influenced by how others perceive and behave towards us. Cooley emphasised that self emerges not just from who we are, but also from what we imagine others think of us, including our appearance, character, behaviour and so forth. For Mead (1934) the emphasis was not just on society generally, but on the strong impact of the views of 'significant others'.

Sometimes an aspect of identity is clearly signalled

How we see others may be influenced by their appearance, age and behaviour. Stereotypes and assumptions of, for example, gender, known abilities and any observable disabilities may guide our expectation of how they will behave. Through verbal and non-verbal communication we may add to our initial impression by evaluating how the person speaks and presents themselves, perhaps taking cues from their accent and assumptions about their cultural heritage and perceived social standing. This is a complex social process. As adults we are often mindful of the impact of first impressions and may choose to dress and behave in accordance with how we evaluate a social situation, such as a job interview or meeting a potential parent-in-law. This process highlights how, as individuals, we take consideration of how we present ourselves socially.

More recent research has explored the impact of social context and culture within a *transactional* perspective (Fuhrer, 2004). A significant feature of this approach is its assumption that individuals alter their social experience by changing their behaviour. According to this approach, close inspection of individual behaviour as well as the social context, other social actors and interactive behaviour is needed to understand a person's identity. For example, five-year-old Fortesa relied on the support of her family and other children when her family left Kosova and became refugees in London.

> 'My name is Fortesa and I am nine years old ... I was born in Prishtina, the capital of Kosova. We had a flat there. We left Kosova in 1995. I was really sad when we had to leave all my friends, but we had to do it. Because I was only five years old when we left, I did not really understand why we had to go. We came to London. But I have also got uncles in Germany and Denmark. This is because of the war in Kosova – they left too. It was not nice to be spread around so much, as Albanians like to have their families near them. When I started school in London, it was hard for me because I did not know any English. But there were children from lots of different parts of the world in my school and we helped each other. When I first came to London, I cried a lot at school, because I remembered the people we had left behind in Kosova. I missed my grandparents a lot. When the fighting started in Kosova, everyone at home was very worried. I started crying again.'
>
> (Davies and Rutter, 2001, pp. 9–11)

Fortesa and her family had to adapt to their changing circumstances as they moved from Kosova to London and, ultimately, back again. We can only surmise how these changes may have impacted on their identities and wellbeing. Less dramatically, the parents of children in our focus group reported how changes over their lifetime had impacted on their identities.

> I am thirty-nine and my name is Veronica. I am married and have three children. I suppose my identity is made up of my many roles, as wife, mother, teacher, friend, daughter. The list could go on, but obviously changed as I change. As a child I was a dancer and this very much shaped my identity at that time. Now, it's more about my role in my family and my job.
>
> (Veronica, aged thirty-nine years)
>
> My name is Malcolm and I am forty-two years old. I was married and I have two boys who live mostly with their mum. I am a sales director. Who am I? Well, I am a son and a father. I am a professional and a friend. I am no longer a husband.
>
> (Malcolm, aged forty-two years)
>
> My name is Grace and I am a teacher. I am Black. I have been married for over twenty years and I have four children – all boys. Just because I was born in Jamaica doesn't mean anything,

well not to me. I am Black and I cannot change that. I wouldn't want
to. But I came to the UK when I was twenty-two. I have lived
here for over twenty years. I feel European. When I came here
I felt I had come home. I have never really identified with my
so-called ancestry. I never have.

(Grace, aged forty-six years)

Thinking point 1.3   Are there any significant differences in how adults describe who they are
in contrast to the children's descriptions?

It is interesting to note how both the children and adults use name, place,
age and social roles, such as friend, sister, brother, wife, to define who they
are. In contrast to the children, the adults can identify their occupational
role and draw on changes they have experienced in their lives to describe
themselves. Veronica indicates how her identity may have changed
throughout her life. Similarly, Malcolm stresses how he is no longer a
husband, marking a change in his circumstances and perhaps a new
dimension to his identity. These extracts may prompt us to question how
these changes may have impacted on the perceived identities of Malcolm's
and Grace's family and friends.

All the children and adults use 'I' to define who they are and Silvia and
Layla use 'we' to denote their membership of a group. For Layla, 'we'
refers to her family, while for Silvia it denotes her relationship with her best
friend. Interestingly, Amy also uses 'me' when she says 'I am me'. The
differentiation of 'I' and 'me' has been a long-standing focus of debate
within psychology and sociology.

William James (1890, 1893), an early twentieth century psychologist, first
distinguished between 'I' and 'me' as aspects of identity, reflecting the
contrast between how we view ourselves as an individual ('I') and in
relation to others ('me'). The distinction between 'I' and 'me' has proved
useful in analyses of identity and continues to be a recurrent theme (Harter,
1999). Wylie (1970) describes the difference between 'I' as observer and
'me' as the observed, a central distinction that encourages us to examine the
different elements of identity: the individual and social.

The early work of Goffman (1959) highlighted the contrasts within our
identity, with particular emphasis on how we present ourselves to the world.
He differentiated between 'performed self' and 'private self' and questioned
whether self description, observation and analysis of how we perform in the
world actually sheds any light onto how we think and feel. He went on to
suggest that there are many parts of our identity which we may prefer
(consciously or unconsciously) to keep private. So, while certain elements
of a person's identity, such as age, are physiological, many more aspects of
self are defined socially and influenced by the complex dynamic between
social context, cultural context and individual thoughts and feelings.

Social identity theory (Tajfel, 1978, 1981) explores how individuals adopt not only a personal identity as unique individuals, but also a social identity, which may reflect their membership of a particular group or groups. While many people may describe themselves as shy or introverted in certain situations, their friends may see them differently in relaxed circumstances where they may exhibit a more confident and extroverted side to their identity. Turner (1982) argues that how we present our identity, either personal or social, at any given time reflects the context in which interaction takes place.

Holloway and Valentine (2000) emphasise the impact of social dynamics on identity formation among children as well as the fluidity of this process, placing particular stress on the impact of place, belonging and children's geographies. Sharing and involvement with others allows us to differentiate ourselves and develop our individual, as well as our collective, identities. This can be taken further to consider how we belong to certain groups (and not to others), and how we may identify with 'place' to infer a sense of belonging. The notion of place encapsulates a whole host of meanings, including the home, school, outside areas for play, leisure, clubs, and so forth. Holloway and Valentine (2000) stress how children's geographies provide arenas for the construction and reconstruction of identity as children move in and out of different contexts. The emphasis here is on how **human geography** may, in some way, alter our behaviour and patterns of social interaction and induce a different side to our identity to be displayed.

Human geography is a branch of geography that focuses on the study of patterns and processes that shape human interaction with the environment, with particular reference to the causes and consequences of the spatial distribution of human activity on the Earth's surface.

This point is exemplified by Oscar's description of how he behaves differently at Scouts from how he behaves at school.

> I love scouts. You can do want you want and nobody really minds. I am shy at school. At scouts I can be as loud as I like, not like at school. Cos there is nobody to tell you off.
>
> (Oscar, aged eleven years)

The focus group extracts offer us glimpses into who the children and adults think they are and the social worlds they inhabit. For Amy, this may be playing with her friend Chantelle. For Berty it may be that he lives in Stroud. Both Oscar and Layla discuss their school lives and their friends as well as their family. Each adult emphasises their position within a family context and their occupational role within society as well as their age, gender and name. This reflects the assertion by Weigert et al. (1986) that our tendency to describe ourselves both individually and collectively is a basic human trait. We see ourselves as unique individuals who nevertheless share specific characteristics with others.

Identities are not fixed or stable, but are socially constructed in response to changing circumstances and the demands of different contexts. In stressing the instability and fragmentary characteristic of identity formation, this

Identity changes as children develop new skills

view challenges the conceptualisation of a unified self (Gayer, 2000) and raises the question of how we can gain insight into something as complex and changeable as identity. This is especially the case when, as we have already established, identity continues to change throughout life and difficulties in describing one's identity are not limited to children.

1.1 Ways of exploring identity

Early investigations of identity focused largely on the content of self-representations and how these changed over time in a developmental sequence (Harter, 1999). Psychologists have also applied attitudinal scales as a means to locate traits and characteristics that both children and adults use to describe themselves in comparisons with others. These methods have, however, been the subject of methodological critique (Fuhrer, 2004; Harter, 1999; Sani and Bennett, 2004).

We asked the children in our focus group 'How can you tell what a person is like?' and 'How can you see who they are?'. The following extracts from the group discussion offer glimpses into the complex world of identity.

> You can tell a person from their name, what they say they like and their friends. Also, it's about how they look. How they dress. Some people have wild hair.
>
> (Jasmin, aged eight years)

> Some of my friends make out they are different to how they really are. Always bragging and pretending. They are different on their own when they are not showing off. I suppose it's about how they feel on the inside.
>
> (William, aged nine years, six months)

I don't really know how much you can tell from what people just say. They could lie. You have to watch them. See how they act. Also ask their friends and teachers. And their family.

(Liam, aged eleven years)

It is evident that children (and, indeed, adults) have multiple identities, which reflect the nature of our being in a social world. Take the case of Layla on page 13, who describes herself as a human, a daughter, a sister and a friend simultaneously. So, added to the issue of the instability of identity, we have the question of how people working with children can consider a multiplicity of identities.

Thinking point 1.4   Think about a child who you know or with whom you currently work. How do they reveal different aspects of their identities in different contexts? What do you do to enable them to explore different aspects of their identities?

It is interesting to note how the younger children, such as Amy, Berty, Jasmin and Silvia, use gender labels to define themselves as girls or boys. Jasmin refers to her bi-cultural background by describing herself as 'half-and-half', while Silvia introduces us to the label 'special needs' in describing the help she receives at school.

Sani and Bennett (2004) have drawn attention to the potential weaknesses of children's self-evaluations. Harter (1999) suggests they are likely to be unrealistic, as young children find it difficult to differentiate between conceptualisations of 'who they are' and 'who they wish to be'.

She notes that young children tend to list a series of attributes that reflect not necessarily aspects of their own identity, but perhaps more of a wish list. In contrast, older children, from approximately eight to twelve years, use vocabulary to describe qualitative features of themselves, such as 'happy', 'sad', 'stupid' or 'silly'. It should not be assumed, however, that when children use descriptors of traits such as 'clever' or 'silly' that these are constant. Sani and Bennett (2004) explore the difficulty that young children may have in describing themselves without relying on categorical labels and public criteria, such as 'learning difficulty', which may not be reliable representations of their true identity.

Blaxter (2004) addresses the question of how we can gain insight into identity in relation to identity and health. She presents identity formation as a life story, drawing on the work of McAdams to explore identity as 'an internalised integration of past, present and anticipated future' (McAdams, 1989, p. 170). The metaphor of 'life story' draws our attention to the importance of self within a context. Our story will have a central character and supporting roles moving in and out of different scenes. The story will have a plot and various contexts in much the same way that our life weaves in and out of contexts with various people and significant others. Blaxter (2004) goes on to stress the importance of drawing together an individual's present and past as well as their social context and culture for a full exploration of their identity formation.

Life story work and the preservation of memories is particularly important for Looked After children (Rose and Philpot, 2005). It has been used to explore identity development and its relationship to health (Kelleher and Leavey, 2004). Barnes (2006) stresses the importance of using children's experiences and representations as a means to explore and understand illness in a way that only an individual can. Barnes notes how many children resist and recast their illness labels. This emphasis on children as active within identity formation is examined in section 2.

If we are to promote children's wellbeing, support healthy development and provide appropriate services for children, we need to gain insight into who they are and who they might become. So, how can we examine identity formations? Should we explore the inner, private worlds of human feelings and thoughts?

Weigert et al. (1986) asserted that effective exploration and theorising on identity warrants analysis in four areas, or levels:

- biographical
- situational
- institutional
- historical and cultural (this pre-dates birth).

Biographical analysis

This provides information about the individual, following them across their lifespan and noting particular life events.

Situational analysis

This level examines the interactive fabric of daily social life as individuals interact and communicate with others, allowing practitioners to contextualise individual experience and place it within a given social dynamic.

Institutional analysis

This level extends situational analysis by examining interaction and experience within any given institution. The values and social norms operating within each institution are crucially important here.

Historical and cultural identity (this pre-dates birth)

All children are born into a pre-defined cultural community with its own history and set of meanings.

In other words, effective exploration and analysis of identity formation involves building up an accurate picture of the *whole child*. In order to reach a level of understanding that reflects the true nature of the child, practitioners must endeavour to consider both the individual child and how she or he behaves within a given social dynamic. Returning to the case of Louis, who we met at the beginning of this chapter, we could apply the Weigert et al. model to develop more of an understanding of who he is and who he may become.

Thinking point 1.5   How might we go about obtaining biographical, situational, institutional, and historical and cultural information to build up a fuller picture of Louis and his identity?

To access biographical information we could talk directly to Louis' family and key people in his life. We might look at his life story book or ask him to draw big events in his life so far. We might be particularly interested in exploring the process by which Louis acquired the 'label' learning difficulty and when, and in what way, his deafness was detected.

To begin a situational analysis we may visit Louis and home or at school or in other locations and watch how he interacts with others. We might also look at the kind of work he is doing in school, or at his art work, or talk to him about his hobbies and interests. Establishing the values and social norms of each institution Louis visits would involve careful observation and discussion with participants, including Louis himself. All of these observations and discussions would also help to gain insights into the historical and cultural communities Louis inhabits.

A biographical analysis revealed that Louis' learning difficulties began along with his hearing loss when he had meningitis. An institutional analysis explained why Louis' family have consistently argued for him to be 'labelled' as having learning difficulties. They believe that, given the current funding strategies in schools, this is the only way to ensure that he will receive the help and support he needs. A situational analysis highlights that while Louis accepts the need for a label, he is at pains to stress that he is 'deaf and not stupid'. In this instance, we can see the paradox of the label that secures the necessary school resources itself creating potential barriers for Louis.

Thinking point 1.6   What strategies do you use to find out about the individual children with whom you work? How might the Weigert et al. model help?

A child's wellbeing, health and development depend on appropriate provision and services, which in turn depend on appropriate assessment of need. Insights into different facets of an individual's identity help with that process. In working with children, we are presented with a challenge: to examine the whole child, considering their individual subjective experience and how this operates within a social and cultural world. This will be discussed in more depth in Chapter 2.

Key points

1   Identity is strongly linked to feelings of wellbeing and self-esteem.

2   Identity is complex and multi-faceted.

3   Identity changes over time and place and in the light of events.

4   Identity appears to be both an individual and a social concept.

5   Effective analysis of identity involves building up a picture of the whole child, which includes exploration of both the individual and how they interact in social settings.

2 Identity development

All children are members of numerous social groupings and each grouping brings with it certain values, norms and expectations. This section explores the relationship between society and the individual by asking when identity development begins, at birth or before birth? The section also considers the importance of an individual's social community and gender and introduces the concept of pre-natal identity (PNI).

A wealth of research focuses on how children acquire an identity through a series of stages (Harter, 1999). However, this section is more concerned with the social construction of identity. To simplify matters we look at the emergence of an individual's identity through an exploration of one feature, gender. In reality, of course, identity formation is a lifelong, complex process in which the 'effects of gender, class and other formative categories overlap, in often very complicated ways, to shape an individual's identity' (Siraj-Blatchford and Clarke, 2006, p. 3).

Weigert et al. (1986, p. 93) stress how most of the research on identity is 'tied to bodies' and the importance of our physiological gender in pre-determining who we are. Our multiple identities of, say, son, brother and cousin may operate before birth, illustrating the transcendent nature of identity development and how our culture and community shape much of how we, and those around us, come to perceive who we are.

Thinking point 1.7   What factors may shape our expectations of a child, prior to its birth?

This question points to the fact that children step into social categories prior to birth, depending on how any given community defines and views factors such as gender, heritage, ability and disability. Furthermore, how we behave and act towards a child may be influenced by how we perceive these factors. These important questions are addressed in subsection 2.1 through an analysis of pre-natal identity.

2.1 Pre-natal identity

A child is born not only into a sociocultural environment, but also into one that is meaningfully organised.

(Fuhrer, 2004, p. 97)

Research in psychology and sociology has examined the emergence of identity from birth. While many authors stress how identity formation is constantly evolving and changing in response to differing circumstances and life events (Fuhrer, 2004), little research has examined how we metaphorically step into much of our identity as it exists within our social and cultural community long before we are born. As the opening quotation emphasises, the attribution of meaning is crucial in the analysis of identity.

The case of Anesha highlights this point. Milesh is awaiting the birth of her baby (Anesha). She already has two sons and the whole family's eagerly awaits the arrival of a girl. The fact that the family have asked about the sex of the unborn child implies much about the importance of gender for them. We may speculate as to what might be influencing the family's desire to have a girl. Milesh describes how she has been 'waiting a long time for a girl' and how important it is for her husband (Bhartej) and two sons (Virdee and Marj). The two boys discuss what their sister will be like.

> She's a girl and so she will like to play girl things. We won't share our toys with her. She wouldn't like them anyway. She will like to play with fairies.
>
> (Virdee, aged four years)

> I play with girls at school. They like pink. Edward in my class likes pink and Joseph laughs at him. My sister already has a room. It's not pink. It's purple. I hate it.
>
> (Marj, aged six years, five months)

Bhartej describes how 'different' it will be to 'have a baby girl amongst a house of boys'. Milesh, on the other hand, is keen to 'even things out'. Anesha already has aspects of her identity mapped out for her. Her parents and siblings have expectations as to what she may like and how she may behave.

The contribution of the environment to an individual's experience is well documented (Durkin, 2005). In western societies, parents view their newborn children differently according to their gender (Sweeney and Bradbard, 1988). They may dress them differently (Shakin et al., 1985), decorate their bedrooms differently (Rheingold and Cook, 1975), provide different forms of non-verbal feedback and use different language terms to define who they are (Sani and Bennett, 2004).

> Identity does not refer to a fixed set of context relationships but rather person and context mutually define each other.
>
> (Fuhrer, 2004, p. 81)

Gender is a distinct quality of an individual, but is very much socially and culturally defined (Weigert et al., 1986; Holloway and Valentine, 2000). Gender identity infers a whole host of social expectations and meanings reflecting gender role stereotypes and sexual identities. Gender identity also tells us much about what is seen as appropriate behaviour, what is expected

An opportunity to try a different identity?

of girls and boys, and how such behaviour may be met with approval or disapproval.

Consider the following interview extracts as pregnant mothers describe the emerging identity of their child and potential name choices.

Susan, choosing a name for her son (Fergus):

> I wanted something that was a bit unusual. Something strong and fairly manly. We know it's a boy. I think we would know anyway ... He is very physical. He drives me mad turning round and round.

Debbie, choosing a name for her daughter (Isobel):

> I love feminine, gentle names. I know my baby is a girl and so I wanted a really girlie name. A name that reflects her femininity. My husband loves the name Marnie. But that just reminds me of Hitchcock films. I wanted a name that we would both like and that other people would like as well.

Rebecca, choosing a name for her son (William):

> All the names we went for are very elegant English names. I suppose they are timeless, quite old, traditional. It has a strong identity. A name for kings. I don't know if we are having a boy or girl. I feel it is a boy. Quite different from my daughter. He is boxing in there (pointing to her tummy).

Celebrating a shared identity; your name can be an important part of your identity

Milesh, choosing a name for her daughter (Anesha):

> It is an Indian name we both loved. It was my great-grandmother's name.

Parents may decide the types of names they like or dislike before conception. Choosing a baby's name is dependent on one's culture and family. For a number of parents, choosing their baby's name demands serious thought. Some parents refuse to choose or disclose their baby's name before birth to prevent them from being influenced by others.

A person's name evokes a range of connotations, including gender, ethnicity, nationality and class, as well as association with others of that same name, a period in time, a character from a film, and so on. It may, further, draw on how the parents and carers wish their prospective child to be perceived and possibly their hopes and aspirations for the future. Where the gender of the unborn child is not known, parents may have two names in preparation for either eventuality. If we consider this simple act of choosing a name, we glimpse the tapestry of social dynamics that directs our feelings and reactions.

The choice of a name is influenced not only by the perceived gender of the unborn child, but perhaps also by the culture of the family, associations, and the desire to select a name which evokes a certain quality. Debbie suggests that she is selecting a name to denote both gender and feminine qualities. Susan, by contrast, is choosing a name which is both 'strong' and 'manly'. By association, Debbie does not like the name Marnie as it reminds her of the Hitchcock film, and Milesh is only too pleased to be reminded of her great-grandmother and Indian heritage.

It is interesting to note how Rebecca and Susan define their unborn babies' behaviour by drawing on perceived gender signals. They use terms such as 'rough' and 'physical' to suggest that these are male as opposed to female attributes. It is impossible to determine from these brief extracts whether Fergus's and William's pre-birth behaviour was overtly physical, or why both mothers chose to use these gender stereotypes to describe their unborn babies. What each extract does demonstrate, however, is the complexity of selecting a name and how we tend to draw on the vast array of social cues to direct us. It is a case of choosing a name not only that you like yourself, but, as Debbie suggests, 'that other people will like as well'. As Weigert et al. (1986) suggest, all individuals are symbolised through such media as personal names, as labels with an individuating content.

The importance of children for families and the potential stress caused by significant changes or loss will be well known to all who work with children. In addition, a child's position within families, how children interact with and respond to siblings, and the significance that this could, or could not have, may be important for identity formation. For some, being

an only child may be important in shaping their identity, while for others it may be that they have half-brothers and -sisters, live with a step-parent or adoptive parents, or live in foster care or other residential care settings (Edwards et al., 2006). It is important that we acknowledge the complexity of family life and the varying forms that families can take.

Christensen et al. (2000) unpack the many assumptions tied to the concept of 'family' and consider the diversity of contemporary demographics and family trends. Wyse and Hawton (2000) note how since the 1990s family life has been characterised by change, diversity and uncertainty. What is important is the way in which children define who they are, in part, in terms of the way they describe their family.

Our focus group did not include children whose family life may be particularly changeable and uncertain, such as children in care and refugees. In exploring the relationship between identity and place, Christensen et al. (2000) challenge the traditional assumption that identity formation is tied to location, boundaries, feelings of attachment and 'belonging'. They chart how movement has become fundamental to modern identity formation and, particularly, the experience of 'non-place' as part of everyday existence for travellers, refugees and migrants. These important issues for practitioners working with children are beyond the scope of this chapter. For a fuller discussion, see Rapport and Dawson, 1998; Wyse and Hawton, 2000; Holloway and Valentine, 2000.

Key points

1   Identity begins to take shape prior to birth and young children step into aspects of their identity.

2   Children develop or resist aspects of gender identity based on how gender is perceived by others and the social/cultural dimensions of gender that surround them.

3   The choice of name for a child can be an important part of identity formation; names may have special significance for the parents or be linked with certain social or emotional characteristics.

3 Children as active agents

The development of identity has been examined in relation to child-rearing processes and also in relation to the impact of the media (Durkin, 2005). Early theoretical explanations tended to ignore the child's own understanding of aspects of their own identity (Aitken, 2000). More recent research has added the significance of the child's own motivating force as they regulate much of their own identity development to support or dispute societal conceptions and expectations (Furhrer, 2004; Holloway and Valentine, 2000; Sani and Bennett, 2004).

In this section we address the position of the child within this process to determine how far children direct their own identity formation.

Thinking point 1.8   How much are children passive recipients of their identity, and how are they active within the process of identity development?

A considerable body of research has examined the role of children in directing their identity development, casting them as more active constituents (Fuhrer, 2004; Sani and Bennett, 2004) than passive recipients. This view draws on the analysis of the child as active agent within their environment. We develop this discussion by exploring key works in the analysis of child as agent and then go on to examine the subsequent relationship between the individual agent and social system. We take the complex process of labelling to demonstrate the importance of this relationship, indicating that while social context is powerful and influential, we cannot ignore the role of the person in actively constructing and reconstructing their identity.

A first step to understanding who we are is the recognition that we exist. William James (1890, 1893) identified this aspect of self as 'I'. It is also referred to as the 'existential self'. Four key elements within the development of 'I' have been identified and can be neatly summarised as an awareness that:

I exist

I am aware (that I am aware)

I am unique (separate)

I can act and I have power (agency).

Infants soon develop a sense of agency and recognise their impact on the environment and the emergence of 'me'.

Lewis (cited in Bennett and Sani, 2004) addressed the early characteristics of a person, such as their gender, name, age, size and social role, as aspects

Becoming a reader changes a child's identity and increases the influences on their identity development

of 'me', defined as 'categorical self'. Aspects of our identity may, though not always, remain fairly constant throughout our lives. Further, they are often presented as a way to compare ourselves to others. The notion of comparing ourselves to others allows us to explore how young children judge themselves as compared to others and what they value. How a care giver interacts with a child can shape the way in which a child comes to develop their sense of agency and their recognition of their impact on and within the world. So, once a child has a degree of self-awareness, they begin to identify themself within an environment. The emphasis on ascribing meaning to one's social world is central here and forms a strong link to the socio-constructionist model.

Rather than define 'identity' as self-contained, independent and consistent across diverse social contexts, social constructionists, such as Bruner (1990), Harré and Gillett (1994) and Shotter (1993), present self as an amalgam of an individual and their social context, with blurred boundaries between each. Within this context, the self is not a concrete, singular, static form, but an ever-changing, multi-dimensional representation that weaves in and out of social life. In this approach, interpersonal communication is the very basis of social meaning. Interaction between self and social context, therefore, works both ways (Harré and Gillett, 1994). Bruner (1990) argues that in defining and exploring who we are, we must consider the meanings, cultures, contexts and social practices of our daily life. If we are to examine how any one individual gives meaning to themself, we must first locate and examine the complex meanings into which the individual is born and raised.

3.1 Labels and labelling

In describing themselves, children and adults will draw on a host of meanings and values embedded within language and cultural representations to present an aspect of their identity.

Children are consistent in drawing on socially constructed definitions of themselves, using language, images and behaviour that reflect the social norms and meanings embedded within any given culture. It follows, therefore, that an individual's identity derives in part from these socially constructed meanings (Weigert et al., 1986) and attributed labels (Hudak and Kihn, 2001). Fuhrer (2004) accepts the impact that any given social situation, context and culture can have on a child's identity development, but he draws on the work of Bruner (1990) to stress that the central focus needs to be meaning and how we construct and reconstruct it throughout our lives.

Thinking point 1.9   Critically address the strengths and limitations of using a label such as 'disabled'.

Labels such as 'disabled' carry with them various connotations and may conjure up stereotypical images. The interpretation of 'disabled' is difficult as it requires us to delve into our own understanding, experience and, often, our prejudices.

Children will draw on a host of meanings to describe who they are. When Louis at the start of this chapter says he is 'deaf', it is important that we look beyond the label to evaluate how he arrived at this description. In the absence of analysing this rigorously with Louis himself, we can perhaps assume that a number of factors have influenced the attribution of this label. Louis may have compared himself with others, perhaps including his family members and friends. No doubt he will have been told by doctors that his hearing and speech have been affected by meningitis. Adults and children in school may have commented on his deafness and suggested ways they could help. Louis may have been bullied by others because of his deafness. He might also have had the opportunity to discuss what his deafness means in institutions such as hospitals, doctors' surgeries, school, clubs and societies. The impact of the media cannot be ignored, as Louis may be aware of the image of deaf people as they are presented in, or omitted from, magazines, comics, books, television and film. The fact that taking up the label 'disabled' has been positive for disabled rights activists and the disabled rights movement may also have had an impact.

Research draws our attention to the ease with which both children and adults use labels to construct meaning within the social world (Asher, 2001; Fuhrer, 2004). The value that labels can offer has been

Disabled, gifted or just different?

considered (Hudak, 2001), in conjunction with the potential barriers that labels can impose in terms of perceiving the whole child (Fuhrer, 2004).

Dimitriadi (2006) provides a rich insight into the lives of disabled children, the labels often used to define their conditions, and how children resist these and develop their own. Taking the example of dyslexia, she shows how children potentially resist identification with disadvantage, choosing rather to take pride in their individual creativity. Rather than this being a compensatory strategy, Dimitriadi states that, quite rightly, some children perceive themselves as gifted in contrast to others' preoccupation with disabled labels. This research explores the accounts of four children with dyslexia and their personalised representations of their identity as individuals with disability. Each child was given a digital camera to narrate their personal story by 'showing people what dyslexia is all about' (p. 148). They were free to choose any representation of their own identity. The background to this research rested on traditional assumptions about disabled children as passive victims to their impairment. This research, by comparison, shows children as active constructors of their own identities.

Dimitriadi notes how, for these children, identity is based not on any single label and comparison between normality and disability, but rather on a collage of experiences and preferences that cross such boundaries. It is not that these children reject their disability, but that this is only part of their identity and they are not consumed or defined by it. However, there is a cautionary note within the account of this research, as Dimitriadi stresses the importance of exploring the origins and development of any social group as a means to unveil identity development. Within this context, disability, or indeed any social label, cannot be understood in the absence of its history and linguistic and social representation. Children and adults will vary considerably in what they gain and lose as a result of being labelled.

Asher (2001) describes how labelling represents a basic human trait that helps us to create order and common groups within our worlds. For example, young children learn to label cats and dogs and they might then go on to learn to label different breeds of dogs. Several of the children in our focus group use labels to define themselves: Jasmin uses 'half-and-half', while Silvia suggests she has 'special needs'. Both Amy and Layla use descriptive labels such as 'pretty' to define their best friends, demonstrating the importance of using social markers and socially constructed labels to tell us about one another.

The everyday normality of labelling means that we scarcely notice its dangers and limitations (Asher, 2001). As Hudak (2001) states, it needn't be negative; it is when labels are used to oppress others that the process can become damaging. The potential impact of labels and how we can work with children to challenge them is discussed at length in Chapter 2.

Hudak (2001) explores the labelling process within educational contexts such as schools. Given that practitioners and peers can sometimes find it difficult to see beyond a label and consider the person, he examines the potential barriers to understanding that labels may induce. He draws attention to how labels have the capacity to become deeply embedded within a child's identity, part of their lived experience that is very difficult to change once the person internalises and lives out the label.

In considering the fluidity and changeable nature of identity, Fuhrer (2004) focuses on the great potential within identity development to creatively pursue one's true self. Yet we must explore the many restrictions that some labels impose, acting as barriers to identity development, change and growth.

Thinking point 1.10   What labels would you use to describe yourself? What labels have you been given and rejected?

Hudak (2001) emphasises the potentially problematic nature of labelling and advocates the need for practitioners to try to search and see beyond the label. Asher (2001) examines how labels potentially become reified to become legitimate ways of knowing. They further allow us to cut corners, to categorise one another based on limited information. We therefore make assumptions based on our understanding of labels.

Earlier we mentioned the paradox of Louis' 'learning difficulties' label: that it opened up the possibility of gaining support while potentially creating barriers to development. The process of labelling has advantages in that it means acknowledging difficulties where difficulties lie. In the case of 'special needs', a label may allow a formal statement of need to be made, which in turn can secure the necessary resources and appropriate support. At the same time, labels can act as a barrier to reaching a full and appropriate level of understanding regarding the whole child.

Althusser (cited in Maas Taubman, 2001) reminds us that it is not just the label that is important. Merely assigning a label to someone is no predictor of performance (Fuhrer, 2004; Sani and Bennett, 2004). Both label *and* action are important. Within this context, a child must in some way connect with and feel inclined to behave akin to their label. The work of social constructionists is important here in addressing the relationship between the individual agent and the social context. A growing number of researchers (Aitken, 2000; Clifford, 1997; Holloway and Valentine, 2000) present identity formation as a contested process in which children actively construct and reconstruct their identities in relation to their life experiences and social and cultural contexts. Consider the following focus group extracts:

> I don't really feel part of the gang. The boys' gang. I never have. I have always enjoyed hanging out with the girls. Julia goes to the same dance school as me. We used to do tap and modern together. We have known each other since I was, well, really very young. We have lots in common. Mostly dance. The boys play football and I can't stand it. I never have. They say I'm a gay-lord. I don't care.
>
> (Joseph, aged eleven years)

> I am not what they call a 'girly girl'. I like playing with boys, climbing trees and stuff. Jo and I are into fantasy stuff, fighting with swords, making up stories of battles. I refuse to wear dresses and pink stuff. Mum and I are always falling out about that.
>
> (Emily, aged eleven years)

These extracts indicate that children identify with labels, rejecting or contesting stereotypical forms. In a similar fashion, Grace, whom we encountered in section 1, says that though she is Black and from Jamaica she does not identify with her cultural ancestry and feels more at home as a European. Grace chooses labels as a means to define her identity, demonstrating that, as individuals, we do not necessarily have to respond to labels ascribed to us. We do have some choice. People can and do construct and reconstruct their identities.

Key points

1   The socio-constructionist model presents the child as active within the identity formation process.

2   Practitioners working with children must be mindful that the labels children use to describe who they are may be imposed, rather than selected, and that labels cannot tell the full story.

Conclusion

Identity is a complex term and process. Influenced by a myriad of social factors, an identity develops and evolves as a life story. Identity formation begins prior to birth and is influenced by social context, interpersonal relationships and the social construction of meaning. An understanding of the complexity and fluidity of identity development can help us to question ascribed labels, which may create barriers for children and between children. The socio-constructionist model builds on previous research in the fields of symbolic interactionism and developmental psychology to present an approach which considers the impact of both the child *and* social context on identity formation. This provides practitioners working with children with a methodological instrument that urges them to examine the importance of the whole child and the whole child in context.

References

Aitken, S. (2000) 'Play, rights and borders. Gender bound parents and the social construction of children' in Holloway, S. and Valentine, G. (eds) *Children's Geographies: Playing, Living, Learning*, London, Routledge.

Asher, N. (2001) 'Checking the box: the label of "model minority"' in Hudak, G. and Kihn, P. (eds) *Labelling: Politics and Pedagogy*, London, Falmer Press.

Barnes, E. (2006) 'Captain Chemo and Mr Wiggly: patient information for children with cancer in the late twentieth century', *Social History of Medicine*, vol. 19, no. 3, pp. 501–519.

Bennett, M. and Sani, F. (2004) *The Development of the Social Self*, Hove, Taylor & Francis.

Blaxter, M. (2004) 'Life narratives, health and identity' in Kelleher, D. and Leavey, G. (eds) *Identity and Health*, London, Taylor & Francis.

Bruner, J. (1990) *Acts of Meaning*, Cambridge, MA, Harvard University Press.

Burns, J.R. and Rapee, R.M. (2006) 'Adolescent mental health literacy: young people's knowledge of depression and help seeking', *Journal of Adolescence*, vol. 29, no. 2, pp. 225–239.

Canino, G., Shrout, P., Rubio-Stipec, M., Bird, H., Bravo, M., Ramírez, R., Chavez, L., Alegría, M., José, J., Bauermeister, J., Hohmann, A., Ribera García, P. and Martínez-Taboas, A. (2004) 'The *DSM-IV* rates of child and adolescent disorders in Puerto Rico: prevalence, correlates, service use, and the effects of impairment', *Archives of General Psychiatry*, vol. 61, pp. 85–93.

Christensen, P., James, A. and Jenks, C. (2000) 'Home and movement: children constructing "family time"' in Holloway, S. and Valentine, G. (eds) *Children's Geographies: Playing, Living, Learning*, London, Routledge.

Clifford, J. (1997) *Routes: Travel and Translation in the Late Twentieth Century*, Cambridge, MA, Harvard University Press.

Cooley, C.H. (1902) *Human Nature and the Social Order*, New York, Scribner.

Davies, H. and Rutter, J. (2001) *Kosovan Journeys: Refugee Children Tell Their Stories*, London, Refugee Council.

Department for Education and Skills (DfES) (2004) *Every Child Matters: Change for Children*, London, DfES.

Dimitriadi, Y. (2006) 'Resistance from within. Children with dyslexia gazing at their disability' in Satterthwaite, J., Martin, W. and Roberts, L. (eds) *Discourse, Resistance and Identity Formation*, Virginia, Stylus Publishing.

Durkin, K. (2005) 'Childhood and adolescence' in Hewstone, M., Fincham, F. and Foster, J. (eds) *Psychology*, Oxford, Blackwell.

Edwards, R., Hadfield, L., Lucey, H. and Mauthner, M. (2006) *Sibling Identity and Relationships: Sisters and Brothers*, London, Routledge.

Fuhrer, U. (2004) *Cultivating Minds: Identity as Meaning-Making Practice*, London, Taylor & Francis.

Goffman, E. (1959) *The Presentation of Self in Everyday Life*, New York, Doubleday.

Harré, R. and Gillett, G. (1994) *The Discursive Mind*, London, Sage Publications.

Harter, S. (1999) *The Construction of Self: A Developmental Perspective*, New York, Guilford Press.

Holloway, S. and Valentine, G. (eds) (2000) *Children's Geographies: Playing, Living, Learning*, London, Routledge.

Hudak, G. (2001) 'On what is labeled "playing": locating the "true" in education' in Hudak, G. and Kihn, P. (eds) *Labelling: Politics and Pedagogy*, London, Falmer Press.

Hudak, G. and Kihn, P. (eds) (2001) *Labelling: Politics and Pedagogy*, London, Falmer Press.

James, W. (1890) *Principles of Psychology*, New York, Holt.

James, W. (1893) 'The stream of consciousness' in *Psychology*, New York, H. Holt and Company.

Kelleher, D. and Leavey, G. (eds) (2004) *Identity and Health*, London, Taylor & Francis.

Kendall, P.C. and Kessler, R.C. (2002) 'The impact of childhood psychopathological interventions on substance abuse: policy implementation, comments and recommendations', *Journal of Consulting and Clinical Psychology*, vol. 70, no. 6, pp. 1303–1306.

Kernis, M.H. (eds) (1995) *Efficacy, Agency, and Self-esteem*, New York, Plenum Press.

Layder, D. (2004) *Social and Personal Identity: Understanding Yourself*, London, Sage Publications.

Maas Taubman, P. (2001) 'The callings of sexual identities' in Hudak, G. and Kihn, P. (eds) *Labelling: Politics and Pedagogy*, London, Falmer Press.

McAdams, D.P. (1989) 'The development of narrative identity' in Bauss, D.M. and Cantor, N. (eds) *Personal Psychology: Recent Trends and Emerging Directions*, New York, Springer.

Mead, G.H. (1934) *Mind, Self, and Society from the Standpoint of a Social Behaviorist*, Chicago, University of Chicago Press.

Rapee, R.M., Abbott, M.J. and Lyneham, H.J. (2006) 'Bibliotherapy for children with anxiety disorder using written materials for patients. A randomized controlled trial', *Journal of Consulting and Clinical Psychology*, vol. 74, no. 3, pp. 436–444.

Rapport, N. and Dawson, A. (eds) (1998) *Migrants of Identity*, Oxford, Pergamon Press.

Rheingold, H.L. and Cook, K.V. (1975) 'The contents of boys' and girls' rooms as an index of parents' behavior', *Child Development*, vol. 46, no. 2, pp. 459–463.

Rose, R. and Philpot, T. (2005) *The Child's Own Story: Life Story Work with Traumatized Children*, London, Jessica Kingsley.

Sani, F. and Bennett, M. (2004) 'Developmental aspects of social identity' in Bennett, M. and Sani, F. (eds) *The Development of the Social Self*, Hove, Taylor & Francis.

Shakin, M., Shakin, D. and Sternglanz, S.H. (1985) 'Infant clothing: sex labelling for strangers', *Sex Roles*, vol. 12, nos 9–10, pp. 55–64.

Shotter, J. (1993) *Cultural Politics of Everyday Life: Social Constructionism, Rhetoric, and Knowing of the Third Kind*, Buckingham, Open University Press and University of Toronto Press.

Siraj-Blatchford, I. and Clarke, P. (2006) *Supporting Identity, Diversity and Language in the Early Years*, Maidenhead, Open University Press.

Strauss, A.L. (1959) 'Mirrors and masks' in Weigert, A.J., Smith Teitge, J. and Teitge, D.W. *Society and Identity: Toward a Sociological Psychology*, Cambridge, Cambridge University Press.

Sweeney, J. and Bradbard, M.R. (1988) 'Mothers' and fathers' changing perceptions of their male and female infants over the course of pregnancy', *Journal of Genetic Psychology*, vol. 149, no. 3, pp. 393–404.

Tajfel, H. (ed.) (1978) *Differentiation Between Social Groups: Studies in the Social Psychology of Intergroup Relations*, London, Academic Press.

Tajfel, H. (1981) *Human Groups and Social Categories*, Cambridge, Cambridge University Press.

Turner, J.C. (1982) 'Towards a cognitive redefinition of the social group' in Tajfel, H. (ed.) *Social Identity and Intergroup Relations*, Cambridge, Cambridge University Press.

Weigert, A.J., Smith Teitge, J. and Teitge, D.W. (1986) *Society and Identity: Toward a Sociological Psychology*, Cambridge, Cambridge University Press.

Wylie, R.C. (1970) *The Self-concept* (vol. 2), Lincoln, University of Nebraska Press.

Wyse, D. and Hawton, A. (eds) (2000) *Children: A Multi-professional Perspective*, London, Arnold Publications.

Chapter 2

Children negotiating identities

Sue Johnston-Wilder and Janet Collins

Introduction

As we saw in Chapter 1, identity is a complex and contested area involving a host of dilemmas and tensions both for individuals and for the wider social groups to which those individuals belong. In this chapter we look at how children find out about, challenge, change and extend perceptions of themselves. We use ideas around identity, self-image, self-esteem, labelling, resilience and belonging to examine how we can support children as they develop and negotiate their identities.

Practitioners face a dilemma around needing to *both* accept *and* change children's perceptions of themselves in order to promote their wellbeing. Developing resilience is also of vital importance if children are to face up to and cope successfully with the challenges that come their way. Other important issues examined in this chapter are: what working effectively with others means; how the relevant skills develop; how children can be enabled to make choices about fitting in; where things may go wrong; and how positive intervention strategies can be applied.

The position taken throughout this chapter is that no aspects of identity are inherently negative or positive. A person's gender, ethnicity and (dis)ability are, of themselves, neutral. These attributes become the basis for discrimination, unfair treatment or, to look at the alternative perspective, a justification of supremacy or preferential treatment, only according to the meanings imposed by individuals and groups; or, as Hamlet puts it, 'there is nothing either good or bad, but thinking makes it so' (Shakespeare, *Hamlet*, Act 2, scene 2, pp. 250–51).

Core questions

- What is self-esteem in relation to children's self-identity and group identity?
- How is self-esteem created and maintained for children?
- What is resilience and how does this relate to children's negotiating identity?
- How can children's resilience be strengthened or increased?
- What are the issues around social skills and fitting in?
- How can practitioners support children's identity negotiation?
- What interventions are useful?

1 Identity and development

I feel confident when it is just one person I know well already but as soon as there is more than one they talk about things that I have no idea about and I feel left out.

(James, aged eight)

I feel unconfident when I don't know what to say when asked a question and I feel confident when I have prepared what to say already.

(Helen, aged ten)

Being shy is normal but you get scared out of your wits.

(Aberash, aged ten)

It is difficult to think about children's wellbeing without some reference to an individual's view of themselves and their place in wider social groups. The children quoted above were part of a focus group the authors contacted through three local primary schools and interviewed prior to writing this chapter. The focus group was made up of eighteen children (eight boys aged between five and eleven, and ten girls aged between four and eleven); five expectant mothers; one family (one male and one female parent and two boys aged four and six); and three other adults (two females aged thirty-nine and forty-six years, and one male aged forty-two). Four children disclosed that they had 'special needs' (one statement for dyslexia, one for cerebral palsy and two for ADHD) and two children made reference to their cultural heritage (Indian and bi-cultural respectively). All details have been changed to ensure confidentiality.

Thinking point 2.1   Which ten words would you use to describe yourself? What are the positive and negative interpretations of each word?

Before discussing how children negotiate identity, it is important to establish what is meant by some useful aspects of identity, self-image and self-esteem. Lawrence (1988) based his counselling work with eight- to eleven-year-old children on a definition of self-esteem as the extent to which we admire or value ourselves. Children and adults with high self-esteem are responsible and self-controlled, perceive themselves realistically, own up (at least to themselves) to some of their strengths and weaknesses, take pride in their accomplishments, and are not often threatened by the successes of others. This is why how we talk to and about children and their strengths and weaknesses is so important. Children can begin to become the people we think they are. (Issues of self-fulfilling prophecy are discussed in more depth in subsection 1.1.)

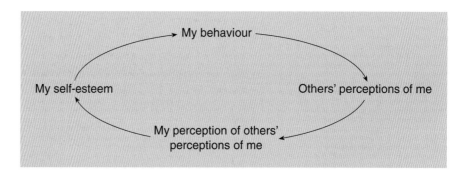

Perceptions and
self-esteem (Owens,
1995, p. 3)

Owens represents the circular nature of self-esteem as shown in the
diagram above.

Attachment theory suggests that children's self-esteem is profoundly
affected by the quality of early relationships between children and their
parents, carers or significant others (Bowlby, 1988; Sroufe et al., 2005).
Longitudinal research completed in the late twentieth century suggests that
early insecure attachments are strongly related to individual differences in
dependency throughout childhood (Sroufe et al., 2005; Urban et al., 1991).
Knowledge of attachment and separation behaviours can be useful in
supporting children who show unusual signs of stress in unfamiliar social
situations, such as the transition to school (Barrett and Trevitt, 1991).
But even exponents of attachment theory recognise that attachment
history is only partially useful in predicting some outcomes for children,
and even these would not be uniquely predicted by attachment history.
Practitioners need to use a range of theories and knowledge to understand
the behaviour of children with whom they work and be tolerant of
individual differences and needs. There can, however, be pressures on such
tolerance: schools, for example, often justify their exclusion policies with
reference to the need to educate *all* children and keep them safe from harm.

Self-image is a multi-dimensional and dynamic system of beliefs (Cole
et al., 2001). Domains of self include one's family, intelligence, body,
behavioural conduct, and social and cultural understanding and integration.
These domains are significantly affected by gender, ethnicity and
(dis)ability, and context. In Chapter 1 a child in our focus group described
herself as 'half-and-half', inheriting some of her culture from her father and
some from her mother. Wardle (1999) emphasises the need for families and
communities to address and develop the identity of 'dual heritage' children.
He argues that the choice of ethnic identity of a 'dual heritage' child is
made more difficult because many practitioners working with such children
have not focused sufficiently on their best interests. Wardle argues that
children should be brought up to have a knowledge and pride in their total
genetic, cultural and historical heritage.

We believe our children are the product of both parents'
backgrounds. And we know they have grown up in an environment
that is uniquely different from that of a single race child. Further,
we believe our children can develop a strong sense of this
combined identity as a positive tool in the difficult task of healthy
development in a narrow-minded, racist society. We believe that
asking our children to deny one side of their parentage is both
unfair to that parent and that parent's extended family, and will
cause the child a great amount of guilt.

(Wardle, 1999, p. 7)

Following this argument, we might agree that all children, including those
with a 'dual heritage' and 'bi-cultural' children, need to be able to negotiate
a strong sense of identity and belonging. They may feel the need to use
labels to define who they are and to answer questions about where they
belong. This process of negotiating identity begins in the family and
community and continues when outside their home. Community
membership involves having various dispositions or habits of mind which
in turn contribute to an individual's self-image.

Thinking point 2.2   How many different communities do you belong to? In what way do these
communities contribute to your definition of yourself?

Not all communities and social groups have a membership as visible and
obvious as that of the football supporter in the photograph below, and
not all communities and social groups are universally welcoming.
Becoming a reader and learning to make meaning from print – following
written instructions and perhaps reading for pleasure – is also to become

Football supporters are
united by their love of the
game, even though they
may be divided by club
loyalty

a member of a social group. Belonging to a social group can bring a certain kind of self-confidence and competence, and feelings of entitlement and empowerment (Greeno et al., 1999). Being excluded from a social group can have the opposite effect, especially if membership is seen to be high status and/or universal.

Schools are a community of which children are expected, and can expect, to feel a part. However, some children spend much of their school life feeling that they do not belong or do not want to belong. Where adults never felt part of the school communities of their childhood, the consequences for them and their children can be immense.

'No one forgets a good teacher'

In the UK, for example, there are identifiable links between illiteracy and dyspraxia and crime, with many long-term prisoners experiencing difficulties with reading and writing (Portwood, 1996; Laszlo and Bairstow, 1985). In addition, many children living away from their parents do not do as well as their peers at school (Jackson, 2001; Sinclair et al., 2005).

In terms of encouraging children to do well at school (however that is defined), the issue is further complicated by the fact that schools themselves are faced with a serious dilemma. In transmitting and explicating the community's interpretation of the world, a school runs the risk of perpetuating, however implicitly, certain views of the world. This can be alienating for those who do not hold those views, such as failing to achieve academically, particularly where a target-driven culture seems to allow for less variation and less scope for creativity. To challenge the dominant views may result in offending others. This is true of all aspects of life, but may be particularly sensitive in terms of morality, culture and religion.

1.1 Labelling and labels

So, how can practitioners work towards practice that reflects an understanding of the multiplicity of a child's identity? How do we get beyond the labels? As Liam, a member of our focus group, observed: 'I don't really know how much you can tell from what people just say. They could lie. You have to watch them. See how they act. Also ask their friends and teachers and their family.'

Labels can enhance or depress self-esteem by extending or limiting an individual's view of their potential. In this subsection we look at what happens when self-esteem is challenged. One of the earliest sociologists (Cooley, 1902) argued that we primarily develop a sense of self from the reactions and behaviours of those around us. However, how people present themselves and what they reveal or hide about their identity, at any given time, reflects the context in which interaction takes place. Goffman (1959) called this the 'performed self' which does not necessarily offer knowledge of the hidden, subjective and very private inner world of identity. Self-representations of identity disclose one aspect of ourselves, yet may not offer any insight into how we feel or reveal anything about the unconscious drives and aspects of ourselves which we choose to keep private.

When people use labels to define themselves, others may focus on the label and find it difficult to perceive the whole person. Labels can become a defining truth, an internalised part of our lived experience and identity that is very difficult to displace. In order to see beyond the label it is useful to separate the label from the image of the person. Thus, prior to learning to read, children might be encouraged to reject any notion that they might be slow, but rather say 'I am clever but I don't read yet'. Similarly, children who are behind with mathematics might be encouraged to say something like 'I can't do numbers, but I am not stupid'. A child labelled 'naughty' because they won't sit still might feel more positive about themselves if they are praised for their energy. Children who find some kinds of schoolwork difficult can have their self-image enhanced within and outside school, with reference to music, art, acting, computer skills, sports or hobbies.

We are asking you to think about both labels and labelling here; both are important. This approach is not, however, without its drawbacks. How might a practitioner respond if a child announces, 'I'm not stupid but I haven't learned to read yet. You must be teaching me wrong.'?

'I can't do maths, but I'm a really fast runner.'

Thinking point 2.3   Think about a child who you know or with whom you have worked. What qualities, skills and talents do they have that should enhance their self-image? How do they respond to complements or praise from you or other people?

To prevent a child adopting damaging labels, or having damaging labels attached to them, practitioners need to know a child as fully as possible. For all children, but especially important to some groups of children, children in care for example, it is also important to develop an understanding of the historical and cultural context of labels and labelling as well as its consequences. It is relatively easy to see, for example, how Black and Asian fostered children may find it hard to develop positive identities if they are completely isolated from Black or Asian communities. However, it may be very difficult to identify and deal with religious, cultural and class issues such as these. An additional challenge for those who work with children is to recognise the impact of their own identity and attitudes on the children with whom they work.

In the late 1960s the concept of the self-fulfilling prophecy was famously demonstrated by Jane Elliott who showed how her class of primary-aged children enacted the expectations their teacher randomly assigned to people according to eye colour (Peters, 1987). In this experiment, when criticised by the teacher, children with blue eyes were alienated, given lower expectations and began to 'underachieve'. The phenomenon whereby some students perform better than others simply because they are expected to has become known as the *Pygmalion effect*, after the character in the Shaw play, or the *Rosenthal effect*, after Robert Rosenthal and Lenore Jacobson who reported on the *teacher-expectancy effect*. Rosenthal and Jacobson (1968) showed that if teachers were led to expect enhanced performance from some children, then the children demonstrated enhanced performance. Carol Dweck (1999) studied pupils' beliefs about their

Is this ADHD Attention Deficit Hyperactivity Disorder or Active, Determined, High curiosity, Different?

abilities, dividing them into those who believed their intelligence was fixed and those who believed their ability could be improved by hard work. The latter appeared to have more reserves or 'resilience' when learning became more difficult and thus achieved more.

Of course, the self-fulfilling prophecy does not deny a child the individual agency to accept, reject or challenge expectations. Moreover, some labels have a higher status or are considered to be less damaging than others. For example, a parent or child may prefer to have the 'label' ADHD than that of 'lazy'. Jenny, a member of our focus group, certainly preferred to be thought of as 'dyslexic', because: 'Now I know there is something wrong and I can get help ... Before I thought I was thick'. Sometimes labels can help to facilitate negotiation between practitioner and child in the context of a recognition on both sides that some things (such as paying attention, making friends, writing and spelling) are harder for that child than for their peers. A label can be used to highlight that, with patience and additional support, physiotherapy or medication the child can continue to improve, though perhaps not in line with age-appropriate expectations. However, other children and adults will want to reject labels based on comparisons with some notion of a 'norm' and the medical model which sees some individuals as less than others. Labels can 'fix' behaviour and pin individuals in ways they cannot or will not change.

Practitioners need to be aware that labels are likely to have consequences. Consider, for example, the case of an educational psychologist who was asked to assess the educational needs of a five-year-old girl, Joanne, who had a mild physical disability. Joanne was coping really well with the social, educational and physical demands of her nursery school, where staff adapted their provision to ensure her full participation in all the activities.

Despite this, the educational psychologist added Joanne to the special needs register so that the primary school on the same site could gain the funding to make the necessary adaptations to the school to enable Joanne to move there with her friends. Staff and parents were delighted with the decision to label Joanne as having 'special educational needs (SEN)'. Joanne's feelings and the positive and negative consequences of the label will become apparent only over time.

Thinking point 2.4   How might an SEN label be an advantage or disadvantage for Joanne?

Whether a child has an SEN label or not, it is important that they are repeatedly offered opportunities to define who they are and how they have come to that understanding.

1.2 Supporting the development of self-esteem

Parental and familial relationships will influence the development of children's self-esteem, but they are by no means the only factor. Relationships with significant others and role models in society, including the media, as well as individual personalities, all contribute to identity formation. Dweck describes how practitioners can foster successful motivational patterns, encouraging children 'to value learning over the appearance of smartness, to relish challenge and effort, and to use errors as routes to mastery' (Dweck, 1999, p. 4).

What an individual defines as success and failure, may be constructed differently by other members of society. Learning to read is an achievement for any child, but school authorities are likely to have strong views as to the most appropriate age for children to learn this. A child who is not a

Aspirations and expectations for children differ significantly and are signed in a number of ways

reader by the age of eight in the UK is likely to be considered slow, while children who enter nursery as readers may well find few reading materials appropriate for their stage of development. Schools are 'where the child first encounters such criteria – often applied arbitrarily. School judges the child's performance, and the child responds by evaluating himself or herself in turn' (Bruner, 1996, pp. 36–37). Moreover, schools that emphasise a child's failings rather than their strengths are likely to be 'rough on children's self-esteem' (Bruner, 1996, p. 37). Take Nick, who was also in our focus group:

> Nick was soon to be ten when he was diagnosed as having ADHD and given medication. In school his teachers say he is restless and seems unable to concentrate for more than a few minutes at a time. Away from school, however, Nick is rebuilding a mini-motorbike with his father. In that context, Nick works systematically and logically through the tasks his father sets. Concentration is not a problem as Nick works for hours at a time to ensure that his bike is ready for the next off-road race.

The development of self-esteem can be measured as an affective process and is a measure of the extent to which the individual cares about the discrepancy between their self-image and their perception of their ideal self. It is worth noting that failure itself does not produce low self-esteem, but rather the way in which people react to the failure. For example, Nick doesn't care too much about his schoolwork and he is likely to respond badly to a teacher's attempt to get him to behave in ways appropriate for classroom lessons. Nick is unlikely to be upset if he is told his schoolwork is poor, as that is what he has come to expect. However, winning races and keeping his bike in good working order means a great deal to him. Moreover, this frequently monosyllabic boy can talk at length and with passion about his bike and how he handles the disappointment of accidents or mechanical malfunction.

Thinking point 2.5   What qualities might Nick show at home that his teachers might not be aware he possesses? What is it about the school environment that blocks the demonstration of these abilities?

Teachers have to cope with classes of twenty or thirty pupils, as well as cover a largely prescribed curriculum, while doing their best to ensure that as many pupils as possible achieve expected standards. In that context it is extremely difficult to find out about the various interests and hobbies of all the pupils in their care. (Meeting the needs and interests of individual children in a family setting can also be difficult.)

If a child is praised for effort and for the strategies they use rather than ability and results, they are more likely to develop robust self-esteem

Learning new skills takes persistence and a level of support

(Dweck, 1999). However, it is also possible that individuals over-generalise and, for example, begin to see failure in one aspect of their life, such as academic work, as failure as a person. Perhaps a child's level of self-esteem may be related to the extent to which the child values the opinions of others. Individuals with high self-esteem are more likely to rely on self-perception, while individuals with low self-esteem are likely to find external sources of feedback more salient (Ilgen et al., 1979).

McDermott (2001) demonstrated that the performance of individual children is greatly affected by the circumstances in which they perform, the level of support they receive and their perceptions of the task and their ability to perform it successfully. Self-belief exerts a powerful effect on persistence and mastery of a range of intellectual and artistic endeavours (Sloboda et al., 1999). The perceptions of others also play a significant role in the development of an individual's self-image. A child who is perceived to have certain skills is likely to be confident of success in that area; a child perceived to be lacking such skills is less likely to receive support.

Strategies for developing an individual's self-esteem are of great importance. Most children evaluate and value themselves in line with the general reactions of others toward them, and practitioners can help by working towards positive relationships that display high levels of warmth and low levels of criticism. An 'unconditional positive regard' kind of acceptance strengthens self-esteem. Even though we may not always approve of a child's behaviour, empathy, respect and responsiveness are important for fostering healthy evaluations of self. The most important strategy for dealing with unwanted, or anti-social, behaviour is to distinguish between the child and the behaviour. Practitioners should try to show that they respect the child while at the same time condemning the behaviour. People also need to model the kinds of attitudes, behaviour and language that they might expect from children.

Self-evaluations are active, dynamic and a more stable source of self-esteem than those that depend on the views of others. Self-esteem can also be supported by giving children opportunities to meet others who share their interests and values, and opportunities to develop skills in areas they are naturally good at and/or enjoy working in.

Having considered ways in which to support the development of self-esteem, we go on to consider the notion of resilience.

Key points

1 No aspects of identity are inherently negative or positive.

2 Identity is related to membership of social groups and communities, some of which have higher status than others.

3 Labels can help enhance or depress self-esteem.

4 Children can become what they are expected to become and this works both positively and negatively.

5 High warmth and low criticism can contribute to strengthening a child's self-esteem.

2 Resilience

One of the mysteries of human development is the way in which seemingly similar experiences can result in radically different responses from different people. Consider, for example, the case of children who are physically abused by their parents. Some develop a tendency towards abusing other children and, when they become adults, to abusing other adults and children, while others, vowing to give their own children a life they wanted for themselves, become loving and caring parents. The willingness and ability to love and nurture others may be seen in children who have never known what it is to belong to a loving family.

The term resilience is used to describe why some people struggle hard to cope with life experiences while others survive with self-esteem, identity and their level of wellbeing intact. The concept of resilience has been used to refer to:

1   a positive outcome despite the experience of adversity;
2   continued positive or effective functioning in adverse circumstances; or
3   recovery after a significant trauma.

(Masten quoted in Schoon, 2006, p. 7)

What constitutes adversity, adverse conditions and trauma varies among individuals and between cultures. Like adults, children vary considerably as to what they find easy, hard or impossible to deal with. When children are exposed to a stimulus that might offer a threat to self-image or self-esteem, they respond differently.

Consider, for example, a queue of children waiting to demonstrate a jump in a local gymnastics competition. Some of the children feel confident that they can jump well; for some the rising tension is an aid to concentration, but one of the girls, Krissie, suddenly bursts into tears and runs to her mother. One might argue that Krissie has become overwhelmed by the challenge of completing the task or the possibility of failure. The decision to encourage her to overcome her fear and have a go at the jump, or to abandon the challenge altogether, will depend on a number of factors. Whatever the decision, Krissie's image of herself as a gymnast may be affected. She might also learn something about her own willingness and ability to overcome fear. A single incident such as this might be quickly forgotten or it might have long-term consequences. How many of us have given up a sport or a particular activity because of an incident which seemed humiliating or traumatic at the time?

Some of the children with whom we work have experienced extremely traumatic events, some of which may be relatively common while others may be outside our common experiences.

> My father gets drunk. He said he was going to kill my mother and me. My mother put me with friends and ran away. I don't know where she is.
>
> (Six-year-old boy)
>
> I have to go to the hospital a lot because I have so many illnesses. I don't know if I will ever get well.
>
> (Ten-year-old girl)
>
> I saw my father get stabbed by a neighbour who was mad at him.
>
> (Six-year-old girl)

(Children quoted in Grotberg, 1995, p. 11)

The long-term effects on the children involved in such situations depends in part on their resilience, that is on their capacity to face, overcome and even perhaps be strengthened by adversity.

Thinking point 2.6   If you were working with one of the children quoted above, how would you be able to judge their level of resilience?

We can consider factors that promote childhood resilience under three headings: the child, the family, the wider environment:

- A child is most likely to demonstrate resilience if they are easy-going, have recognised aptitudes, good social skills and personal awareness of their own strengths and weaknesses, feelings of empathy, a belief that their efforts can make a difference and a sense of humour.

- A child is most likely to demonstrate resilience if they come from a supportive family with communicative relationships, harmony and offering a valued social role within the family group.

- A child is most likely to demonstrate resilience if they have successful school experiences, a close relationship with a mentor, and experience of extra-curricular activities (Newman, 1999).

Thinking point 2.7   How could resilience be better promoted with children in schools?

Grotberg identified specific factors that are important in the formation of resilience, including:

> trusting relationships, emotional support outside the family, self-esteem, encouragement of autonomy, hope, responsible risk

> taking, a sense of being lovable, school achievement, belief in God and morality, unconditional love for someone.
>
> (Grotberg, 1995, p. 10)

Rutter (1987) observed that where appropriate protective processes such as those discussed in the next section are present, a large proportion of children recover from brief childhood adversities with little long-term impact. On the other hand, there is also evidence that a focus on the identification and elimination of risk factors may weaken the capacity of children to overcome adversity. Practitioners need to consider promoting children's ability to resist adversity as well as reducing risk factors. Resilience may be partially inherent, but it can also be developed through exposure to difficulty. Resilience, both physical and psychological, can develop through gradual exposure to difficulties at manageable levels, with appropriate support and at appropriate points in the child's development. Where difficulties are sustained or too hard, damage rather than resilience may be the outcome.

Resilience should be viewed as something we foster throughout children's development by strengthening protective processes at critical moments in their lives. When resilience is viewed as a developmental process that can be fostered, strategies for change can be directed toward practices, policies and attitudes among practitioners. It is important to realise, however, that even when practices, policies and attitudes are changed, the result is not automatically a community of fully resilient children. Within every young person there is, during critical life events, a delicate balance between the protective processes and risk factors that originate both internally and externally. Protective processes have to be reinforced constantly so that the potential for young people to be resilient, when faced with risk factors and vulnerabilities, remains intact. Young people also need opportunity to practise and develop their coping strategies in challenging situations (Newman, 2004).

> The three characteristics of the process of fostering resilience are as follows:
>
> 1   The process is long-term and developmental.
> 2   The process views children with strengths rather than with deficits/risks.
> 3   The process nurtures protective processes so that children can succeed, by changing systems, structures, and beliefs within schools and communities.
>
> (Winfield, 2001, webpage)

In the following practice example members of a multi-agency team work together to nurture protective processes and to support children at risk of exclusion from school.

Practice box 2.1

Excluded Children's Project, Rochdale

The aim of the project in Rochdale was to develop a multi-agency team to intervene with children under twelve at risk of and experiencing school exclusion. The team is based within the Child and Adolescent Mental Health Services (CAMHS) in Rochdale and comprises a team leader, community psychiatric nurse, two social workers and an educational psychologist.

The ethos of the team is to ensure that those children who have experienced an exclusion from school gain access to a multi-agency assessment of their needs so that an appropriate package of support can be offered to them and their family. The project had initially aimed to work in a preventive way with children at risk of developing mental health problems. However, their experience to date has been that those children who are particularly at risk of exclusion are children with multiple needs, who have often previously been in contact with a range of agencies.

The team completes a full social, personal, educational and family history for each referred child. In addition, there are discussions with the school about the child's reason for exclusion and the behaviour problems. The child is given a simple educational screening to determine whether there is a need for a further, more detailed educational assessment. A meeting is then held with the school, family and other professionals to decide the most appropriate intervention.

The options are:

- cognitive behavioural therapy;
- behaviour modification;
- brief family intervention;
- education inputs in targeted areas;
- nurture approaches;
- play therapy;
- counselling;
- social skills training/group;
- experience therapies;
- parent management training.

The project's main focus is to work with the child and family, outside the school environment, offering a range of behavioural and therapeutic interventions in order to help the child and family address their behaviour and underlying causes of this. In addition, the team works with the school, helping them further develop their skills and practices in relation to working with the excluded child, raising such questions as: What sorts of supports are available within the school? How is the child's behaviour being managed?

This two-pronged approach appears to be being extremely well received by the schools – and by the children and families. The team has been providing a detailed multi-disciplinary assessment of the children's needs and has been quite successful in reintegrating children into school, enabling behaviour to settle and be managed. The presence of an educational psychologist on the team has meant that statementing issues can be addressed. Social workers have also been able to address wider home issues affecting the children. Health professionals have been helpful in identifying undiagnosed mental health problems like ADHD, which has been assessed in a number of the children, enabling them and their parents to receive appropriate support from the CAMHS team.

It has been stated that those schools that have worked with the project can see a real gain. They are gaining definite help with managing and supporting pupils with complex needs and they can see a positive impact through the project on the behaviour of the children. As the project said:

> This multi-disciplinary approach has provided a more holistic assessment of the child's needs, which in the vast majority of cases appears to be successful and the children are functioning better with no further exclusions. We await with interest whether we have made any difference to their mental health.
>
> (Teachernet, 2007, p. 53)

Protective interventions might involve reducing risk, interrupting negative chains of events, establishing and maintaining self-esteem or creating opportunities for change. Preserving continuity can be important. For example, when a child is being moved from one foster placement to another, attempts are made, where possible, to allow for maintaining contact with parents and friends, attendance at the same school, taking personal clothes and toys, and retaining religious affiliations and food choices. In such situations, life story work can be especially valuable (Rose and Philpot, 2005). However, any intervention may do harm as well as good, so services should not seek to provide unnecessary help. 'Gains made by removing risk factors should be greater than any negative unintended consequences that may occur through intervening' (Newman and Blackburn, 2007).

The table below outlines examples of interventions that can promote resilience and will, if successfully implemented, result in a range of benefits for children.

Intervention	Benefit to child
If children have opportunities to take part in demanding and challenging activities then …	… they will become less sensitive to risk and more able to cope with physical and emotional demands.
Where children are in situations of conflict at home, contact with a reliable and supportive other will …	… reduce exposure to, and impact of, parental conflict.
Facilitating contacts with helpful others or networks who can provide activities or opportunities for work will …	… help break the sequence of negative 'chain effects' that occur where children are in highly vulnerable situations.
If children are exposed to manageable demands and opportunities to succeed in valued tasks, then …	… they will develop more competencies and their competencies and self-esteem will grow.
Exposure to people or events that contradict risk effects will compensate for previous bad experiences and …	… help counter the belief that risk is always present.
Opportunities for careers or further education will …	… result in a greater likelihood of adult stability and increased income.
Teaching coping strategies and skills and being helped to view negative experiences positively will result in the child having …	… a capacity to re-frame experiences and be an active rather than a passive influence on their own future.

Intervention and benefits to child (Rutter, 1977)

It is worth noting that the theme of supportive networks is a recurring one in promoting resilience. Given the importance to developing resilience of belonging to and maintaining networks, we look further at the issue of belonging in section 3.

Key points

1   Resilience refers to positive functioning despite adverse circumstances or trauma.

2   Resilience can be developed and supported.

3   The factors which promote childhood resilience can be considered in terms of the child, the family and the wider environment.

3 Children's wellbeing and social groups

It is important not to expect all children to fit in all of the time. We need to consider how we can help children to develop their identities to the point where they have choices about how much to fit in and how much to be different. Our aim in this section is to discuss support whereby children can choose which aspects of their identity they want to highlight and consequently which social groups they might wish to be a part of, challenge and try to change, or not join. Developing skills for dealing with others can be linked to success in education and in the workplace and thus to life chances. Poor social skills are related to under-achievement (see, for example, Kohn, 1977).

Practice box 2.2

Azkar and Kieron join a football team

The importance of social skills and a willingness to 'fit in' was highlighted when Azkar and Kieron both joined a football team at their local community centre. Azkar quickly made friends with everyone on the team and tried hard to do what the team coach asked. He soon became popular and enjoyed teasing the team coach. He rarely misjudged a social situation and rarely upset the coach by taking a joke too far. By comparison, Kieron found it hard to make friends. Most of the time he was quiet and did not talk to his team mates. Envious of Azkar's popularity, Kieron tried to join in with the teasing, which always seemed to land him in trouble. The coach tried to distance himself from Kieron by putting him in the reserve team. After a little while Kieron stopped going to practice sessions.

Jasminda's drawing

Jasminda's anxieties about fitting in took a different form. In school she was given a task she felt unable to accomplish. She took her piece of paper and pencil to the corner of the table and sat covering her paper with her left arm as if to prevent someone from seeing. She blinked away tears and looked very sad indeed. A teaching assistant went to sit with Jasminda and asked what she was drawing. 'We have to draw our family, but I don't have a dad. It's just me and mum.' With gentle questioning, Jasminda began to cheer up as she drew her grandparents, aunties, cousins, friends and pets. 'I have a great big family,' Jasminda later explained to a classmate.

Self-identity is related to a person's position and role within the communities or societies to which they belong, or would like to belong. For the majority of children, their family is their first experience of belonging. They are part of a family which may be extended or reconstituted. A minority of children's experience may be with adoptive or foster families, or in a care home. Families, in turn, may belong to a number of wider neighbourhoods or communities related to any number of shared interests and beliefs, including age, friendship, religion, culture, geography, leisure and hobbies. Added to this, the majority of children have to attend some form of compulsory education where schools, classrooms and playgrounds offer a dazzling array of groups and communities to which they may want to belong. However, other groups, communities and spaces may be closed to some children for some or all of the time.

Belonging is a two-way process between individuals and the communities or groups to which they belong. It involves an interaction between the expectations of others and the degree to which an individual shares, or is willing and able to fit in with, those expectations. In order to maintain membership of a group or community, an individual needs to be able to modify their behaviour in the light of feedback from others and also to communicate feedback to them. Feedback comes in a variety of forms, including language, body language and group behaviours. Before we look in detail at these feedback mechanisms, let us reflect on the social groups or communities to which children might wish to belong.

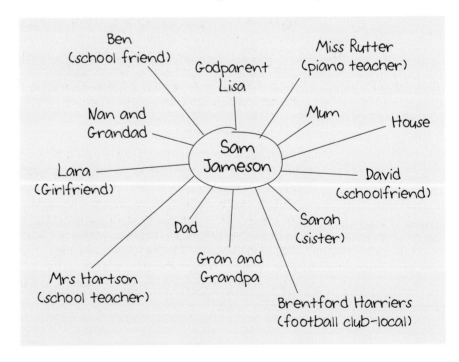

Ecomap diagram

Children relate to others in a variety of different settings: home, extended family, neighbours, school, the wider community, and other formal and informal settings. In each setting, adults and other children have different expectations of how children should behave, and children can be expected to adjust their behaviour appropriately. This often means having to intuit what is expected in different settings, using the behaviour of others to provide clues. In today's western societies children spend most of their days in public institutions such as schools, and fitting into school communities has implications for children's identity construction.

3.1 Fitting into a school community

As education is a universal experience for children, learning to 'fit in' in classrooms and schools is an important aspect of almost every child's life. It has been recognised for some time that the degree to which a child is able to 'fit in' with the expectations of others can have significant implications for their learning. For example, in the 1930s the psychologist John Dewey (1934, 1939) considered that social interactions were an essential stimulus for any individual to learn. Dewey's view that learning has its origins in social situations and their demands on the individual was echoed and developed in the work of Lev Vygotsky. For Vygotsky, learning originates in interactions between people and then develops within the mind of the individual.

> Any function in the child's cultural development appears twice, or on two planes. First it appears on the social plane, and then on the psychological plane. First it appears between people, as an interpsychological category, and then within the child as an intrapsychological category. This is equally true with regard to voluntary attention, logical memory, the formation of concepts, and the development of volition. ... Social relations or relations among people genetically underlie all higher functions and their relationships.
>
> (Vygotsky, 1979, p. 163)

Vygotsky and social constructivism

An important consequence of Vygotsky's theory is that an individual who experiences difficulty in operating in what he calls 'the social plane' might be expected to suffer some disadvantage in terms of learning. For, as Vygotsky wrote, 'human learning presupposes a specific social nature and a process by which children grow into the intellectual life of those around them' (Vygotsky, 1978, p. 88). Successful participation in social interaction and engagement in social discourse are seen within Vygotsky's theoretical framework as providing essential stimulation for the individual to develop higher cognitive functions.

Indeed, this view of learning lies at the core of social constructivism, a theory about how learning occurs, that places emphasis on the environment, especially the social context, within which learning interactions take place. Learning, in or out of school, for child and adult, involves interactions between a learner, a teacher and the material to be learned. These interactions take place within an environment, or *milieu* as Brousseau calls it (1997). Recognition of the importance of the social milieu within which learning takes place leads to awareness of the importance of the social practices and cultural norms that shape our interactions with one another, and the central role played by language as a mediator of such practices and norms. Individuals who lack awareness of the social and cultural norms, or who do not use language successfully in social interactions with teachers or other learners, might be disadvantaged as learners.

Social constructivism received closer attention and detailed analysis in the more recent work of social psychologist Etienne Wenger. Although the implications of limited 'social skills' are not spelled out explicitly, Wenger's clear summary of the central processes of learning in a social context leaves little room for doubt that fitting in with others, and adapting to changing social circumstances, are essential ingredients for successful learning.

> *Learning is fundamentally social* ... What both drives and enables [learning] is the increasing possibility of participating in [social] activities ... The most private thoughts we think use images, words, and concepts that reflect our social participation. ... learning is most effective when it is integrated in a form of social participation.
>
> *Learning changes who we are* ... By transforming our relations with the world and with others, learning transforms our identities as social beings.
>
> *Learning is a matter of engagement in practice* ... It implies the ability to engage in the world in certain ways, so as to recognize oneself and to be recognized as a member of a community.
> It is a matter of competence, of being able to participate in socially defined activities and to contribute to a community and its enterprise. It is this engagement in practice, not some abstract notion of membership, that determines what we learn and that empowers us to be who we are. ... it is our ability to participate in and contribute to a shared enterprise that defines our experience of identity in practice.
>
> (Wenger, 1996, webpage)

Social intelligence:
Howard Gardner
(1993) argued that
there are various types
of intelligence, hence
the *theory of multiple
intelligences*. Social
intelligence can be
defined as the
intelligence that lies
behind group
interactions and
behaviours.

All of this strongly suggests that learning is more likely in an individual who is socially competent, who is able to adjust successfully to a variety of different social norms, and who is able to participate effectively in social exchange. The ability to work with feedback mechanisms as part of social exchanges is a key element of what has been called '**social intelligence**'.

Children within families are aware of themselves as, for example, the youngest or the oldest, but it is not until they start nursery or school that development of self in relation to peer group begins. Typically, before they start school, children spend time with accommodating adults and small numbers of other children, as Will Hadcroft did.

> Like most boys, I was fascinated by trains. The track of this miniature railway line went round in a large circle, with a straight piece veering off into the centre where a couple of sheds housed the carriages and the engine. Such was my fascination that every morning at eight o'clock, I was escorted from the hotel by Grandad or my father to 'help' the driver set up the carriages and bring them out of their shed. He let me sit with him in the engine free of charge as he tested the track, and then rewarded me with a lollipop for my invaluable help. I loved that train, and would spend most of the time, when I wasn't actually on it, looking forward to the next time that I would be.
>
> Again, words like 'obsessed' and 'fixated' were never used by adults at this stage, probably because no one had come to appreciate just how obsessed with it I actually was. They just thought it was cute.

(Hadcroft, 2005, p. 21)

Once a child starts school, labelling and comparisons with other children in a peer group are almost unavoidable, and this can be a very negative experience for some children.

To be a 'good' pupil, young children quickly learn to live up to, but not exceed, the norms of the school community as decreed by teachers or fellow pupils. They may, for example, think it is good to be better at football than at singing (if you are boy) or better at singing than at football (if you are a girl). Children learn very quickly not to ask questions in school for fear of being thought a nerd or attracting too much teacher praise. It may not be acceptable to be clumsy or not to understand jokes, but it may be acceptable to be the class clown.

3.2 Reading social situations and understanding others

> I am aware that lots of people worry about how they fit in and how they are perceived by other people. Most of the time I am not aware of thinking about this and if I do catch myself thinking about what

other people think of me I try to suppress the thoughts. I cannot understand why other people do not do the same. It makes life a lot easier.

(Paul)

I am constantly feeling that I do not fit in and that I am doing something wrong, but I don't know what it is.

(Sarah)

Autistic spectrum disorders (ASD) (sometimes referred to as the autism spectrum disorders) are a developmental and behavioral syndrome that results from certain combinations of characteristically autistic traits. Although these traits may be normally distributed in the population, some individuals inherit or otherwise manifest more autistic traits than the majority of the population.

Having established the need for effective social communication and understanding in learning, it is important to consider children for whom levels of social communication and understanding are not sufficient to sustain effective learning and induction into communities. One way of looking at the **autistic spectrum disorders** (**ASD**) is to see them in terms of:

- those who do not know they are not fitting in
- those who know they are not fitting in but are not bothered about this
- those who know they are not fitting in and are vulnerable to being negatively affected by this.

Children with ASD have been diagnosed as having extreme difficulties with three aspects of social functioning:

1 social communication – knowing what to say to other people and what they are saying to you
2 social understanding – knowing what to do when you are with other people
3 imagination – pretend play, make believe and fantasy.

Studying children diagnosed with ASD, and children with some related symptoms, can help us come to a better understanding of why things can go wrong for a wide range of pupils.

Many people who do not have ASD may also find some aspects of social functioning difficult, especially when they are young. They may find it difficult to make and keep friends; to understand what others think, feel and want; to choose a response to others; and to understand the consequences. They may be negatively affected by feeling different in some way, or attract attention by use of negative processes. They may not ask for help when needed. They may be bullied. Their difficulties may have a significant, and occasionally catastrophic, effect on home life where the demands on parents exceed the parents' ability to meet the need and there is insufficient support. According to Roger Elliot (2007), some useful social skills include:

- the ability to remain relaxed, or at a tolerable level of anxiety, while in social situations
- listening skills, including letting others know you are listening
- empathy with and interest in others' situations

- the ability to build rapport, whether natural or learned
- knowing how, when and how much to talk about yourself – 'self-disclosure'
- appropriate eye contact.

There is also a need to adapt to changing social contexts and to pick up implicit clues about such changes. Practitioners should not assume that children of a certain age have gained certain social skills, but be ready to support their development. Many social skills can be taught explicitly to those who do not learn them spontaneously. For example, 'look at me when I am talking to you' may not be an appropriate thing to say to a child, depending, for example, on their culture or their place on the autistic spectrum. You may need to say – 'look as if you are listening by looking in the direction of my face'.

Children with ASD may, through no fault of their own, fail to meet targets based on age-group norms. We need to begin by challenging those norms and establishing individual or personal learning targets. If children who need extra support, for example with coordination, visual tracking or working in groups, do not receive it at key points in their school career, then intervention to maintain resilience may be needed. Among these kinds of interventions, circle time has a strong following, even though research evidence as to its efficacy is not conclusive (Mosley and Tew, 1999; Lloyd and Munn, 1998).

Given the importance to children and young people of what they imagine others think of their appearance, character, behaviour and so on (see Chapter 1), many children need feedback about the impact they make on others so that they can make informed choices about the impact they may wish to have. Other children intuit this for themselves and do not need it spelling out explicitly. Circle time can be one mechanism for providing such feedback directly by providing a space to:

- share thoughts and feelings in a place where you feel safe
- feel you belong in a group you can trust
- have more confidence and feel good about yourself
- get things off your mind and say what your worries are
- talk about things that are important to you – good or bad
- learn to listen and take turns
- respect what other people have to say
- build friendships and relationships
- learn to talk about your feelings calmly
- work together to solve problems and learn from your mistakes
- know that you do not need to be angry to solve problems
- give positive messages to others and share praise

- hear good news about yourself
- thank others for helping and supporting you
- help others to feel good about themselves
- co-operate with others and accept each other's differences
- make a difference to the behaviour and learning in your school
- celebrate success and achieve your goals.

(Learning and Teaching Scotland, 2007, webpage)

Practice box 2.3 introduces another strategy used to help develop fitting-in behaviour.

Practice box 2.3

Carol Gray (1994) developed some very specific rules for writing effective social stories to help children develop fitting-in behaviour. A social story contains more informative statements (explaining social cues or providing reasons) than directive statements (telling the child what to do and say). Directives are stated positively as 'do' statements rather than 'don't' statements.

Here is one example of a social story, written to help a child learn appropriate behaviour in the cafeteria at school.

Eating in the school cafeteria

When it's time for lunch, my teacher tells the class that it is time to go to the cafeteria.

I walk to the cafeteria with all the other kids. I try to walk slowly.

We have to wait in line for our food. I wait my turn to get my lunch. It is important to wait my turn. Other kids don't like me if I push ahead of them. I want other kids to like me.

The lady behind the counter is very nice. She asks me what I want. I get to choose a main course, a vegetable, a dessert, and a drink. I point to each food, and she puts it on my tray.

I can have only one dessert. If I have too much dessert, I might feel sick.

I say 'thank you' to the lunch lady.

I push my tray to the end of the line and give my lunch card to the person at the cash register. She punches a hole in it. This hole tells them that I paid for my lunch.

(Ozonoff et al., 2002, p. 203)

Ideally, practitioners would develop as much consistency as possible in their communication about the routines in their settings. More specific training for practitioners and shared definitions and procedures within multi-agency teams may be an important first step. Nikopoulos and Keenan's (2007) *Video Modelling and Behaviour Analysis: A Guide for Teaching Social Skills to Children with Autism* has some useful advice about how to teach social skills effectively. Video modelling is a technique that uses video-taped scenarios for the child to observe, thus allowing the adult to focus the attention of the child on specific aspects of a social situation and repeating as often as needed.

Another strategy which might be worth considering, especially in extended and out-of-school settings, is where children study in mixed age groups much as they do in New Zealand. The effect of this is to reduce the sense of difference among a class of children as there is greater variety of ages in the first place. A third strategy, discussed below, is to offer activities in which a range of different skills is needed and collaborative team work is effective.

Collaborative work

Collaborative tasks can be designed such that different skills are required. One good current example of this is the UKMT mathematics team challenge where, as part of an after-school club, pupils come to appreciate that being fast at mathematics is not the be all and end all, provided there is one fast person in the team. Other skills, such as being able to work spatially, become appreciated in a new way.

Practice box 2.4

In the Robotics work promoted by RoboCupJunior, an international competition, pupils of different strengths take different roles in the team: programmer, builder, designer, choreographer, reporter, etc. As a result, pupils with different strengths and weaknesses, e.g. in reading or in social skills, tend to recognise each other's strengths and potential areas of contribution and learn to work in teams. Here is a description of one example of collaborative work resulting in appreciation of an otherwise alienated child.

> John has difficulties with social interaction. Before the project started, Jane found John annoying. Jane wrote in her diary "This week. I did all of the programming. We checked to see if the music went with the steps we had done. Altogether we had 44 steps. I made all of the steps 2.5 seconds.

John fixed arms onto the robot and he got them working!!!!" A later week she wrote: "The hall floor was the best for the robot as we had a lot of room and it was a lovely smooth service. As we couldn't reach the "Run" button, John rearranged the design so we could do so."

(Johnston-Wilder et al., 2006, p. 3)

Thinking point 2.8   How could you establish a collaborative activity with or between the children with whom you work on a regular basis?

Key points

1   Identity is related to a person's position and role within groups or communities and their sense of belonging.

2   While children have some choice about which social groups they choose to belong to, most children have to learn how to 'fit in' with or survive compulsory education.

3   Some children, may need additional support to help them to develop the social skills they need from the practitioners who work with them.

Conclusion

The chapter began by considering how children find out about themselves. It then examined labels, the process of labelling, the development of self-esteem, resilience and related issues. In this chapter we have emphasised the role of practitioners in supporting children in developing the ability to choose to 'fit in' or not, and to exhibit appropriate behaviour in a range of social circumstances. Children's wellbeing is connected to finding out about themselves and who they want to be. In the light of a child's right 'to preserve his or her identity' (*United Nations Convention on the Rights of the Child*, United Nations, 1989), practitioners have a responsibility to ensure that the children with whom they work can develop an identity in an atmosphere that challenges discrimination and prejudice. In order to do this, adults need to know the children with whom they work, to work to build positive relationships with them and between children themselves, understanding and respecting their individual and emerging frames of reference.

References

Barrett, M. and Trevitt, J. (1991) *Attachment Behaviour and the Schoolchild: An Introduction to Educational Therapy*, London, Routledge.

Bowlby, J. (1988) *A Secure Base: Clinical Applications of Attachment Theory*, London, Tavistock/Routledge.

Brousseau, G. (1997) 'Theory of didactical situations in mathematics: didactiques des mathématiques, 1970–1990' in Balacheff, N., Cooper, M., Sutherland, R. and Warfield, V. (trans., eds) *Theory of Didactical Situations in Mathematics*, Dordrecht, Kluwer Academic Publishers.

Bruner, J. (1996) *The Culture of Education*, Cambridge, MA, Harvard University Press.

Cole, D.A., Maxwell, S.E., Martin, J.M., Peeke, L.G., Seroczynski, A.D., Tram, J.M., Hoffman, K.B., Ruiz, M.D., Jacquez, F. and Maschman, T. (2001) 'The development of multiple domains of child and adolescent self-concept: a cohort sequential longitudinal design', *Child Development*, vol. 72, no. 6, pp. 1723–1746.

Cooley, C.H. (1902) *Human Nature and the Social Order*, New York, Scribner.

Dewey, J. (1934) *Art as Experience*, London, Allen & Unwin.

Dewey, J. (1939) *Freedom and Culture*, London, Allen & Unwin.

Dweck, C.S. (1999) *Self-Theories: Their Role in Motivation, Personality, and Development*, Philadelphia, Taylor & Francis.

Elliot, R. (2007) *6 key social skills*, available online at <http://www.self-confidence.co.uk/social_skills.html>, accessed 16 October 2007.

Gardner, H. (1993) *Frames of Mind: The Theory of Multiple Intelligences* (2nd edn), London, Fontana Press.

Goffman, E. (1959) *The Presentation of Self in Everyday Life*, New York, Doubleday.

Gray, C. (1994) *Social Stories*, London, Future Horizons Incorporated.

Greeno, J.G., Pearson, P.D. and Schoenfeld, A.H. (1999) 'Achievement and theories of knowing and learning' in McCormick, R. and Paechter, C. (eds) *Learning and Knowledge*, London, Paul Chapman.

Grotberg, E.H. (1995) 'A guide to promoting resilience in children: strengthening the human spirit' in Cesarone, B. (ed.) (1999) *Resilience Guide: A Collection of Resources on Resilience in Children and Families*, Champaign, IL, ERIC Clearinghouse on Elementary and Early Childhood Education, available online at <http://www.eric.ed.gov/ERICDocs/data/ericdocs2sql/content_storage_01/0000019b/80/15/f8/05.pdf>, accessed 22 August 2007.

Hadcroft, W. (2005) *The Feeling's Unmutual: Growing up With Asperger Syndrome (Undiagnosed)*, Gateshead, Athenaeum Press.

Ilgen, D.R., Fisher, C.D. and Taylor, M.S. (1979) 'Consequences of individual feedback on behavior in organizations', *Journal of Applied Psychology*, vol. 64, no. 4, pp. 349–371.

Jackson, S. (2001) *Nobody Ever Told Us School Mattered: Raising the Educational Standards of Children in Care*, London, British Agencies for Adoption and Fostering.

Johnston-Wilder, S., Sheehy, K., Hirst, T. and Green, A. (2006) 'Learning through Robotics', paper presented at This Learning Life Conference, at the University of Bristol, 20 April.

Kohn, M. (1977) *Social Competence, Symptoms, and Underachievement in Childhood: A Longitudinal Perspective*, New York, Wiley.

Laszlo, J.L. and Bairstow, P.J. (1985) *Perceptual Motor Behaviour: Developmental Assessment and Therapy*, London, Holt, Rinehart and Winston.

Lawrence, D. (1988) *Enhancing Self-Esteem in the Classroom*, London, Paul Chapman.

Learning and Teaching Scotland (2007) *Health promoting schools: circle time*, available online at <http://www.healthpromotingschools.co.uk/children/factfiles/circletime.asp>, accessed 16 July 2007.

Lloyd, G. and Munn, P. (eds) (1998) *Sharing Good Practice: Prevention and Support for Pupils with Social, Emotional and Behavioural Difficulties*, Edinburgh, Moray House Publications.

McDermott, R.P. (2001) 'The acquisition of a child by a learning disability' in Collins, J. and Cook, D. (eds) *Understanding Learning: Influences and Outcomes*, London, Paul Chapman.

Mosley, J. and Tew, M. (1999) *Quality Circle Time in the Secondary School: A Handbook of Good Practice*, London, David Fulton Publishers.

Newman, T. (1999) *Highlight 170: Evidence Based Child Care Practice*, London, National Children's Bureau/Barnardo's.

Newman, T. (2004) *What Works in Building Resilience?*, Ilford, Barnardo's Policy and Research Unit.

Newman, T. and Blackburn, S. (2007) *Transitions in the lives of children and young people: resilience factors*, available online at <http://www.scotland.gov.uk/Resource/Doc/46997/0024004.pdf>, accessed 22 August 2007.

Nikopoulos, C. and Keenan, M. (2007) *Video Modelling and Behaviour Analysis: A Guide for Teaching Social Skills to Children with Autism*, London, Jessica Kingsley.

Owens, K. (1995) *Raising Your Child's Self-Esteem*, London, Plenum Press.

Ozonoff, S., Dawson, G. and McPartland, J. (2002) *A Parent's Guide to Asperger Syndrome and High-Functioning Autism: How to Meet the Challenges*, London, The Guilford Press.

Peters, W. (1987) *Frontline*, available online at <http://www.pbs.org/wgbh/pages/frontline/shows/divided/etc/friday.html>, accessed 13 July 2007.

Portwood, M. (1996) *Developmental Dyspraxia: A Practical Manual for Parents and Professionals*, Durham, Durham County Council.

Rose, R. and Philpot, T. (2005) *The Child's Own Story: Life Story Work with Traumatized Chilldren*, London, Jessica Kingsley.

Rosenthal, R. and Jacobson, L. (1968) 'Pygmalion in the classroom', *Urban Review*, vol. 3, no. 1, pp. 16–20.

Rutter, M. (1977) 'Protective factors in children's responses to stress and disadvantage' in Kent, M.W. and Rolf, J.E. (eds) *Primary Prevention of Psychopathology. Vol. III: Social Competence in Children*, Hanover, NH, University Press of New England.

Rutter, M. (1987) 'Psychosocial resilience and protective mechanisms' in Rolf, J., Masten, A., Cichetti, D., Nuechterlein, K. and Weintraub, S. (eds) *Risk and Protective Factors in the Development of Psychopathology*, New York, Cambridge University Press.

Schoon, I. (2006) *Risk and Resilience: Adaptations in Changing Times*, Cambridge, Cambridge University Press.

Sinclair, I., Baker, C., Wilson, K. and Gibbs, I. (2005) *Foster Children: Where They Go and How They Get On*, London, Jessica Kingsley.

Sloboda, J., Davidson, J.W. and Howe, M.A.J. (1999) 'Is everyone musical?' in Murphy, P. (ed.) (1999) *Learners, Learning and Assessment*, London, Paul Chapman.

Sroufe, A., Egeland, B., Carlson, E.A. and Collins, W. (2005) 'Placing early attachment experiences in developmental context: the Minnesota longitudinal study' in Grossmann, K.E., Grossmann, K. and Waters, E. (eds) *Attachment from Infancy to Adulthood: The Major Longitudinal Studies*, London, The Guilford Press.

Teachernet (2007) *Promoting children's mental health within early years and school settings*, available online at <http://www.teachernet.gov.uk/_doc/4619/mentalhealth.pdf>, accessed 16 July 2007.

United Nations (1989) *United Nations Convention on the Rights of the Child (UNCRC)*, Geneva, United Nations.

Urban, J., Carlson, E., Egeland, B. and Sroufe, L.A. (1991) 'Patterns of individual adaptation across childhood', *Development and Psychopathology*, vol. 3, pp. 445–60.

Vygotsky, L.S. (1978) *Mind in Society: The Development of Higher Psychological Processes*, Cambridge, MA, Harvard University Press.

Vygotsky, L.S. (1979) 'The genesis of higher mental functions' in Wertsch, J. (trans., ed.) *The Concept of Activity in Soviet Psychology*, New York, Sharpe.

Wardle, F. (1999) *Tomorrow's Children: Meeting the Needs of Multiracial and Multiethnic Children at Home, in Early Childhood Programmes and at School*, Denver, CO, Centre for the Study of 'Dual Heritage' Children.

Wenger, E. (1996) *Communities of practice: the social fabric of a learning organization*, available online at <http://www.ewenger.com/pub/pubhealthcareforum.htm>, accessed 16 July 2007.

Winfield, L. (2001) *NCREL monograph: developing resilience in urban youth*, available online at <http://www.ncrel.org/sdrs/areas/issues/educatrs/leadrshp/le0win.htm>, accessed 16 July 2007.

Chapter 3

Health matters

Pam Foley

Introduction

Children's health and wellbeing is a matter of personal and political significance. The motivation of policy makers and service providers involved with children's health can be profoundly influenced by ideas about a nation's standing, conceptions of responsibility and risk (see also Chapter 5), and wide-ranging debates around just what and who contribute to a healthy and safe environment for children (see also Chapter 6). The politics and economics of childhood mean that children's health will continue to hold a place at the top of governments' lists of priorities.

The prevailing contemporary view of health is that it should be viewed broadly, to include emotional and mental or psychological health as well as physical health. Equally, it should, as far as possible, recognise the many and varied interrelationships between the emotions, the body and the mind, and have regard to an individual's environment. This will be our approach here. It is also necessary to retain an awareness of how much 'health and wellbeing', and associated terms such as 'health needs' and 'health outcomes', are caught up in political, economic and ideological conventions.

The chapter opens with an international profile of contemporary children's health and wellbeing. It then examines some of the issues and debates that feature in children's health policy and asks how a child's physical, mental and emotional health can be protected and promoted by those adults who care for and work with them. It examines healthcare and health promotion interventions and their impact on children's lives. Finally, the chapter discusses children's health promotion in a multi-agency context.

Core questions

- What are the key issues for children's health across the UK today?
- How are decisions made about health interventions and what impact do they have?
- How can practice and practitioners contribute to a healthy environment for children?
- What influences the development of health education and health promotion policy and practice for children?

1 The development of child health policy

According to the United Nations Children's Fund, among the rich countries of the industrialised world the UK appears to have been, overall, the worst place to be a child in 2007 (UNICEF, 2007). The UNICEF report focused on six areas: material wellbeing, health and safety, educational wellbeing, family and peer relationships, behaviours and risks, and young people's own perceptions of their wellbeing, with the stated purpose 'to encourage monitoring, to permit comparison, and to stimulate the discussion and development of policies to improve children's lives' (p. 2). It drew on a multi-dimensional approach to child health and wellbeing, making it clear its emphasis was on:

> the importance of growing up in a happy and loving family environment, on the child's right to an adequate standard of living, to social security, to protection from violence and exploitation, to the highest attainable standard of health care, to social services and to equitable access to educational opportunity.
>
> (UNICEF, 2007, p. 40)

UNICEF described itself as informed by the *United Nations Convention on the Rights of the Child* (United Nations, 1989), including the participation rights of the child, and so incorporated a dimension solely based on children's own sense of wellbeing.

International comparisons such as these indicate a country's strengths and weaknesses, showing what is achievable in practice and providing information to argue for, and work towards the fulfilment of children's rights and the improvement of their lives (UNICEF, 2007). Disparities between countries, such as those graphically indicated in this report, are not inevitable but are susceptible to priorities and choices expressed through national and local policies. Child health and welfare remains at the top of government agendas both nationally and internationally, fed and driven by a range of rationales. Kamerman and Kahn (2003) highlight seven such rationales that are active in health and welfare policies for children in the industrialised nations:

- there is the view that promoting child welfare is an investment in 'human capital' and that effective children's services contribute to a productive adulthood

- there is a high female labour force participation that needs to be supported by policies to support childcare and maternity and paternity leave

Dimensions of child wellbeing	Average ranking position (for all 6 dimensions)	Dimension 1 Material well-being	Dimension 2 Health and safety	Dimension 3 Educational well-being	Dimension 4 Family and peer relationships	Dimension 5 Behaviours and risks	Dimension 6 Subjective well-being
Netherlands	4.2	10	2	6	3	3	1
Sweden	5.0	1	1	5	15	1	7
Denmark	7.2	4	4	8	9	6	12
Finland	7.5	3	3	4	17	7	11
Spain	8.0	12	6	15	8	5	2
Switzerland	8.3	5	9	14	4	12	6
Norway	8.7	2	8	11	10	13	8
Italy	10.0	14	5	20	1	10	10
Ireland	10.2	19	19	7	7	4	5
Belgium	10.7	7	16	1	5	19	16
Germany	11.2	13	11	10	13	11	9
Canada	11.8	6	13	2	18	17	15
Greece	11.8	15	18	16	11	8	3
Poland	12.3	21	15	3	14	2	19
Czech Republic	12.5	11	10	9	19	9	17
France	13.0	9	7	18	12	14	18
Portugal	13.7	16	14	21	2	15	14
Austria	13.8	8	20	19	16	16	4
Hungary	14.5	20	17	13	6	18	13
United States	18.0	17	21	12	20	20	–
United Kingdom	18.2	18	12	17	21	21	20

An overview of child wellbeing in rich countries (UNICEF, 2007, p. 7)

- there are moral dimensions to child health since children have no control over the families they are born into; some will find themselves born into a poor family and will be adversely affected

- there is concern to increase social solidarity across generations and classes

- there is clear evidence that income inequalities have serious implications for children's health and wellbeing

- there exists a strongly pro-natalist (encouraging births) element in some countries

- there is a focus on children as direct beneficiaries of social, health and economic policies rather than as a part of a family unit in some countries.

Rationales such as these are threaded through a wide range of health and wellbeing policies aimed at children across the UK. Some of them can be seen in, for example, Al Aynsley-Green's foreword to the National Service Framework for Children, Young People and Maternity Services, a ten-year programme to stimulate long-term and sustained improvements in children's health in England, setting standards for children's health and social services and the interface of those services with education. Aynsley-Green, subsequently the first Children's Commissioner for England, was writing as the National Clinical Director for Children.

> Children and young people are important. They are the living message we send to a time we will not see; nothing matters more to families than the health, welfare and future success of their children. They deserve the best care because they are the life-blood of the nation and are vital for our future economic survival and prosperity.
>
> Healthy mothers produce healthy babies who become healthy children and adults; much preventable adult ill health and disease has its roots during gestation, infancy and childhood. Children's vulnerability and the inability when young to articulate what they feel pose a challenge for all those involved in delivering health and social care services to meet their individual needs and those of their carers.
>
> Improving the health and welfare of mothers and their children is the surest way to a healthier nation – the best way to achieve a fairer society for the future is to improve health and tackle inequalities in childhood.
>
> (Aynsley-Green, 2004, webpage)

Thinking point 3.1   Within this quote, can you detect one or more of the rationales that Kamerman and Kahn identified above?

Some of the most common policy trends and the rationales that underpin them can be found in Aynsley-Green's foreword: the impact of poverty and inequalities and the moral dimension of child health policy, the emphasis on early intervention and preventative measures, and the importance given to child health as a national investment for the future. The link with our collective futures is perhaps the most consistent policy rationale to feature in child health and wellbeing.

Children as 'human capital' have been crucial to the 'social investment state' approach identified by Giddens as having become dominant in British politics (Giddens, 1998). In essence this has meant an emphasis on investing in human capital, meaning lifelong learning, family-friendly workplaces, entrepreneurial initiatives, the strengthening of communities and public project partnerships. It also involves a different contract between the individual and the government in which the expansion of individual responsibility is the prime focus (Giddens, 1998). Giddens summed up his vision for the social investment state by inverting the five 'wants' on which Beveridge founded the welfare state in the 1940s:

> Positive welfare would replace each of Beveridge's negatives with a positive: in place of Want, autonomy; not Disease but active health; instead of Ignorance, education, as a continuing part of life; rather than Squalor, well-being, and in place of Idleness, initiative.
>
> (Giddens, 1998, p. 128)

Lister (2003) argues that for children the influence on policy of the 'social investment state' is critical and its key features are repeatedly explicit in major policy speeches and policy documents that impact on children's services and children.

Key features of the social investment state

- Investment in human and social capital and community as emblems.
- Children prioritised as citizen-workers of the future.
- Future-focussed.
- Redistribution of opportunity to promote social inclusion rather than of income to promote equality.
- Adaptation of individuals and society to enhance global competitiveness.
- Integration of social and economic policy, but with the former still the 'handmaiden' of the latter.

(Lister, 2003, p. 459)

The social investment state paradigm may prove a helpful analytical tool to examine developments in children's services. Children have a particular iconic status, but:

It is the child as 'citizen-worker' of the future rather than the 'citizen-child' of the present who is invoked by the new discourse of social investment. Thus despite the prioritising of children, the quality of their childhood risks being overshadowed by a preoccupation with their development as future citizen-workers.

(Lister, 2003, p. 459)

This aspect of the social investment paradigm, its prioritising children but as 'citizen workers' of the future, is increasingly critiqued within policy and practice from the 'new sociology of childhood' approach, with its emphasis on the present wellbeing of children.

On its own a focus on futurity is unbalanced and needs to be accompanied by a concern for the present well-being of children, for their participation in social life and for their opportunities for human self-realisation.

(Prout, 2000, p. 464)

A focus on futurity can be discerned within many central and local programmes within children's health.

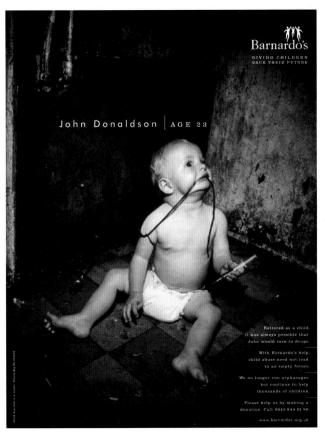

Adult problems are widely understood as being rooted in childhood adversity

If you were to adjust the focus of child health policy from the future of children to their present, which issues might recede, which might come to the fore and which would be looked at differently?

Housing, transport, poverty, wide income differentials, healthy schools, healthy cities, feeling safe, feeling part of a society, being supported in having aspirations, having positive relationships with other children and adults, benefiting from social action programmes that address inequalities, and well-judged interventions in the lives of individuals, all of these affect children in the here and now as well as in the future. We now discuss some of these in more detail.

1.1 Key determinants for child health

Most healthcare and health outcomes are still rooted in individual and family life, and parents will certainly retain the primary responsibility to meet the full range of needs of their children. Trends in children's health, such as the increase in childhood obesity, can cause an extensive amount of media coverage and the media has become a formidable influence on political health issues. However, emerging public health problems are likely only to increase the focus on preventive health measures and therefore on the individual and the family.

Improving childhood for children will always require some collective initiatives and solutions to protect children's health, provide for children's healthcare and support children's participation in and growing level of responsibility for their own health. This will, of course, involve working with parents to support children's healthcare and health choices. It will also involve direct work with children, causing different agencies and organisations to come together and to work in different settings.

Practice box 3.1

In 2003 in Scotland the Minister for Education and Young People announced a free fruit scheme for schoolchildren. Funding meant that 99 per cent of schools in Scotland were supplied with fresh fruit at least three times a week.

In Glasgow, every child between three and twelve in all 381 primary schools, council managed nurseries, and special educational needs establishments were provided with free fruit every day during the school terms. The initiative is part of the Food and Health Framework developed by the Glasgow Healthy City Partnership to promote healthy eating. Partners include Glasgow City Council and the Greater Glasgow NHS Board.

(Scottish Executive, 2007a)

Direct work with children to improve health: free fruit has been given to children in schools

Health inequalities returned to the political agenda following the election of the Labour government in 1997. The effects of class differentials are played out in where you live, where you work, what your income is and in your health. In an era of mass communication, every individual can see how others live, what others buy and what she or he cannot. Poverty not only affects employment and income, but it makes for a deprived and possibly miserable childhood affecting health, wellbeing, education and aspiration. Essentially, poverty can still undermine anything health, social and educational systems attempt to do, and it can overpower good parenting.

Poverty can be rooted in a range of factors: in the actions of individuals; in social factors (those characteristics that define groups of people and/or make them vulnerable to other poverty-inducing factors); in political factors (the extent to which a government is prepared to intervene to tackle poverty, or discrimination, for example); and in economic factors (for example, the strength of the economy and the distribution of income) (McKendrick and Dickie, 2007). Here, for example, are some of the factors that can make certain groups of children particularly vulnerable to poverty.

Life cycle	*children:* limited ability to earn money to lift themselves out of poverty; poverty status dependent on parents
Families and households	*lone parents:* cost and availability of childcare; work–life balance; mismatch between school hours and working hours *partnered parents:* unequal distribution of income among households
Social	*work status:* low-paid jobs; costs associated with 'flexible' workforce *gender:* costs associated with being primary carers of children; gender segregation in labour market; over-concentration of women in lower paid jobs; gender gap in pay; intra-household distribution of income *ethnicity:* language barriers during transitional phases for immigrants; racial harassment and victimisation and stereotyping; tendency to work in low pay sectors of economy *disability/illness:* extra costs associated with managing disability or illness; higher costs associated with shopping locally; costs of caring; discrimination based on stereotyping; disabling environments hampering access
Place	*rural area:* lack of public transport, fewer public services, lower pay, higher cost of living, more restricted employment opportunities

(Adapted from McKendrick and Dickie, 2007)

Of course, some children's lives will be affected by several of these factors simultaneously.

Inequalities are marked, begin before birth and are set to continue. The Millennium Cohort study is following 18,000 babies born in 2000. One of its first measures, taken from the babies' personal child health record at around nine months, was that of 'positive health status', which involves being breast fed for at least one month, having had the immunisations recommended for their age and living with a non-smoking mother during infancy. These factors are recognised as important health indicators for children across Europe (Dex and Joshi, 2005).

In the UK overall, only a third of the babies (37.7%) could be considered to have positive health status according to this measurement. There were marked differences in the percentage with positive health status in different parts of the UK: Northern Ireland 24.1%, Wales 31.9%, Scotland 37.3% and England 42%. Maternal education was also highly significant: the babies of 71.9% of graduate mothers, 50.9% of mothers educated to A/AS/S levels and 19.4% of mothers educated to O levels or equivalent were assessed as having a positive health status. There was already a greater than two-fold difference between babies at nine months whose mothers were in routine and semi-routine occupations and those in managerial or professional occupations (Dex and Joshi, 2005). Moreover by the age of three their cognitive development assessments showed marked differences

Policies have to address many issues affecting children starting any 'race of life'

between children from advantaged and disadvantaged backgrounds. Significantly higher scores were achieved by children with two working parents with high levels of education and higher incomes (Institute of Education, 2007).

There is firm evidence that rates of low birth weight, infant mortality, child mortality, most morbidity (including dental health), child mental health, youth suicide and smoking among girls are all much higher among poor children (Bradshaw, 2003). However, other child health indicators that have worsened, such as asthma and alcohol and illegal drug consumption, do not appear to be associated with poverty (Bradshaw, 2003). There are a mix of explanations for the relationship, or lack of it, between child poverty and health: poor children may be unhealthy because they are genetically less healthy, because the environments in which they live are less healthy, because their behaviour and that of their parents puts them at greater risk of being unhealthy, or because they have less access to health and other services that would enable them to maintain their health (Bradshaw, 2003).

Ridge's study (2006) looked at the effects of children's poverty on their lives, notably participation in social activities, sustaining networks and friendships and being included in the social environment. She found that hiding poverty was especially difficult for children to whom consumer goods, especially clothing and personal accessories, are markers both of individuality and belonging. In childhood, feelings of exclusion can be experienced acutely:

> This is Lewis talking about how he felt when his mum was out of work and his friends were off doing things at the weekends without him:

> Couldn't do nothing on the weekends, just stayed in, couldn't go out with my friends and go to the shop or anything like that, so ... bit boring.

... Alfie is 12 years old ... Although he did not work at the time of the interview, he was very keen to do so. His reasons were clear:

> Then I'll be able to go skating every week, I'll be able to go swimming with my friends. I'll be able to do that.

> (Ridge, 2006, pp. 26, 32)

And lack of money causes problems in the family itself:

> This is Zoe talking about the rise in tensions in her house during the summer holidays:

> We always start rowing all the time 'cos I always ask for money all the time nearly, 'cos I want to go to town and there's nowt else to do ... just to go to town. And every time you go to town you need money.

> ... and children like Hester are struggling to ensure that they are able to conform to their schools' clothing codes:

> My dad he didn't really help with it because he was being a bit nasty at that time. So he was a bit, like, not helping my mum with the money so I was trying not to get my school uniform ripped or dirty or try not to grow so the trousers would get too small or something you know.

> (Ridge, 2006, pp. 27, 30)

The alleviation of child poverty

The alleviation, or even elimination, of child poverty was a highly symbolic and significant aim of the post-1997 Labour governments. After many years of political denial, these governments were the first not only to acknowledge the scale of child poverty, and that children had replaced pensioners as the poorest group in UK society (Brewer and Gregg, 2003), but to take direct responsibility for its abolition. A focus on child poverty was a logical part of central government policy once it decided to move from a more egalitarian model to a discourse of opportunity and social inclusion (Lister, 2003).

The majority of the reports coming from the Social Exclusion Unit in the late 1990s focused on children and young people. Social exclusion describes what happens when people or places encounter a series of combined problems such as unemployment, discrimination, poor skills, low incomes, poor housing, high crime, ill health and family breakdown. According to the Social Exclusion Unit (Cabinet Office, 2006), a child born into the lowest social class is more likely to leave school with no qualifications, to live in relative poverty and to live seven years less than a peer born into the professional classes.

As Platt observed, this area of government policy, like much that had gone before, explicitly drew on the rationale of human capital:

> All children, especially those who are disadvantaged or deprived, need to be equipped properly for the challenges of the new century, so they can achieve their potential (DfEE, 2000, p. 9).

> It is possible to observe in such statements continuing overtones of the tension between childhood as something to be valued in its own right, and children as primarily incipient adults. Moreover, the stress on 'those who are disadvantaged or deprived' indicates that this tension is more palpable in relation to children from poor backgrounds. Their construction as children is subservient to their role as workers and citizens of the future.

> (Platt, 2005, p. 118)

Child poverty was certainly an important issue for the governments led by Tony Blair and Gordon Brown since it led to a commitment to halving child poverty by 2010 and ending it by 2020. The strategy to abolish child poverty had three main components: raising direct financial support to families with children, reducing worklessness in households with children and ameliorating the long-term consequences of child poverty (Brewer and Gregg, 2003). This constituted one of the most ambitious commitments of the New Labour governments. The flagship of their social programmes was an increase in 'child contingent' resources and services, primarily through the Sure Start programme for families with children under four years of age (reshaping and coordinating local services to deliver early intervention services to children and their families) alongside the Children's Fund (launched in 2000 to tackle disadvantage among children and young people through prevention of social exclusion, partnership working and participation).

This level of commitment grew out of an acceptance of the evidence of how the British economy had adversely affected the ability of some adults to secure incomes above the poverty level, the particularly marked deterioration of the position of British children in relation to other groups, and the evidence that deprivation in childhood adversely affected a person's long-term outlook (Brewer and Gregg, 2003). However, policies directed at alleviating child poverty have focused on support through the education system, particularly in the early years, support for parents, primarily to get back into work, no matter how badly paid, and changes to fiscal support for families, and these have been criticised as being misdirected in addressing the real needs, primarily direct financial support, of the poorest of children (Ridge, 2006).

While poverty remains the primary determinant of health, including children's health, this is not necessarily addressed, as Platt points out, when decisions are made about interventions and support for children and families:

> Policy change itself fed into an increasing concern with the situation of the child, which then prompted mobilisation of activity around the issue of child welfare, itself resulting in policy changes and shifts ... Nevertheless, while this marking out of children involves the gradual recognition of children as 'children' first and 'poor' second, such recognition does not result in an unequivocal response to child poverty. The prevailing ideologies of the day, the perception of children as primarily the responsibility of their parents, and the emphasis on engendering a responsible public means that active measures to ameliorate the poverty of children can be resisted.
>
> (Platt, 2005, p. 120)

As Platt suggests, the priorities to be addressed by social programmes are constantly redefined. Children, as both a private and a public responsibility, remain both an immediate and long-term issue for British (and all other) governments. As we have seen, the concept of social exclusion has been fundamental to post-1997 Labour government policy and service development to address the interlocking problems of unemployment, environmental degeneration, poor public services and inequalities in health. The anti child poverty approach in Britain has been firmly part of the government's 'opportunity' agenda (Brewer and Gregg, 2003; Lister, 2003).

Targeted interventions

The explicit linking of certain problems – poor child health, poor educational achievement, anti-social behaviour, limited employment opportunities and a poor neighbourhood – led to an analysis focused on problems as concentrated in certain geographical areas. This, in turn, indicated intervention based primarily in localities. However, Barnes and Prior (2000) identified a fundamental weakness of this analysis:

> It is this [analysis] which provides the impetus for the Labour government's attempts both to achieve institutional change in government responses to problems and to encourage agencies in both the public and private sectors at the local level to work together to address the cross cutting issues involved. What is not clear in the government's analysis of the localised character of social exclusion is whether it is the characteristics of particular localities which give rise to this, or whether the exclusionary

impact of broader social and economic change (globalisation for example) is experienced inequitably within different localities.

(Barnes and Prior, 2000, p. 96)

Barnes and Prior went on to identify three key changes to welfare provision that arose from this kind of analysis. First, that service delivery had to become issue- and locality-based. Second, that there needed to be an increased focus on people as members of communities and communities as places in which people enact their citizenship, receive welfare and create the conditions for their own wellbeing. Third was the identification of communities as deliverers of public policy and creators of solutions, as well as the location within which interacting problems can be understood and addressed.

A primary example of this was the Sure Start local programme. Sure Start was inspired by Head Start in the USA, which, from the 1960s, developed into an extensive programme to open out poor communities to social action, offering healthcare, job training and other resources, and aiming to raise the achievement of three- and four-year-olds in poor neighbourhoods to the level of their middle-class counterparts. Sure Start (Children and Youth Support Fund in Wales) brought together early education, childcare, health and family support in designated areas, delivering them through a network across the UK. Its efficacy and cost-effectiveness in reaching its stated goals is undergoing thorough evaluation.

The interactive dimensions of child health

Child health involves constants, such as the social determinants and distribution of health, recent developments such as the growth in the incidence of childhood obesity, issues rooted in the choices people can make and issues rooted in the environments of childhood.

Thinking point 3.3   Can you identify other constant and new issues for children's health? Why are some of the main issues constant? What brings one of these issues as opposed to another to the top of a government's agenda, leading to new policies and the allocation of resources?

The Commission for Healthcare Audit and Inspection offered this snapshot of the situation and issues:

Children are healthier than ever before and death in childhood is rare. The rate of infant death in England and Wales fell to its lowest recorded level in 2004, and there have been considerable reductions in unintentional injury, which is the most common cause of death among children ...

There remains, however, a substantial difference in the rates of death in children from different social classes. The rise in the prevalence of childhood obesity is well-documented, and Britain has among the highest percentages of children who consume alcohol in the world. The number of children with disabilities also increased by 62% between 1975 and 2002. This is, in part, associated with the increasing number of infants surviving premature birth, birth with abnormalities, or other health problems.

(Commission for Healthcare Audit and Inspection, 2007, p. 8)

Within healthcare there is a constant tension; health and health care are at one and the same time private and public, and at one and the same time the domain of individuals and of governments. There is an interplay between, on the one hand, children, their parents and carers and what they understand the issues to be and how they see the responsibilities of themselves and others, and, on the other, how a particular society at a particular time sees fit to invest in child health and wellbeing. There may be a genuine concern for the plight of poor children, but the response judged appropriate will be influenced by, for example, the extent to which parents are considered responsible for the family income. There have been high levels of political will and consensus concerning the importance of children's welfare at other times, most notably in the years following the Second World War, but political will can dissipate without fundamental change having taken place (Platt, 2005).

While child poverty has been a specific target of government policy and resources, other factors may prove a counterweight to any achievements in this area. Social mobility, for example, where children from the most and least affluent families begin and end up in the earning or income distribution of adults, has fallen in Britain. A study by Blanden et al. (2005) showed intergenerational mobility was less for the generation born in 1970 than the generation born in 1958. Because we are comparing the earnings or incomes of one generation with those of their parents, it takes a minimum of thirty years to measure social mobility, so the decline in social mobility we see in the first decade of the twenty-first century is a reflection of influences on children from the 1970s and 1980s. The Blanden et al. study found social mobility to be primarily the result of the link between family income and educational attainment, as the expansion of higher education since the 1980s has disproportionately benefited those from more affluent families.

Health contributes to *human*, *social* and *identity* capital. Individuals and governments have vested interests in all three (Schuller et al., 2004):

  human capital – the knowledge and skills possessed by individuals that enable them to function economically and socially;

social capital – the networks and norms by which people contribute effectively to common goals;

identity capital – the characteristics of the individual that define his or her outlook and self-image, including ego strength and self-esteem, but recognising that many of the components of individual capital are socially shaped and not inherent personality traits.

The relationship between health and healthcare and human, social and identity capital can be detected and improved at various levels. At an individual level, for example, children can be routinely given the information, power and choice they need to see themselves as active partners in their own healthcare rather than passive recipients of services. At the family level, for example, intervention or targeted services can and do deliver improvements for the poorest sections of the community. The majority of poor children do not, however, live in poor communities, but are distributed, less visibly, across many communities, so public health measures need to work through universal services. At the level of communities and neighbourhoods, children's physical health and activity needs to be supported by nice, safe environments for children to walk, cycle and, perhaps most importantly, play in.

At the level of services, these have to respond to the concept that health and wellbeing have different interactive dimensions. Universal services need to be capable, resourced and committed to contributing to children's health and wellbeing. Preventative and early intervention based on timely and comprehensive assessment is believed to be essential (DH, 2005; Scottish Executive, 2007b; Office of the First Minister and Deputy First Minister Northern Ireland, 2006). This needs joint assessment records and plans,

Play makes an important contribution to children's overall level of health and wellbeing, but places to play can be difficult to find

skills development and more information for parents and practitioners. Health is a multi-layered, multi-faceted concept, so children's services need to be integrated, coherent and cohesive; barriers between the voluntary, independent and public sector services need to continue to be broken down (DH, 2005; Scottish Executive, 2007b; DfES, 2005).

An approach to children's health through multi-agency working and working towards common outcomes will most benefit children's wellbeing. This is variously defined but includes being healthy, enjoying, learning and achieving, living in safety and with stability, experiencing economic and environmental wellbeing, contributing positively to a community and society, and living in a society which respects children's rights (Office of the First Minister and Deputy First Minister Northern Ireland, 2006). England's Change for Children programme and Wales's Children First are based on similar goals, which have become the focus of all policy and service development at national and local level.

Key points

1 An international perspective on children's health and wellbeing supports comparison and motivates the development of policies to improve children's lives.

2 Children's health and wellbeing policy and practice need to be as much about the here and now as the future.

3 Health and healthcare are at one and the same time private and public, the domain of individuals and of governments.

4 Poverty remains the key determinant of health.

5 It has become an explicit aim of national governments in the UK to reduce child poverty and social exclusion in order to improve children's health.

2 Child health: protection, participation and provision

Recognition of the contexts in which healthcare takes place has been very much part of public health and public health policy since the late 1990s. The model in the 'policy rainbow' diagram may help us to think through the interactivity between the different determinants of health. Dahlgren's model illustrates a series of factors both within and beyond an individual's control.

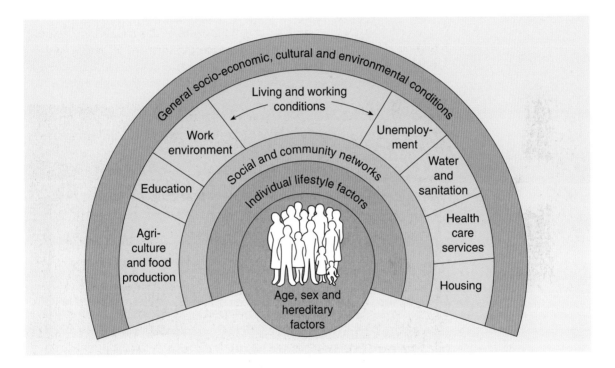

The policy rainbow (Dahlgren, 1995, in World Health Organization, 2004, p. 10)

The ways in which people make decisions about their individual lifestyles, how they look after their health and what they do when they believe they are ill are affected by a number of factors, including: the messages they are given about their health; what health and illness means to them; and the personal resources they have to support their health and health behaviour (Barnes and Prior, 2000).

Public health measures generate considerable capacity for debate and disputation. The public health and medical professions have been joined by the media in offering an extensive amount of guidance and information on health and healthcare, including that for parents of young children.

The 'new public health' has also been considered as an example of 'a new morality' (Peterson and Lupton, 1996) which operates in a rather different way from the old public health with its emphasis on explicit regulation and control. The new morality operates through mechanisms based in consumerist notions of choice – 'we will give you the information, it's up to you to make use of that information in order to choose the healthy option'.

(Barnes and Prior, 2000, p. 68)

Health education and health promotion combine in this 'consumerist notion'. While education provides information on which decisions may or may not be made, health promotion is a more active process, engaging people, including children, as individuals and groups to improve their own health.

Health, within health promotion and within health policy more broadly, is frequently expressed as contributing to personal lives through a positive sense of self and, often explicitly, the individual's capacity to be an employed, active citizen. This approach to health relies primarily on the element of self-regulation, which needs to operate within the domestic,

The internet offers new ways for children to access information, including health-related information

personal and intimate lives of individuals. A prominent feature of a primarily self-regulated relationship between the state and the citizen relates to personal responsibility to minimise risks to one's health and that of one's children. (See Chapter 5 for further discussion of risk in the lives of children.) This approach can, however, exhibit an element of coercion, for example in the representation of obesity as an unacceptable loss of self-control (Barnes and Prior, 2000). There also needs to be an awareness of the medicalisation of certain emotional difficulties, behaviours and needs, for example with regard to the debate around the diagnosis and medication of children with ADHD.

People can also hold a notion of a 'right' to health, but this too can be a complex idea:

> The notion of an individual 'right to health' sits uneasily alongside an acknowledgement that improving public health requires action designed to create the conditions in which the collective health of the population can be ensured. The concept of 'health' is also acknowledged to be a socially constructed and contested one. Defining an objective measure of health status to which citizens, individually or collectively, could be entitled may be impossible. There is also the question of whether the state should force people to be healthy – should there not also be an equivalent right to be unhealthy if that is the choice of the individual?
>
> (Barnes and Prior, 2000, pp. 65–66)

The idea of good health as an entitlement for all raises some difficult questions. More difficult questions arise if we consider that some children may lack the power to make choices for themselves. Should children be allowed to choose to be unhealthy? Should we focus only on giving information and advice? We argued in section 1 that the child as a social investment is a forceful rationale underpinning a range of children's health and wellbeing policies and practices. Perhaps what is more workable is a clear and concerted focus on what we can do to contribute to a healthier environment for children.

2.1 Healthy environments for children

Homes, schools, nurseries, hospitals, after-school clubs, a childminder's house, playgrounds – these are the kinds of 'human geography' most prevalent in childhood. As Gallagher reminds us, places are as much social as physical phenomena:

> A central idea in human geography is that spaces, bodies and identities are mutually constitutive, and children's geographers have attempted to demonstrate not only the difference that space

and place make to childhood, but also the difference that children make to the spaces and places in which they live.

(Gallagher, 2006, p. 160)

Thinking point 3.4   Can you think of some ways in which children's spaces and places are, or should be, 'mutually constituted'?

Human geography, a useful element of childhood studies, can contribute significantly to the development of practice and healthy environments for children. Analysis using a human geography approach will encourage reflection on how decisions are made about resourcing and developing children's services.

The creation of spaces by adults *with* children rather than *for* them may also usefully be related to the classic sociological approach of agency and structure:

> Agency, understood as the ability to rule oneself autonomously by acts of will power, can no longer be seen merely as part of human nature. Rather, it is the outcome of the processes of subject formation carried out by institutional structures – particularly through their spatial practices. ... The power of structures ... depends on the agencies of all individuals involved. Understood in this way, the power of agents and the power of structures appear not as mutually exclusive opposites, but rather as entirely co-dependent.
>
> (Gallagher, 2006, p. 164)

Recognition of the power of children as agents can be of immense benefit to the development of good practice and quality services. Many academics and practitioners have emphasised the importance of listening to children about the quality of services, and this is reflected in much ongoing reflective and responsive practice.

Moss (2006) sees listening to children as part of ethical practice:

> my argument has been that listening is an expression of rights, and that rights have an important part to play. But listening, I think, is also an expression of an ethical practice. Listening is the ethics of an encounter. It is also the expression of democratic practice. Because if we are able to recognise difference, to accept different interpretations and engage in dialogue, then we are conducting democratic practice. And if we bring listening into our work and our practice, then we are making ethics and politics first practice in early childhood education.
>
> (Moss, 2006, p. 23)

Practice box 3.2

The Bog Standard Awards

Through listening to children, the Healthy School Team in Sandwell, Birmingham found that school toilets were a major concern. Criteria include children should be able to use the toilet whenever they need to, toilet cubicles must be private and have doors that lock, toilets must be free from bullies and smokers, toilets must be looked after properly and not smell, warm water and soap must be provided, as well as towels or hand dryers.

(Bog Standard, 2007)

A prize winner in the National Bog Standard awards

Moss is here specifically talking about rooting rights and ethics as complementary approaches within early years work, but these principles are equally important for those working with children in all settings. There may be a long way to go. In hospitals, for example, the level of skills in communication and choice for children remains poor given the large number of children who come into contact with hospitals each year, primarily through accident and emergency departments (nearly three million, more than 28 per cent of all children in England) (Commission for Healthcare Audit and Inspection, 2007):

> The level of training in communication with children is poor, especially in outpatients' departments and among surgical and anaesthetic staff. Effective communication between health professionals and children is extremely important. If children understand their treatment, they will be less scared and more able to cope. If professionals are trained to understand the way children, even those unable to talk, communicate, they will be able to provide better treatment, including more appropriate pain relief. Being able to communicate effectively with children also helps staff to fulfil their responsibilities for safeguarding children.

The *United Nations Convention on the Rights of the Child* states that children have a right to be involved in decisions about their care.

(Commission for Healthcare Audit and Inspection, 2007, p. 34)

Reflective, participative and ethical practice: these approaches are vital to health promotion and healthcare with children. Children's involvement, on both a rights and an ethics basis, in choice, individual decision making and collectively making judgements on the quality, planning, delivery and evaluation of health promotion and health services is vital to children's quality of life.

> I don't like coming into hospital. It can be scary and I want my mum and dad. It would be good to have new books and toys for older children. I would also like to see a nicer football table.
>
> (Katie, 9)
>
> I like push-along toys and having a dolly with me. I don't like going into the clinic. It makes me scream.
>
> (Alicia, 3)
>
> I like it that people keep me informed of what's happening. It is easy to get around, but the canteens and shops aren't always open. The hospital should have a room for older children and older toys because the ones they have are too babyish. It should also have more Playstations, TVs, DVDs, and videos.
>
> (Catherine, 11)
>
> I like painting and using the computer. I didn't get much sleep in hospital because babies were crying.
>
> (Michael, 9)

(Children quoted in *Children Now*, 2004, p. 21)

A review of children's participation in health policy development and practice (Franklin and Sloper, 2005) concluded that although the involvement of children is recognised, on the basis of the growing body of evidence demonstrating children's competence to be involved in decision making about their own health and care, there was no evidence yet to suggest this was widespread practice. Competence is dependent on relationships; healthcare decisions and the involvement of children in them will reflect the accompanying information and support (Alderson and Montgomery, 1996). Franklin and Sloper (2005) identified the following as important to the success of participatory work with children in healthcare:

- clarity of purpose and honesty about what participation will involve and achieve

- staff training and development, particularly concerning communication skills and recognising evolving competency

- using flexible and appropriate methods;

- changes to organisational cultures and structures;

- assessments of the evidence and impact of children's participation.

2.2 Health behaviour

The health behaviour of school-aged children is the subject of a long-running study by the World Health Organization (2004). The study has conducted cross-national research with children aged eleven, thirteen and fifteen at four-yearly intervals. About 1500 respondents in each of the three age groups are involved in each of thirty-five countries. The data yields some fascinating material, not least in observing the way certain dimensions of children's wellbeing come to the fore at different points in time. Children's friendship groups, for example, have become part of the study, recorded through questions about how many close friends children had, how many days a week they spent time with friends after school, how many evenings a week they spent out with their friends, and how often to they talked to friends on the phone or sent them text messages or emails.

The survey noted childhood as a period of increasing health inequalities (WHO, 2004). The report also highlighted the following key issues for those creating policy or implementing policy into practice with regard to children's health and health behaviour.

- While evidence suggests that most young people perceive themselves as healthy and are satisfied with life, significant proportions ... are engaged in lifestyle behaviour that can harm their health.

- The survey demonstrates a number of gender and age differences in health experience ... Age and gender-specific polices and programmes would enhance the possibility of promoting equal opportunities for young people to secure and maintain health and wellbeing.

- Life circumstances – including the wealth and structure of the family and social support from the family, peers and the school environment – influence health. Over 70% of what determines health is estimated to lie outside the scope of health services and can be attributed to demographic, social, economic and environmental conditions.

- The improvement of health and the reduction of health inequalities can only be brought about by concerted effort at a number of levels.

The report also emphasised that a shift in thinking is needed to prioritise gathering the views of young people and involving them in the process. It argued that research has increasingly demonstrated that young people do not react passively to health behaviour they witness, or that forms part of their education, but rather they have well-defined attitudes and clear views about health and social inequality and see themselves as capable of being actors in working for change (WHO, 2004).

Backett-Milburn's (2000) research into lay accounts of health and illness among children and parents demonstrated the engagement of children and young people in negotiating those tensions that arise between current understandings of healthy lifestyles and their enactment in everyday life. Adults and children both appeared to use activity levels as the main means of conceptualising the healthy body. The active body was also clearly linked with social functioning. Backett-Milburn's study suggested that while all members of the family were familiar with the main messages of the healthy lifestyle advice, more complex issues arose in the translation of these into day-to-day life. Children knew about healthy food, for example, but didn't connect it easily with benefits to themselves. And there was uncertainty about what it meant to be healthy (as opposed to being unhealthy), or what resulted from positive health behaviours.

Backett-Millburn concluded that children, like adults, made day-to-day decisions partly through negotiations with adults, but also using their own conceptualisations of health and their own lived experience.

> Like adults, many of their decisions about body management were also made pragmatically and for non-health-related reasons. Thus, for example, almost all identified fruit and vegetables as good for health and the body, but only a few claimed either to like vegetables or to eat them regularly. Similarly, exercise of the body was seen to have as much of a social as a health payoff, and decisions about eating the contents of a school packed lunch were affected by time availability, the lure of playtime and the approval of certain foods by friends.
>
> (Backett-Millburn, 2000, p. 98)

People's knowledge of health behaviour has a complicated relationship with their health-related decisions and the places where these decisions are made. Rhiannon Oldershaw, a researcher at the Open University Children's Research Centre, carried out a research project to find out whether children eat a balanced diet, looking at packed lunches and using food diaries, and found that crisps rather than fruit or vegetables were the most popular food item.

As a child herself, Oldershaw's contribution illustrates another point: children can be the subjects rather than the objects of research and thus make another contribution to their own healthcare.

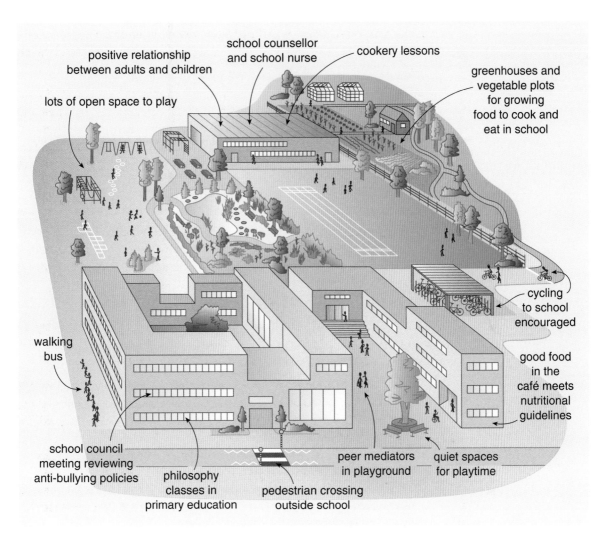

positive relationship
between adults and children

school counsellor
and school nurse

cookery lessons

greenhouses and
vegetable plots
for growing
food to cook and
eat in school

lots of open space to play

walking
bus

cycling
to school
encouraged

good food
in the
café meets
nutritional
guidelines

school council
meeting reviewing
anti-bullying policies

philosophy
classes in
primary education

pedestrian crossing
outside school

peer mediators
in playground

quiet spaces
for playtime

In the 21st century a 'healthy school' needs a broad application

Practice box 3.3   Healthy schools

The National Healthy Schools Programme in England has four themes:

- personal, social and health education (PSHE), including sex and relationships (SRE) and drugs education
- healthy eating
- physical activity
- emotional health and wellbeing, including bullying.

The four core themes relate to both the school curriculum and the emotional and physical learning environment in school. Each theme includes a number of

> criteria that schools need to fulfil in order to achieve National Healthy School Status. Although each theme covers a different area, they are all delivered using the whole-school approach, so the basic requirements are the same.
>
> (Healthy Schools, 2007 webpage)

Children's services, particularly universal services such as schools, have the capacity to contribute to children's health, resilience and emotional wellbeing and they are increasingly explicit in addressing these outcomes. However, health education is still not a part of the national curriculum. Schools have been criticised for not giving enough priority to looking at the extent to which personal, social and health education is changing attitudes and behaviour, and too few schools involve children in the type of policy development that would enable them to better meet children's needs (OFSTED, 2005).

Practice box 3.4

Schools may further develop their skills and model behaviour that can address the mental and emotional dimensions of children's health. Ofsted urges schools and other settings to:

- use the DfES national guidance on mental health difficulties to develop clear procedures that are known and used by all staff, for identifying and supporting pupils

- ensure that issues concerning mental health are tackled successfully. Either through the National Healthy School Standard (NHSS) programme or the PSHE curriculum

- establish arrangements for preventing bullying and promoting positive relationships and monitor their effectiveness

- work together to ensure that the DfES guidance is disseminated to all staff.

(Ofsted, 2005, webpage)

Most people would agree that young children need a sustained, positive relationship with at least one adult carer, but those who work with children can also make a significant contribution to promoting their mental and emotional wellbeing. Children's mental health and emotional health is a widespread issue for practitioners and one which more practitioners need an understanding of; one in ten children in England and Wales – over a million – has a mental health disorder, with prevalence rates significantly higher for some vulnerable groups (DH, 2005).

Schools can, for example, address why children within schools become so socially stratified, with some children being pushed to the margins of a predictable social circle which constitutes acceptability and popularity

Schools are now directly addressing social and emotional wellbeing through ideas such as friendship benches in playgrounds

(Billington and Pomerantz, 2004). Circle time, buddy schemes and other similar strategies in schools have directly tried to strengthen children's resilience and reduce bullying (see Chapter 2). Emotional exploration and support has evolved from listening to stories, for example, to circle time, which is a ritual that involves encouraging children to talk about issues relating to their peer and family relationships and encouraging them to listen, be open with each other and empathise with others. Buddy schemes offer peer support to children who are dealing with potential traumas such as starting a new school, bullying and difficulties with friendships.

How much these strategies are related to the development of positive relationships between children and between children and adults will remain debateable. There are, or should be, accompanying doubts about how children actually experience methods such as circle time; it may be found by some children to be boring or intrusive and might give rise to feelings of pity rather than empathy. And some issues such as homophobic bullying remain unaddressed by too many schools. Homophobic bullying can be dealt with in exactly the same way as racial bullying – a zero tolerance policy backed with legislation and education programmes for practitioners in how to deal with homophobia.

Schools specifically impact on children's health and this impact may be increased if and when schools become multi-agency settings. The New Community Schools initiative in Scotland was among the first to grasp multi-agency work: social work, health, psychology and other professionals came together in selected schools, nurseries and family centres from 1999 (Literacy Trust, 2007). Multi-agency working out of multi-professional settings, with an emphasis on early intervention, is seen as a crucial way to tackle the effects of social deprivation and prevent failures of child protection. This model was picked up by the Department for Education and Skills in England, who set up a strategy to implement the government's goal that, over time, every primary school will be able to offer childcare from 8 a.m. to 6 p.m. all year round, a wide range of study support activities, parenting support opportunities and swift and easy referral to a wide range of specialist support services for pupils (DfES, 2005).

A range of children's health services are increasingly working from school sites, with an emphasis on early preventative work. The driving idea behind extended schools is to provide a range of support schemes such as out-of-hours childcare, healthcare for children and their families, and adult education. So a school-based community worker, a nurse, a police officer, a community link worker, a mental health adviser, a student services manager, an attendance manager and a learning mentor can together discuss a child they are worried about. The idea is to build a complete picture of the problems children face in and outside of school.

Thinking point 3.5   What are the advantages and disadvantages of schools providing more health and social services to children?

Schools, it could be argued, are singularly ill-equipped to tackle inequalities in health, since education often reflects wider inequalities rather than diminishing them. Middle-class parents, for example, have been much more able to manipulate the education system to their advantage (Blanden et al., 2005). For those children who are not at school, making schools the conduit of health and social services will present further difficulties: how will children who live a long way from school, who are excluded, or who are home educated, use services if they have to go through schools?

Home schooling is an increasingly favoured option for children who have difficulties with ordinary school

There is considerable debate, for example, around whether schools are the appropriate place to help children with family and behavioural problems as these children are quite likely to be dissatisfied with school. So, as Craig pointed out, developments in schools should raise some questions:

> When we talk about the 'extended school' what is being extended? By whom, to who? Does our vision of what we can offer match their vision of what they need? It turns out that, in our fragmented and diverse society, the very notion of a community to extend into is not as simple as it seems. The central challenge of extended schooling is legitimacy – it is about engaging with a community, and with the other agencies inside the community, in a manner that invites their participation, ownership, even leadership.
>
> (Craig et al., 2004, p. 2)

Taking a broad perspective, good schools can contribute to children's health through their core purpose, education. In a study of adult learners, Schuller et al. (2004) came to the conclusion that education can enhance all health outcomes through enabling individuals to see, perhaps understand, their lives in a broader context:

> This is achieved through raising self-esteem and feelings of efficacy, broadening people's knowledge, understanding and attitudes, providing alternatives and opportunities ... generating a sense of purpose and future, and through greater social integration. There is an expansion from looking inwards to looking outwards, which has positive effects on health along the whole of the mental health continuum and enables individuals to cope more effectively with ill-health and other types of adversity. Perhaps this conclusion is what one would expect, because learning must always be about questioning and extending boundaries. Nevertheless, it is an important one because it is a crucial aspect of learning in relation to the generation of wider benefits, and one that distinguishes it from other activities.
>
> (Schuller et al., 2004, p. 56)

Thinking point 3.6   Could these points be equally applied to children?

Through education children gain a broader and deeper level of knowledge, understanding and attitudes with which to make sense of the world, including the issues associated with health, health behaviour and health outcomes. It might also be possible to see education as an important component of a child's identity capital, since education comes next to family and occupation in people's understanding of and confidence in their own identities (Schuller et al., 2004).

Key points

1   To be able to achieve their optimum health and wellbeing, including developing healthy lifestyles, children need education about health as a social as well as an individual phenomenon. They need to experience health promotion and prevention of ill health and this has to be backed by good preventive and treatment services.

2   Healthier environments for children can result from reflective, participative and ethical practice.

3   Preventative work, early intervention and multi-agency working are explicit across the policy trends for children's health across the UK. Schools are increasingly identified as prime sites to improve children's health, but there will be disadvantages as well as advantages to this strategy.

Conclusion

Each child's health is a product of a personal, social, economic and environmental context, but there is a question over whose overall responsibility it is: the child and the parents, or the government and its agencies. The solutions to health issues will depend on which questions are asked and when. Analysis of children's healthcare policies and services can reveal how much they are the product of competing and changing factors, but also how much they are influenced by the status of childhood and of children. Healthcare and health behaviour will remain very much part of people's private lives, despite professions having been very successful in colonising a broad range of human experience as territory about which they have knowledge (Barnes and Prior, 2000).

Undoubtedly, many people and many settings are contributing consistently and fundamentally to children's quality of life. These contributions have involved choices; these choices and decisions shape childhood services (Moss and Petrie, 2002). This may be a good sentence to end with; it is from the report we began with, from UNICEF:

> A true measure of a nation's standing is how well it attends to children – their health and safety, their material security, their education and socialization, and their sense of being loved, valued and included in the families and societies into which they are born.
>
> (UNICEF, 2007, p. 1)

References

Alderson, P. and Montgomery, J. (1996) *Health Care Choices: Making Decisions with Children*, London, Institute of Public Policy Research.

Aynsley-Green, A. (2004) *Foreword to the national service framework for children, young people and maternity services*, available online at <http://www.devonchildrenstrust.org.uk/nsf_child_exec_summary.pdf>, accessed 4 June 2007

Backett-Milburn, K. (2000) 'Children, parents and the construction of the "healthy body" in middle-class families' in Prout, A. (ed.) *The Body, Childhood and Society*, Basingstoke, Macmillan Press.

Barnes, M. and Prior, D. (2000) *Private Lives as Public Policy*, Birmingham, Venture Press.

Billington, T. and Pomerantz, M. (2004) 'Resisting social exclusion' in Billington, T. and Pomerantz, M. (eds) *Children at the Margins: Supporting Children, Supporting Schools*, Stoke on Trent, Trentham Books.

Blanden, J., Gregg, P. and Machin, S. (2005) *Intergenerational mobility in Europe and North America*, available online at <http://cep.lse.ac.uk/about/news/IntergenerationalMobility.pdf>, accessed 4 June 2007.

Bog Standard (2007) *Promoting better toilets for pupils*, available online at <http://www.bog-standard.org/index.aspx>, accessed 14 August 2007.

Bradshaw, J. (2003) 'Child poverty and child health in international perspective' in Hallett, C. and Prout, A. (eds) (2003) *Hearing the Voices of Children: Social Policy for a New Century*, London, Routledge Falmer.

Brewer, M. and Gregg, P. (2003) 'Eradicating child poverty in Britain: welfare reform and children since 1997' in Walker, R. and Wiseman, M. (eds) *The Welfare We Want? The British Challenge for American Reform*, Bristol, The Policy Press.

Cabinet Office (2006) *Social exclusion*, available online at <http://archive.cabinetoffice.gov.uk/seu>, accessed 14 August 2007.

Children Now (2004) 'Children's voices', 25 February–2 March.

Commission for Healthcare Audit and Inspection (2007) *Improvement review into services for children in hospital*, available online at <http://www.healthcarecommission.org.uk/serviceproviderinformation/reviewsandinspections/improvementreviews/servicesforchildreninhospital.cfm>, accessed 21 May 2007.

Craig, J., Huber, J. and Lownsbrough, H. (2004) *Schools Out: Can Teachers, Social Workers and Health Staff Learn to Live Together?*, London, Demos.

Dahlgren, G. (1995) *European Health Policy Conference: Opportunities for the Future. Vol. 2. Intersectoral Action for Health*, Copenhagen, WHO Regional Office for Europe.

Department for Education and Skills (DfES) (2005) *Common core of skills and knowledge for the children's workforce*, available online at <http://www.everychildmatters.gov.uk/deliveringservices/commoncore>, accessed 14 August 2007.

Department of Health (DH) (2005) *Choosing health: making healthy choices easier*, available online at <http://www.dh.gov.uk/en/publicationsandstatistics/publications/publicationspolicyandguidance/dh_4094550>, accessed 10 October 2007.

Dex, S. and Joshi, H. (eds) (2005) *Children of the Twenty-first Century: From Birth to Nine Months*, Bristol, The Policy Press.

Dudley Children's Fund (2007) *Ask Me!*, available online at <http://www.askme.org.uk/nsd/search/child/nsdDudley.aspx>, accessed 15 August 2007.

Franklin, A. and Sloper, P. (2005) 'Listening and responding? Children's participation in health care within England', *International Journal of Children's Rights*, vol. 13, pp. 11–29.

Gallagher, M. (2006) 'Spaces of participation and inclusion?' in Tisdall, E.K.M., Davis, J. M., Prout, A. and Hill, M. (eds) *Children, Young People and Social Inclusion: Participation for What?*, Bristol, The Policy Press.

Giddens, A. (1998) *The Third Way: The Renewal of Social Democracy*, Cambridge, Polity Press.

Healthy Schools (2007) *National healthy schools programme*, available online at <http://www.healthyschools.gov.uk>, accessed 5 July 2007.

Institute of Education, University of London (2007) *Millenium cohort study* (2nd survey), available online at <http://ioewebserver.ioe.ac.uk/ioe/cms/get.asp? cid=6194&6194_0=8239>, accessed 14 August 2007.

Kamerman, S.B. and Kahn, A.J. (2003) 'Child and family policies in an era of social policy retrenchment and restructuring' in Vleminckx, K. and Smeeding, T.M. (eds) *Child Well-being, Child Poverty and Child Policy in Modern Nations* (revised edn), Bristol, The Policy Press.

Lister R. (2003) 'Investing in the citizen-workers of the future' in Hendrick, H. (ed.) (2005) *Child Welfare and Social Policy: An Essential Reader*, Bristol, The Policy Press.

Literacy Trust (2007) *Integrated (new) community schools – Scotland*, available online at <http://www.literacytrust.org.uk/Database/community.html>, accessed 5 July 2007.

McKendrick, J.H. and Dickie, J. (2007) 'Factors leading to poverty' in McKendrick, J.H., Mooney, G., Dickie, J. and Kelly, P. (eds) *Poverty in Scotland 2007*, London, Child Poverty Action Group (CPAG).

Moss, P. (2006) *Let's Talk About Listening to Children: Towards a Shared Understanding for Early Years Education in Scotland*, Edinburgh, Learning and Teaching Scotland.

Moss, P. and Petrie, P. (2002) *From Children's Services to Children's Spaces: Public Policy, Children and Childhood*, London, Routledge Falmer.

Office of the First Minister and Deputy First Minister Northern Ireland (2006) *Children and young people's unit*, available online at <http://www.allchildrenni.gov.uk>, accessed 30 May 2007.

Ofsted (2005) *Healthy Minds: promoting emotional well-being in schools*, available online at <http://www.ofsted.gov.uk/assets/3954.pdf>, accessed 10 October 2007.

Peterson, A. and Lupton, D. (1996) *The New Public Health: Health and Self in an Age of Risk*, London, Sage.

Platt, L. (2005) *Discovering Child Poverty: The Creation of a Policy Agenda from 1800 to the Present*, Bristol, The Policy Press.

Prout, A. (2000) 'Children's participation: control and self realisation in British late modernity' in Hendrick, H. (ed.) *Child Welfare and Social Policy: An Essential Reader*, Bristol, The Policy Press.

Ridge, T. (2006) 'Childhood poverty: a barrier to social participation and inclusion' in Tisdall, E.K.M., Davis, J.M., Prout, A. and Hill, M. (eds) *Children, Young People and Social Inclusion: Participation for What?*, Bristol, The Policy Press.

Schuller, T., Preston, J., Hammond, C., Brassett-Grundy, A. and Bynner, J. (2004) *The Benefits of Learning: The Impact of Education on Health, Family Life and Social Capital*, London, Routledge Falmer.

Scottish Executive (2007a) *Fit futures: focus on food, activity and young people. Research paper 2. Childhood obesity in Scotland*, available online at <http://www.investingforhealthni.gov.uk/documents/Scotland.pdf>, accessed 31 July 2007.

Scottish Executive (2007b) *Delivering a healthy future: an action framework for children and young people's health in Scotland*, available online at <http://www.scotland.gov.uk/Publications/2007/02/14154246/0>, accessed 5 July 2007.

UNICEF (2007) *Child Poverty in Perspective: An Overview of Child Well-being in Rich Countries*, Innocenti Report Card 7, Florence, UNICEF Innocenti Research Centre.

United Nations (1989) *United Nations Convention on the Rights of the Child (UNCRC)*, Geneva, United Nations.

World Health Organization (WHO) (2004) *Young People's Health in Context: Health Behaviour in School-aged Children*, Copenhagen, World Health Organization.

Chapter 4

Play matters

Doug Springate and Pam Foley

Introduction

There remains a general acceptance in western societies that play is vital for the wellbeing and healthy development of children. It is understood to be an essential part of human life, particularly early life, leading to learning and development. However, it is its value in relation to children's wellbeing rather than its function that is our primary focus here. The first and second sections of this chapter give an overview of the main theories and debates around play and their relationship to policy and practice development. The second half of the chapter discusses the social and cultural aspects of play. Here, we take a comparative approach, comparing and contrasting work in the UK with another Western European country to enable examination and consideration of the importance of play to present and perhaps future children's services.

Core questions

- What are the common threads within the leading theories and debates around play?
- What is the relationship between play and children's emotional and social wellbeing?
- What characterises and influences play?
- How can practitioners support play and its contribution to the wellbeing of children?

1 What is playing about?

Play is clearly something of great importance to children, but it can be difficult for adults to grasp fully its function and value. Adults may have a well-founded nervousness of making incursions into the worlds children inhabit through play. While the worlds of children are sometimes startlingly opened out to observers as they play, observing, participating, researching and analysing children's play is difficult since both adults and children live with powerfully informed definitions of 'adult' and 'child'. Some significant thinkers, most prominently perhaps Piaget, focused on children's play. He carried out some incisive experiments and analysis, drawing on historical, anthropological, sociological, linguistic and literary approaches and understandings, and on the experimental methods of the behavioural sciences (Piaget, 1962; Bruner et al., 1976). By the 1960s and 1970s much had emerged from a variety of disciplines about the significance of play. The Opies' extensive studies of children's play and children's games, for example, provided some fascinating insights into the distinctive value of play.

> Play is unrestricted, games have rules ... it will be noticed that when children play a game in the street they ... seldom need an umpire, they rarely trouble to keep scores, little significance is attached to who wins or loses, they do not require the stimulus of prizes, it does not seem to worry them if a game is not finished ... They like games which restart almost automatically, so that everybody is given a new chance. They like games which move in stages, in which each stage, the choosing of leaders, the picking-up of sides, the determining of which side shall start, is almost a game in itself. Adults do not always see ... that many of these games, particularly those of young children, are more akin to ceremonies than competitions. In these games children gain the reassurance that comes with repetition, and the feeling of fellowship that comes from doing the same as everyone else.
>
> (Opie and Opie, 1976, pp. 40–41)

Children's play, as 'the principal business of childhood, the vehicle of improvisation and combination, the first carrier of rule systems through which a world of cultural restraint is substituted for the operation of impulse' (Bruner et al., 1976, p. 20), has raised many questions for a wide range of researchers about its purpose and nature. A breadth of methodologies and methods has been necessary to investigate this area of children's lives and these bring researchers into contact with ethical dilemmas and ethical debates. Most research with children is through participant observation and interview, as these are frequently seen as gaining the most accurate data. This can be supplemented by artefacts such as diaries, drawings and maps, but when techniques such as these are used they involve interpretation and inference (Lewis and Lindsay, 2000). To be able to observe children at play leads to issues for adults outside the family related to privacy and protection. Children also need to understand what is being asked of them and agree to take part and to be able to use the required reporting format, which could well demand a level of literacy or numeracy that they might not yet have. Relying on self-reporting raises a range of issues relating to inclusion, understanding and communication skills.

It is also important for practitioners, researchers and other observers to pay critical attention to the question 'What is an adult?' when carrying out research into aspects of children's lives such as play. This may involve a shift towards engaging with children's own cultures, including the context and timing of communications that are crucial to the process (Christensen, 2004).

Difficult questions for practitioners and adult researchers include: Why should children give information about their play? How is this going to be affected by the power differentials between adults and children? How will the adult use this information? What is in this for the child or children?

Practitioners and researchers may need a variety of tools to find out what it's like to play

The Mosaic approach for listening to children consists of a series of elements: a multi-method approach to recognise the different voices or 'languages' of children, participation, reflection, adaptability, focusing on children's lived experiences and being embedded in practice (Clark, 2005). Clark used the Mosaic approach to focus on a particular children's playhouse that children had indicated was an important space for them:

Henry   This is where we play and talk and cook.

Bob   And sit on the chair. Henry and I can whistle.

Jim   When it's night time it gets dark. Bats are hanging on the windowsills. I love staying there, all there.

Robert   I don't like playing doggies in here – it's too noisy too many in here some of the teachers gets one of them out.

(Clark, 2005, p. 40)

The research tools used to find out about what it's like to play in a playhouse included observation, cameras and book making, tours and map making, practitioners, parents and child interviews. Listening, using the Mosaic method, plays to children's strengths rather than to adults, and shows how listening can work at different levels and in different contexts.

It is possible to draw on some key concepts from the theoretical strands within play to help us understand its value. Brown (2006) summarised the contemporary thinking about play and its value thus:

- play is a stimulus seeking activity and it should contain elements of uncertainty

- play encourages self-initiated, free-flowing activity with a reduced fear of failure

- play is more about process than outcomes as play is inherently flexible and responsive to contexts

- play makes a significant contribution to social development and the acquisition of social skills, including an understanding of customs, rules and power relationships

- play, when physical, develops motor skills and creates a sense of wellbeing

- play contributes to cognitive development
- play enables the exploration of ideas and the development of creative problem solving
- play, through externalising feelings, contributes to emotional health and wellbeing
- play enables the development of the self through exploration of culture and social roles.

As Brown observes, some of these components appear contradictory; play seems to be both a means of expelling excess energy and a means of reinvigorating energy levels through creativity. But it is with an understanding of such complexities of play that we can really value the true nature of play to people whatever their age.

Thinking point 4.1   What distinguishes play from other activities? Are there fundamental differences between the value of play to adults and the value of play to children?

Play is an essential learning tool, but it is more than that. Play, in its widest sense, can make a significant contribution to people's quality of life and to their physical, social and emotional wellbeing. Children and adults have play and playing in common; although routinely associated with children, play can be applied to much of human activity:

> Although the noun 'play' is associated with trivial, childish things and contrasted with the serious worlds of school and work, when we use the word to describe actions it can apply to almost any human activity; recreation, sport, being part of the action, fun, drama, music, gambling even sex. To see play as peripheral and unreal is to miss the point that it is central to all human culture. It is the source of learning, sociability, language, art, intervention and science. It structures experience and leads to understanding, for adults as well as children.
>
> (Ennew, 1994, p. 139)

Play is also a 'layer of living' where children, and children and adults, can connect (Giulbaud, 2003, p. 17). While it is likely that play will remain understood as a fundamental part of learning, it is also a means of understanding the developing self and others, a means of building rapport and developing relationships between children and between adults and children, and is vital to the collective experience of childhood.

The 'otherness' or strangeness of play, even its inaccessibility to those not directly playing, should not detract from our perception of its value:

> research styles and techniques may help a move towards the richness and otherness of children's worlds. But, as I see it, they cannot and should not aspire to move to the very centre of those worlds. If you happen to eavesdrop on a group of children playing and talking freely, you might find yourself knowing what they are saying and doing, and you could even ask them afterwards to reinterpret, but to grasp what the *meaning and feeling to them at the time* is entirely another matter.
>
> (Jones, 2001, p. 178)

Key points

1   Play is of crucial importance to children's wellbeing, and play-related skills are therefore important for all practitioners.

2   Play is crucial to children's wellbeing as a form of learning, development, expression and investigation of identity, communication and connection with other children and with adults.

2 Does play matter?

Here's one definition of play, used by the Children's Play Council:

> Play is intrinsic to children's quality of life: it is how they enjoy
> themselves. It is also a key component of a healthy lifestyle,
> enabling good physical, emotional, mental and social development.
> Strong, vibrant communities have at their heart a variety of places
> to play. Children and young people should feel confident and safe
> to play freely – indoors and out – in a manner appropriate to their
> needs and interests.
>
> While it is a central part of children's own culture, play is different
> from structured cultural activities like sport, art, music, and dance.
> Given the opportunity, children play wherever they are. It is what
> they do when they are allowed free time and space to use in their
> own way, for their own reasons and for no external outcome,
> reward or goal.
>
> (National Children's Bureau (NCB), 2005)

Definitions such as this draw out some crucial aspects and characteristics of
play and pull together the reasons why play matters to children. It is
essential to their quality of life. We could probably stop right there with our
answer to whether or not play matters, but, as this definition makes clear,
play also makes a significant contribution to physical, cognitive and social
development. It is related to physical and emotional health. Its free-flowing
nature also links with creativity and problem solving. And it is central to
children's own culture.

Influential educational pioneers built their philosophies on unsystematic
observations of children at play rather than through formal research
procedures; early nursery education radical Margaret McMillan, for
example, was able to establish nursery schools as distinctly different in that
they were all about play and all about experiencing the outdoors (Bradburn,
1976). These were open air schools, essentially huge gardens with shelters,
the outside space being the prime environment, a true 'children's space'.

During the 1960s and 1970s play became an important part of learning in
schools as influential reports, such as the Plowden Report, emphasised play
as the principle means of learning in childhood (Central Advisory Council
for Education, 1967). However, this philosophy of the value of play was
later to be outflanked by some very powerful lobbies with some very adult
agendas – health and safety, after-school care and curriculum-based
education.

Margaret McMillan's nursery schools (this is one) were based on a radically different view of what children needed

The valuing of play within early years education and care and within primary education came under threat from a focus in the 1980s and 1990s on national tests, inspections and universal curricula. Many teachers now feel unsure about their ability to make room for free play even if they agree that for young children there is a need for it. Older children, who already have in the UK one of the longest school days in Europe, can experience such an overloaded curriculum that playtimes, even lunchtimes, can shrink. After school there may be a range of activities and homework; 'extended schools' take up more of the day by offering a range of services and activities, and are likely to become more widespread since their early evaluation points to benefits for children (Ofsted, 2005).

Yet play remains a vital means of connecting with children and an important means of communication for practitioners. Play therapy, for example, can help practitioners understand and support troubled children. By using play in a safe space, as an alternative to talk, it can help children to try to make sense of things and address areas of emotional turmoil (Brandon et al., 1998). The value of play to children in hospital has also been widely understood for some time. More than being a nice way to pass the time, it is now widely recognised as something that can:

- increase the child's ability to cope with a hospital admission
- facilitate appropriate channels of communication between the child, the family and health care professionals
- create an environment where stress and anxiety are reduced
- provide the child with the means with which to cope with diagnosis, illness and treatment

- reduce developmental regression
- promote confidence, self esteem and independence
- assist in the assessment and diagnosis of illness
- offer the child coping strategies for managing pain and invasive procedures
- prepare the child and family for medical and surgical procedures.

(NCB, 2005, p. 1)

While some free time for play for young children is still widely implemented, this is not the case for older children, who can find their forms of interaction, or play, can be more problematic for adults. Practitioners with a strong play perspective have much to offer children; a play perspective can form a positive approach to those aspects of children's lives that are often seen as problematic, such as taking risks or 'acting up', viewing these as the basis for emotional and social development rather than behaviour to be eliminated. It is important to hold on to the ways in which play expands children's choices and abilities, fosters their self-esteem and respect for others and, perhaps most distinctively, encourages exploration of boundaries.

Not only could time and space for play contribute to healthier, stronger children and communities, but space and time to play is recognised in Article 31 of the *United Nations Convention on the Rights of the Child* (United Nations, 1989) as every child's entitlement.

Coram's Fields, a children's outdoor space in the middle of central London, has been in existence for seventy years. It has a pets corner, play equipment, open spaces, sand, water, and a garden, and adults are allowed in only if they are accompanied by a child.

United Nations Convention on the Rights of the Child: Article 31

1   State parties recognise the right of the child to rest and leisure, to engage in play and recreational activities appropriate to the age of the child and to participate freely in cultural life and the arts.

2   State parties shall respect and promote the right of the child to participate fully in cultural and artistic life and shall encourage the provision of appropriate and equal opportunities for cultural, artistic, recreational and leisure activities.

(United Nations, 1989)

However, childhood constitutes a primary site for managing the tensions between conformity and autonomy, and the social control of children increasingly tightened during the 1990s (James and James, 2001). Early years education, childcare services and primary schools were widely criticised for becoming increasingly formalised and over-structured, with children funnelled through a series of tested, sequential stages of prescribed learning. As children's lives in the UK have become more constrained and pressurised, voices have been raised concerning the importance of time and space for playing.

A positive play perspective and a commitment to play across the wide range of children's services would lead to emphasis on children's appetite for experience, their response to challenges and freedom and their ability to capitalise on what is on offer. Whether in designated play settings, in public spaces, in schools or in other contexts, the importance of play needs to be acknowledged in practice and policy. Wales was believed to be the first country in the world to launch a national play strategy in 2002. The Welsh Assembly Government produced a clear statement that it believed play to be the elemental learning process (DfTE, 2006). Play was defined as freely chosen; personally directed and intrinsically motivated; critically important to the development of physical, social, mental, emotional and creative skills; first and foremost the process of a child's own self-directed learning; and it was the very freedom and child centredness of play that made it such an effective and comprehensive learning process.

The Welsh Assembly identified the following benefits to having a national policy for play:

> The play policy will:
>
> > be an unequivocal statement of the vision for a future where all children of Wales, and their play needs, are given the highest regard and they are provided with play opportunities of quality.

- articulate an agreed definition of play and provide a framework of values and principles that are consistent across Wales.

- raise awareness and contribute to a shared understanding of the fundamental value of children's play and the integral role of play in all children's well-being, learning and development.

- contribute to the creation of an environment of change where all with an interest in the play needs of children, and those whose work has an impact on children's lives, share an understanding of both the contribution that they make, and also the contribution of others.

- provide the context in which the focus of government's vision for the play needs of children is realised through change, innovation and long term strategic development.

- promote a new way of thinking about and working with children. This includes defining their play needs and identifying ways of meeting them, providing the basis for the development of a strategy for the allocation of resources, to deliver both a universal entitlement to play and also strategically in response to identified play needs.

(Welsh Assembly Government, 2002, p. 11)

Commitment at 'top level', that is, national policy, can make a significant difference. It places a duty on local authorities to address the play needs of local children, using an agreed definition of play, and clarifies the essential role of play in children's wellbeing, learning and development. It gives some practitioners the opportunity they have been waiting for to expand resources to support play. It can also bring together these practitioners to work together.

Children are quite capable of structuring their own play and can plan and see the consequences of what they are doing. However, quality play experiences are more common in places where practitioners have had some training in the support of play. Some play workers may, however, find it difficult to reconcile their commitment to maintain children's sense of autonomy and control over their own play, with an increased level of adult involvement (Conway, 2003). And over-intervention can stultify the very things that play should engender; knowing when and how to support or intervene is important for practitioners.

Play and learning are understood to be inextricably linked. With play, children's cognitive, social and physical abilities are developed through making choices, generating decisions, negotiating, using ideas and imaginations, exhibiting motivation and perseverance, setting their own

Given an opportunity, children play wherever and whenever they can

goals, using a range of social and interpersonal skills, and functioning symbolically (Moyles, 2005). While there may remain a residual level of doubt that play provides 'real' learning, play has re-emerged in some major policy initiatives for children's services. In *Every Child Matters* (DfES, 2004), for example, key outcomes for all children included the need to access a range of recreational activities including play, and for children who are Looked After and children who have learning difficulties and or disabilities to be included.

2.1 Inclusive places to play

A child's free choice of their own play is seen as a critical factor in allowing play to make its contribution to enriching their learning and to their wellbeing and development (DfTE, 2006). Choice within play depends on an inclusive context, an inclusive space. Gallagher gives this definition of an inclusive space:

> Let us define an inclusive space as a space that has been, and continues to be, produced and reproduced so as to reflect the various interests of all those who might wish to use that space. If all children were able to participate in the production and reproduction of a particular space, it should reflect the interests of all those involved, and it would thus be inclusive according to the definition just given.
>
> (Gallagher, 2006, p. 171)

As Gallagher goes on to point out, social spaces tend to reflect the social relations through which they are produced. Girls and boys, for example, scan play facilities for what can be done there and what can be done by whom. Children frequently actively uphold traditional notions of gender and can vigorously maintain very separate gender categories. Even in settings that are radical in some other ways, gender as a dominant discourse that shapes children's lives can be ignored by those adults who work there (Browne, 2004). Even when this is recognised and challenged by practitioners, this can meet with mixed success, as Browne discovered.

> The view that girls and boys learn what is 'acceptable' or 'appropriate' for them to play with as girls and boys through observing others and absorbing social messages is weakened by the fact that children clearly do not uncritically learn or accept patterns of appropriate behaviour. This is evidenced by the lack of success educators and parents have had in changing gender-based patterns of children's play, and the way in which children will sabotage educators' strategies aimed at involving children in less gender-stereotyped activities ...

It seems likely that children's choices of playmates and activities are part of their exploration of different styles of femininity and masculinity.

(Browne, 2004, p. 69)

Children can be ruthless in maintaining gender categories; so as well as introducing different role models, it may also perhaps be more effective to work with children to positively identify and reinforce different dimensions of masculinity and femininity.

More inclusive places can result when a commitment to rights to inclusion is overt and becomes a practical basis for action in an organisation or agency that is open to it. Every setting, mainstream and specialist, can, as a matter of routine, create more inclusive play. Regularly asking children about what they want and what they enjoy doing, and asking them to evaluate what they do and what they have to play with, will be an invaluable basis for inclusive play.

According to the National Children's Bureau (2004a), practitioners can encourage inclusive play by:

- observing the free play of children; recording and discussing with colleagues

- encouraging children to talk by paying attention to what they say

- using games: under-fives may enjoy 'introducing' a soft toy to the setting – saying who's who, good points, bad points, what the rules are

- using art and craft: drawing, painting or modelling favourite activities or ideal play spaces, ideal play workers

- using photography or video to record the good and bad aspects of an environment or neighbourhood

- using songs, poems and stories to express feelings about play settings

- using photos of current attractions or possible attractions from a catalogue

- using tape recorders: children can interview each other about likes and dislikes

- using a graffiti board for opinions

- using a suggestion box

- using questionnaires: some children like filling in forms!

Play needs to be given time, to be free play and to be part of local provision, but it needs to be inclusive too. It is through play that children can learn how to negotiate, take risks and overcome obstacles. It is through play that

An inclusive environment, such as a sensory garden, can be enjoyed by all children

children develop friendships and a sense of belonging to a group; this is particularly essential for disabled children as they are frequently marginalised and/or overprotected (NCB, 2006). Beresford (2002) identified three factors as important to inclusive play services in relation to disabled children:

- *Resources*: adequate staffing is needed to support inclusive practice and services.

- *Training*: staff need knowledge of conditions and practical issues, and all staff need to be trained.

- *A suitable environment*: the physical environment can enable and include as well as disable and exclude. An inclusive environment is one that is barrier free and blurs the differences in the abilities of the children.

Practice box 4.2

PLUS is a charity based in Stirling established by a group of people who believe children with disabilities have as much right as anyone else to an ordinary social life. Playplus provides a range of play, social and leisure opportunities for children with disabilities.

Daniel doesn't see very good, but when he goes out to meet the kids in PLUS, he listens to every voice and as soon as they say 'Hello Daniel', he recognises who it is right away.

He loves making cakes and when he goes, the first thing he asks is, 'Are we baking today?' They play pool, they make Christmas cards, Easter cards. They have computers, games, playstations. They take them to the pictures, Burger King, bowling ... they have a lot of outside activities if it's good weather. It's great to get him out of his bedroom, in the fresh air, mixing with people. If Daniel didn't have PLUS, it would be a big empty space in his life.

(Jim and Thilda, parents)

(Bard, no date)

Children's participation in designing children's spaces is vital to the development of places where care is provided for them; this is a children's hospital

Thinking point 4.2   How many children's play places have been developed and established by children themselves? What would such places look like if children were consulted and involved in their development more? Would they look different if designed by, for example, disabled children?

Some children from minority ethnic groups do not use out-of-school play provision as much as other groups, and refugee and asylum-seeking children can find these activities difficult to access because of their circumstances or because they perceive them as not welcoming (Hood, 2001). O'Brien (2000) found that children from minority ethnic groups have more restrictions placed on them concerning the spaces they can use out of school. Frank (2004), of the Children's Research Centre at The Open University, found that the most popular activity on the estate her research centred on was to play with friends as children feared being bullied. Casey (2005) identified a number of significant characteristics of a play environment that contributed to an atmosphere of acceptance: flexibility, shelter, centres of interest, natural features, sensory elements, accessibility, risk and challenge, and continuity between indoors and out. These factors need to be underpinned by a commitment and capacity for all children to have their views and decisions sought and acted upon.

Part of the 'problem' of children is that they are still in the process of acquiring values, norms, meaning and identities (James and James, 2001). Fostering inclusion capitalises on the potential to bring into settings diverse skills, cultures, backgrounds, experiences and languages at a time when norms are in a state of flux. Good quality play-work practice has to be inclusive practice, but, despite a range of legislation and guidance supporting children's right to play and to be included, disabled children particularly still face barriers of access, information and lack of funding. Some practitioners are wary of including disabled children because they lack experience or training, fear the unfamiliar, or are worried about the attitudes and anxieties of other parents and carers (NCB, 2004b).

Key points

1   Play is essential to learning and development; it is also a vital part of children's identity, culture and quality of life, but it can struggle to be given priority over other items on an adult agenda.

2   A positive perspective on play could be seen as an essential component of a debate about what services and practitioners can try to offer to all children to improve their quality of life.

3   Play needs to be inclusive.

4   Play is a vital means of communicating with children on a day-to-day basis, but is also an important way for practitioners to connect with children at times of trauma or stress.

3 Where can children play?

Moss and Petrie (2002) have suggested that a rethinking of public provision for children and their concepts of children's services and children's spaces is particularly apt for any consideration of play and children's services:

> Both concepts – 'children's services' and 'children's spaces' – can be applied to a wide range of institutions, including schools, nurseries and centres providing for school-age children outside school hours. What distinguishes these concepts are different understandings of children and the purposes of these institutions, from which other things flow: the two concepts produce different practices, different relationships, different ethics and different forms of evaluation. The concept of 'children's services' ... is ... a very instrumental and atomising notion, in which provisions are technologies for acting upon children, or parts of children, to produce specific, predetermined and adult-defined outcomes. The concept of 'children's spaces' understands provisions as environments of many possibilities – cultural and social, but also economic, political, ethical, aesthetic, physical – some predetermined, others not, some initiated by adults, others by children: it presumes unknown resources, possibilities and potentials.
>
> (Moss and Petrie, 2002, p. 9)

Thinking point 4.3   Might play be particularly fundamental to the concept of children's spaces?

It seems to us that play, with its elements of unpredictability, its links with children's social and cultural lives, its connection with exploration of dimensions of the self and its vitality would make the inclusion of time and space for play an effective means of creating many more children's spaces. Children need children's spaces in homes, early years settings, nurseries, schools, parks and playgrounds, but they also need informal, inclusive, spontaneous, flexible and private places to play.

School playing fields, while giving dedicated pitches for football, rugby, and so on, have much undeveloped flat space that provides no additional play opportunities. Were this space developed to provide a range of opportunities for children to play and experience appropriate risk and challenge, it would represent an increased investment for children.

Playday (2007) is an annual celebration of children's play when children from all four nations can join in hundreds of play events in their neighbourhoods. Their survey (London Play, 2006) found that:

- 80% of children (aged 7 to 14) preferred playing outside to inside

It is a constant challenge for designers of public spaces to create places to be shared, as opposed to prioritising one age group over another

- 72% would like to play outside more often

- 82% would rather play in natural spaces such as gardens, parks and local fields instead of places like streets or car parks

- 86% prefer outdoor activities, including playing outside with their friends, building dens and getting muddy to playing computer games.

In the UK, the voices of those children and adults making the case for more play, and specifically more outdoor play, have been increasingly heard and sometimes responded to. The recognition of the value of outdoor play is growing, and play is understood as making a major contribution to children's overall level of physical activity (DH, 2005). However, outdoor games in the UK are often restricted to certain times of the year, and children are normally outside only in months of warmer weather and longer daylight hours.

The **forest school** approach, based on a Scandinavian idea, incorporates significant outdoor learning experiences into normal school life.

Children's spaces should be challenging, confrontational, complex, diverse, amazing and open to manipulation and development. Adults can play roles as encouragers and extenders and can support play's contribution to children's wellbeing through valuing play. Molly, a nursery class teacher, was influenced by **forest school** ideas to the extent that she began to take children weekly to a forest:

'We took ropes and tunnels and a groundsheet and together we constructed an obstacle course. ... On another session it was raining and we were going to do Noah's ark for assembly. I had read them the story so we went into the forest and built a Noah's ark out of logs ... I took loads of photographs and ... they loved to talk about it and I wrote down what they said and they drew pictures and we made books.'

(Maynard, 2005, p. 78)

Molly went on to describe her practice developing as she reduced her direction and control of the forest sessions, finding children preferred to invent their own games rather than engage with her activities. She started to think more in terms of offering resources than activities:

'I take buckets and spades down; we've got rucksacks and I take lots of things, string, scissors, bags, wet wipes. They know what's in the rucksack now so if they want things ...'

(Maynard, 2005, p. 79)

This is the life. I'm going to sleep here tonight

(Rhys)

My shelter is good now it's tidied up. It was quicker with everyone working together.

(John)

I enjoyed chopping the trees down most.

(Steffan)

I just liked building the den, it's good fun.

(Alice)

My favourite bit was being put in charge of the food. I am a master chef.

(Lisa)

(Children quoted in Sayers, 2006, p. 23)

The Forest School in Bridgewater's goal is to offer a setting for children to experience using tools, making fires, and so on

As well as the fact that many children's outdoor play areas have been steadily eroded, there remains the perennial problem of adults who are not comfortable with children playing outside. A survey of over 2600 children aged seven to sixteen across the UK found that children experienced a high level of hostility and were frequently told off by adults when playing outside; a third of children aged seven to eleven said that being told off stopped them from playing outside (Gill, 2003). Children also cited other barriers to outdoor play, such as traffic, bullying and parents' fear of strangers, but adult intolerance was one of the key factors that meant their use of space was significantly reduced.

Ten-year-olds now spend only a quarter of their out-of-school time out of doors (Hadler-Olsen and Springate, 2003), boys spend more time than girls. O'Brien (2000) found that children aged ten to fourteen in a London satellite town had greater freedom to cross the road on their own, play in the street outside, ride a bike on the main road, and walk alone to a friend's house than children in London.

Good spaces to play need to achieve a balance between challenge in physical play and exciting activities.

Practice box 4.3

The Play Rangers Scheme in the Vale of Glamorgan offers unstructured play opportunities to children aged between five and fourteen. The play workers decided to let children take the lead and go to the places where children already play: a river bank, a village green, or a park. Travelling with trailers, the rangers can offer fire, den and hammock building, as well as building boats out of scrap.

(Johnson, 2006, p. 30)

Whenever possible, evaluations of play spaces can be made *with* children rather than *for* them. This may involve adults making a clear distinction between an adult's fears and a child's fears: for example, this could be a matter of choosing certain phrases over others, such as 'I'm concerned that is too high for you' as opposed to 'Don't you think that's too high for you?' (to which the child is very likely to answer 'no') (Lindon, 2003).

While access to some places to play has decreased (most notably the streets), other places have emerged, reflecting the technological changes that affect most Western European children. New technologies and the media have become a part of everyday play and of the fabric of daily life for many children and have considerable influence on their understanding of the world. Adult anxieties around some aspects of these changes – playing computer games, for example – may be rooted in disquiet about the computer as a symbol of the future transformation of society (Valentine and Holloway, 2001). In Marsh's (2005) study of the media practices of two- to four-year-olds, specific material from various media was seen to be embedded in children's play: they could perform particular scenes and plots and they explored aspects of characters' identities, including their gender. Characters from different media can become part of family discourse and permeate various aspects of daily life: play (related to televisual narratives), shopping trips (in which children asked for particular food, such as Bob the Builder pasta), visits to town (in which children pointed out texts and images relating to their favourite characters) and family celebrations (at which children would often be given further items which reinforced interest in these televisual discourses). But Marsh has a positive attitude to the engagement of children with children's media and sees it as not passive but active:

> In relation to the lives of the young children ... popular culture, media and new technologies were not providing a parallel reality but, rather, interacted with daily individual and social practices in complex and significant ways. ... What weaves its way throughout the data is a clear sense that the children were active agents in these processes of meaning-making, a useful counter to those who emphasise children's consumptive practices at the expense of their cultural production.
>
> (Marsh, 2005, pp. 45–46)

Children will want to play in and out of school, at home, in friends' houses, in the street, in parks and open places and in 'virtual' places, but what places and times are possible for play remain very much under the influence and subject to the control of adults.

Key points

1 Places to play, outside and inside, are still very important to children's quality of life.

2 More *children's services* could become *children's spaces*.

3 For play to be effective, children must be given sufficient time to immerse themselves, or 'wallow', in it, and as well as time, children need children's spaces.

4 A comparative view

In much of continental Europe and Scandinavia, practices and settings are informed by the 'pedagogical model'. This has been described by Moss and Petrie as follows.

> Importantly, the pedagogue does not see him/herself as an isolated worker, working *for* children, carrying out actions *on* children. The approach is relational. The child is not regarded as an autonomous and detached subject, but as living in networks of relationships, involving both children and adults.
>
> The pedagogue has a relationship with the child which is both personal and professional. S/he relates to the child at the level of a person, rather than as a means of attaining adult goals. This interpersonal relationship implies reciprocity and mutuality, and an approach that is individualised but not individualistic – the pedagogue most commonly works with groups of children and the value of the group and the needs of the group are given prominence.
>
> (Moss and Petrie, 2002, p. 143)

In Scandinavia, children's services and practices reflect both the application of the pedagogical model and a different philosophy of childhood. A Scandinavian view of childhood is that it is a life phase with an intrinsic value of its own. The child is more seen in a 'here-and-now' perspective, and it is thought important that children are given the possibility to grow at their own pace. Play has a central place in Norwegian kindergartens and it is understood as an important way of learning and a way of life for children.

Thinking point 4.4   What do you think are the most important experiences young children should have access to through children's services? And if you, as a practitioner or parent, were asked in a survey what are the most important values young children need to develop, what would be your response?

Parents and practitioners asked these questions in Denmark thought that children should have experience of and in nature, experiences with animals and experience of peace and tranquillity. The values they most desired to be developed in children were self-worth, independence, consideration for others and tolerance (Williams-Siegfredsen, 2007). This stems in part from a knowledge base that has evolved in Denmark and other Nordic countries which supports the belief that the outdoor environment significantly contributes to the wellbeing of children socially and physically. Children are understood as able to develop their social competencies and to play more cooperatively outdoors as the space encourages children to engage positively with others (Williams-Siegfredsen, 2007).

A belief in the outdoor environment's contribution to children's wellbeing is still strong in Nordic countries

There is also a long tradition of combining children's education with care, and Norwegian preschools look to British eyes more like houses than schools. Those who work in preschools have as long and as rigorous a training as those who work with older children. Practitioners in preschools are less interventionist than their counterparts in the UK, allowing the children to choose and frame their activities freely. In this way play is undirected and is not seen as primarily an opportunity to teach.

There are three types of early childhood institutions in Norway: ordinary *barnehage*, family day care, and open day care (*åpen barnehage*). They are all co-educational and children may attend full-time or part-time. The sizes of the institutions vary according to local needs and priorities and there are no formal links between early childhood institutions and primary schools. Outdoor day care centres emphasise outdoor activities as a feature of the pedagogical approach. The basis of the curriculum is play as it is seen as vital for the development of social and learning skills. Children have a daily routine of free time to play, outdoor activities, playing in groups, supervised activities, meals and circle time with reading or storytelling and singing. The hours spent on the different activities and the order of the activities vary.

The primary school curriculum is more formal and similar to curricula in the UK, but twenty per cent of the time in school for primary-aged children must be spent outdoors. Outdoor play is a central part of Norwegian schooling and there is no such thing as 'wet playtime', merely unsuitable clothing. Outdoor experience is thought important to a child's development and is valued as contributing to their motor skills, self-confidence, social interaction, language, communication, curiosity, fantasy, concentration, independence and knowledge. It is also seen as creating less conflict than indoor activities and is enjoyed more by children. There is also the desire to provide children with play space and apparatus that the children can influence; fixed apparatus is accompanied by more stimulating, moveable apparatus. Adults allow and encourage children to take risks; it is somewhat shocking to adults from the UK to see small children whittling sticks with knives, cooking on open fires and climbing rocks and trees.

In a Norwegian primary school playground in the company of the headteacher, one of the authors pointed out that a boy was a considerable distance up a tree and that this would contravene health and safety regulations in the UK. The headteacher replied that the boy liked to climb and would only go as high as he felt comfortable. She then shouted to the boy, 'Well done Jonas, higher than yesterday'.

Thinking point 4.5   Are children too protected in UK institutions and in their everyday lives in the UK? Do children need more time to play not being overseen by an adult?

Table 4.1 shows the clear differences that Hadler-Olsen and Springate found between London and Bergen, Norway, in the time ten-year-old children spent in their out-of-school activities alone, with other children and with adults.

Table 4.1   Who children in London and Bergen spend their time with

% Time spent	Alone	With children	With adults
London	30%	23.5%	42.5%
Bergen	35%	35%	30%

(Hadler-Olsen and Springate, 2003, p. 31)

There is more colonisation of children's lives by parents and other adults in the UK, which is maybe based on a desire to keep children safe but which affects the crucial times they need on their own and with their peers:

Adult control is a crucial factor in the lives of children especially at this age where being allowed to do something is a recognition of maturity. The London children made more mention of family gatherings which kept the children in the adult domain more. Both groups had some experience of travel within and beyond their home city, but always with their families. This reinforces the greater adult control of what the children do and where they do it. We see these family dynamics as fundamental to the lives of the

> selected groups of children and evidence of continued reduction of their time in activities with their peers in an unsupervised way.
>
> (Hadler-Olsen and Springate, 2003, p. 31)

Free time can be as precious a commodity to children as to adults. Children can find it difficult to find time to play beyond the demands, restrictions, protection and control of adults. In both public and commercial play areas and play schemes there are often as many adults as children present and chances for children to be with their peers or alone is decreased. Parents may seek to improve and expand their children's experience and skills beyond those offered by their school. This may mean musical instrument lessons or Saturday schools that enable children to gain an understanding of their own cultural origin, religion and home language, but less free time.

Free time is essential to free play and free play has to be a fundamental part of play itself. But free play can reflect aspects of the adult world; it takes place within the relationships between adults and children which determine how much time adults allow children to spend playing and the results playing is meant to produce. In the UK today there is perhaps an over-emphasis on the view that children must be supervised and in sight of adults for most of their time, primarily to keep them safe.

Hadler-Olsen and Springate's (2003) research into the lives of ten-year-old children in Bergen and London used a weekly diary to take a snapshot of how children spend their free time. Table 4.2 shows the activities the children mentioned and the number of children mentioning the same activity. In all, ninety-three activities were mentioned, but only thirty-four were common to both groups.

Table 4.2   Children's activities in Bergen and London

Bergen only		Activities common to both			London only	
6	TV games	21	TV	21	1	noughts and crosses
5	cinema	7	shopping	9	1	Hangman
5	jumble sale	12	home with a friend	0	4	play in park
1	running	5	swimming	5	1	fishing
2	mountain walk	8	after-school club	2	1	played in playground
6	read magazines	5	read books	11	1	bible study
5	to town	10	visits	12	1	preaching
3	interviews	20	homework	8	1	drama lesson
2	play instrument	3	housework	5	1	errand

Bergen only		Activities common to both			London only	
4	raffle sale	6	football	2	1	karate
4	football club	1	radio	1	1	fireworks
2	ballet	2	scout/guides	3	2	soccer match
3	baking	8	video	3	1	alternative school
1	basketball	7	CD/tapes	7	1	bobbing apples
3	cycling	8	games	5	2	telling stories
1	roller skates	2	phoning	3	2	dressing up
2	concert	2	sibling care	3	1	photography
1	dancing	2	church	2	1	making a mask
2	crochet	1	PC	2	1	fighting
1	billiards	3	dog/pet care	3	1	washing
2	role play	2	writing	1	1	puzzles
2	talking	1	riding	1	1	Subbuteo
2	dolls	5	drawing	2	2	packing
1	cars	1	trains	1	1	doggy spots
1	figures	1	library	1	1	fighter heads
1	counting	1	party	3	1	toys
1	bored	2	ill in bed	1	1	run outs
1	thinking	4	sleep/naps	3	1	ball
1	knitting	5	eat out	7	1	visit from friends
10	unspecified play	2	Lego	1	1	nothing
9	'at home' unspecified	1	hairdressers	1	2	coming home
2	dress	5	bath/hygiene	13		
4	arts course	1	sewing	1		
2	drama course	10	outside play	10		
1	weekend trip away					

(Hadler-Olsen and Springate, 2003, p. 27)

It can be difficult for children to be adult-free in the UK. They have to adapt to a crowded and restricted timetable with little scope to be private in their play. It is becoming harder to find suitable play areas outside the home, and private space at home is not always available. Some adults appear not to have time for children's play, do not value it and try to remove the risk elements from it. However, adults can choose to support children's play. Where practitioners do take part in children's play, they could take account of the following guiding principles:

- value children's play and talk to them about it; ask questions about what the child has played as well as what the child has learnt in class

- prioritise children's play so that they get the message that play is valuable

- choose to make time and space for play

- consider how to make play more inclusive and act upon those considerations

- intervene to ensure safe play, but know when to intervene and support, and try to ensure play offers flexibility, challenge and, at times, an element of risk.

Key points

1   Different approaches to children and childhood lead to different approaches to children's play.

2   Adults could choose to give play a greater priority in children's services.

3   Play should not be marginalised in children's lives.

4   Adult attitudes, particularly to risk and supervision, can limit the contribution of play to children's quality of life.

Conclusion

Play is under the influence of many things within and beyond the control of the children and adults involved, including the social, economic and material circumstances of the child and their family. However, adults can support play through contributing to environments that give children choice, and that may include companions to play with, and by supplying time and space for play. We can always rely on children for the motivation and means to play, but they need to be able to rely on adults to protect and provide time and space for play.

Children will always find a way to play; it's that necessary to them. To end on an optimistic note, Judith Ennew reminds us that:

> There is a school of thought that claims that children no longer play, that their games are all computer games, their lives too serious or they spend too much time passively watching television. The ... apparently total curricularization of their lives might indicate that they have no time for independent or creative play. If that were so, then human society, at least in developed countries, would develop no more for lack of creative impulse in future generations. However, there is some evidence that, despite the oppression of adults and social imperatives, childhood resistance and creativity is still alive and well.
>
> (Ennew, 1994, p. 140)

References

Bard, J. (no date) *PLUS Comes of Age*, Stirling, PLUS.

Beresford, B. (2002) 'Preventing the social exclusion of disabled children' in McNeish, D., Newman, T. and Roberts, H. (eds) *What Works for Children? Effective Services for Children and Families*, Buckingham, Open University Press.

Bradburn, E. (1976) *Margaret McMillan*, Redhill, Denholm House Press.

Brandon, M., Schofield, G. and Trinder, L. (1998) *Social Work With Children*, Basingstoke, Macmillan Press.

Brown, F. (2006) *Highlight 223: Play Theories and the Value of Play*, London, National Children's Bureau.

Browne, N. (2004) *Gender Equity in the Early Years*, Maidenhead, Open University Press.

Bruner, J.S., Jolly, A. and Sylva, K. (eds) (1976) *Play: Its Role in Development and Evolution*, London, Penguin.

Casey, T. (2005) *Inclusive Play: Practical Strategies for Working with Children Aged 3 to 8*, London, Paul Chapman Publishing.

Central Advisory Council for Education (1967) *Children and Their Primary Schools (The Plowden Report)*, London, HMSO.

Christensen, P. (2004) 'Children's participation in ethnographic research: issues of power and representation', *Children & Society*, vol. 18, no. 2, pp. 165–176.

Clark, A. (2005) 'Ways of seeing: using the Mosaic approach to listen to young children's perspectives' in Clark, A., Kjørholt, A.T. and Moss, P. (eds) *Beyond Listening: Children's Perspectives on Early Childhood Services*, Bristol, The Policy Press.

Conway, M. (2003) 'Professional playwork practice' in Brown, F. (ed.) *Playwork: Theory and Practice*, Buckingham, Open University Press.

Department for Education and Skills (DfES) (2004) *Every Child Matters*, available online at <http://www.everychildmatters.gov.uk>, accessed 18 July 2007.

Department of Health (DH) (2005) *Choosing Activity: a Physical Activity Action Plan*, London, DH.

Department for Training and Education (DfTE) (2006) *Play in Wales: Play Policy Implementation Plan*, available online at <http://www.learning.wales.gov.uk/pdfs/play-policy-implementation-plan-e.pdf>, accessed 14 August 2007.

Ennew, J. (1994) 'Time for children or time for adults?' in Qvortrup, J., Bardy, M., Sgritta, G. and Wintersberger, H. (eds) *Childhood Matters: Social Theory, Practice and Politics*, Aldershot, Avebury.

Frank, E. (2004) *How children feel about their local housing estates*, available online at <http://childrens-research-centre.open.ac.uk/research/Local_Housing_Estate_Feelings_Eleanor_Frank_11.doc>, accessed 19 July 2007.

Gallagher, M. (2006) 'Spaces of participation and inclusion?' in Tisdall, E.K.M., Davis, J.M., Prout, A. and Hill, M. (eds) *Children, Young People and Social Inclusion: Participation for What?*, Bristol, The Policy Press.

Gill, T. (2003) 'Playday get out and play', *Children Now*, Autumn, issue 18.

Guilbaud, S. (2003) 'The essence of play' in Brown, F. (ed.) *Playwork: Theory and Practice*, Buckingham, Open University Press.

Hadler-Olsen, S. and Springate, D. (2003) 'Children's free time activities: an exploratory study of English and Norwegian children's out of school activities' in Hall, N. and Springate, D. (eds) *ETEN 13: The Proceedings of the European Teacher Education*

Network, London, European Teacher Education Network (ETEN) and University of Greenwich.

Hood, S. (2001) *The State of London's Children Report*, London, Office of the Children's Rights Commissioner for London.

James, A. and James, A. (2001) 'Tightening the net: children, community and control', *British Journal of Sociology*, vol. 52, no. 2, pp. 211–228.

Johnson, M. (2006) 'Special report – excellence in play: super spaces', *Children Now*, 26 April–2 May.

Jones, O. (2001) '"Before the dark of reason": some ethical and epistemological considerations on the otherness of children', *Ethics, Place and Environment*, vol. 4, no. 2, pp. 173–178.

Lewis, A. and Lindsay, G. (2000) *Researching Children's Perspectives*, Buckingham, Open University Press.

Lindon, J. (2003) *Understanding Children's Play*, Kingston-upon-Thames, Nelson Thornes.

London Play (2006) *Children want more natural outdoor play, says Playday survey*, available online at <http://www.londonplay.org.uk/document.php?document_id=381>, accessed 8 May 2007.

Marsh, J. (2005) 'Ritual, performance and identity construction' in Marsh, J. (ed.) *Popular Culture, New Media and Digital Literacy in Early Childhood*, London, Routledge Falmer.

Maynard, T. (2005) '"Making the best of what you've got": adopting and adapting the Forest School approach' in Austin, R. (ed.) *Letting the Outside In: Developing Teaching and Learning Beyond the Early Years Classroom*, Stoke on Trent, Trentham Books.

Moss, P. and Petrie, P. (2002) *From Children's Services to Children's Spaces: Public Policy, Children and Childhood*, London, Routledge Falmer.

Moyles, J. (2005) 'Introduction' in Moyles, J. (ed.) *The Excellence of Play* (2nd edn), Maidenhead, Open University Press.

National Children's Bureau (NCB) (2004a) *Children's Play Information Service Factsheet: Consulting Children About Play*, London, NCB.

National Children's Bureau (NCB) (2004b) *Play in Coordinated Children's Services*, London, NCB.

National Children's Bureau (NCB) (2005) *Children's Play Information Service Factsheet: Play in Hospital*, London, NCB.

National Children's Bureau (NCB) (2006) *Children's Play Information Service Factsheet: Inclusive Play*, London, NCB, available online at <http://www.ncb.org.uk/dotpdf/ open%20access%20-%20phase%201%20only/ factsheet_inclusiveplay_cpis_20061020.pdf>, accessed 19 July 2007.

O'Brien, M. (2000) 'Childhood, urban space and citizenship: child sensitive urban regeneration', *Children 5–16 Research Briefing*, July, no. 16.

Ofsted (2005) *Extended schools: a report on early developments*, available online at <http:// www.ofsted.gov.uk/assets/4158.pdf>, accessed 18 July 2007.

Opie, I. and Opie, P. (1976) 'Street games: counting-out and chasing' in Bruner, J.S., Jolly, A. and Sylva, K. (eds) *Play: Its Role in Development and Evolution*, London, Penguin.

Piaget, J. (1962) *Play, Dreams, and Imitation in Childhood*, New York, Norton.

Playday (2007) *What's Playday?*, available online at <http://www.playday.org.uk/ about_playday/whats_playday.aspx>, accessed 19 July 2007.

Sayers, J. (2006) 'Forest schools: education outdoors', *Children Now*, 19–25 July.

United Nations (1989) *United Nations Convention on the Rights of the Child (UNCRC)*, Geneva, United Nations.

Valentine, G. and Holloway, S. (2001) '"Technophobia": parents' and children's fears about information and communication technologies and the transformation of culture and society' in Hutchby, I. and Moran Ellis, J. (eds) *Children, Technology and Culture: The Impacts of Technologies in Children's Everyday Lives*, London, Routledge Falmer.

Welsh Assembly Government (2002) *Rationale for a National Play Policy for Wales*, Cardiff, National Assembly for Wales, available online at <http://www.playwales.org.uk/downloaddoc.asp?id=2&page=76&skin=0>, accessed 17 July 2007.

Williams-Siegfredson, J. (2007) 'Developing pedagogically appropriate practice' in Austin, R. (ed.) *Letting the Outside In: Developing Teaching and Learning Beyond the Early Years Classroom*, Stoke on Trent, Trentham Books.

Chapter 5

Anxieties and risks

Mark Gladwin and Janet Collins

Introduction

Children offer countless opportunities for anxiety, especially for parents and carers. Like adults, children are exposed to a range of dangers; however, children, who are relatively small and powerless, can be especially vulnerable. Climate change, pollution, conflict, poverty, ill health and accidental injury or death are risks and anxieties to adults and children. In addition, the upbringing of children is itself potentially a major source of anxiety. Parents and carers worry about the most appropriate ways to bring up children to best ensure their healthy development and wellbeing. As adults we are morally, legally and practically responsible for the wellbeing and safety of children in our care. Individuals, families and societies are judged by the way they protect and nurture their children.

Of course, childhood has always been a time of risk and vulnerability. Today, as at any time in the past, there are many real risks facing children, affecting their healthy physical and emotional growth and development, their ability to cope with the demands of society and the economy, their resilience in the face of change and adversity, and their personal happiness and fulfilment. It is not the purpose of this chapter to list or evaluate these risks – the nature and sources of risk change over time and in different contexts. Rather, the chapter seeks to examine the nature of anxieties about risk, and the effect of that anxiety on the wellbeing of children. The perception of risk in contemporary society, and the propensity of this perception to create a generalised anxiety, is the focus of the first section of this chapter. Section 2 considers why children are such a source of anxiety for adults. Section 3 looks at children's safety from the perspective of practitioners. The chapter concludes with a discussion of play and risk-taking in children's lives.

Core questions

- Is there evidence that we are unusually anxious about children today?
- How does contemporary society perceive and manage risk?
- Is risk-taking important to children's development?
- What is the effect of adult anxieties on children's lives?

1 The perception of risk in contemporary society

In everyday conversation, the word 'risk' is often used loosely as a synonym for 'hazard' or 'danger', but this usage obscures the element of uncertainty that is risk's essential characteristic. A hazard is simply a feature of the physical or social environment that is capable of causing harm: almost anything can be a hazard to somebody. Risk, on the other hand, is a double estimate of probability: how likely is it that something will happen, and what are the likely consequences if it does? Risk has been defined mathematically as the product of the probability and the utility of a possible future event (Adams, 1996). Beck (1992) argues that risk is socially defined and constructed and as such is malleable and changeable. Theoretically, risk can be positive or negative – so that we can talk about the 'risk' of, for example, winning the Lottery – but in everyday usage risk usually has a negative connotation.

Depending on how much is known about the characteristics of a future risk event, it may be possible to calculate the probability of its occurrence or non-occurrence. Experts in many fields are called on to attempt such exercises. Meteorologists, for example, typically assign a percentage figure to the chances of rain at a specified place and time. Geologists make predictions about the likelihood of earthquakes, while astronomers calculate the probability of the Earth being struck by an asteroid. Economic and political pundits make their predictions about the stock market or the result of the next election. Adults working with children carry out detailed 'risk analyses' of planned activities to assess potential risks and suggest strategies for dealing with risks should they occur. Such predictions, if accurate, can be an important planning tool for government, business, organisations and individuals.

Levels of knowledge, however, do not always allow a useful degree of predictive precision, especially in the case of rare but catastrophic occurrences. Regularly occurring events provide ample opportunities for study and are therefore easier to predict with accuracy. The chance of rain tomorrow can be estimated with much greater accuracy than the chance of an earthquake this year, or an asteroid this century. The other part of a risk assessment concerns the probable consequences if the event in question materialises. This evaluation depends very much on the point of view of the person who makes it. A seventy per cent chance of rain might mean much more to a farmer, who could lose a day's work in consequence, than to a city commuter, who just needs to take an umbrella. For practical risk management strategies, the severity of possible consequences is of equal importance to the probability of occurrence of an event.

Thinking point 5.1   What kind of risk analysis might you carry out in your own home prior to a visit from a toddler? How might that differ for your own children?

1.1 Historical approaches to risk analysis and risk management

Attitudes to determining, assessing and minimising risk have undergone significant changes. Three broad historical stages of risk definition and management may be distinguished: pre-modern, modern, and postmodern or contemporary.

Pre-modernism usually refers to the pre-industrial era in Europe when most people's knowledge and understanding of the world were derived from tradition and religious or mythological explanations. Knowledge was communicated through basic texts and oral tradition.

Modernism describes the era (from the sixteenth century onwards) when pre-modern knowledge and understandings were replaced by empirical and rational explanations. It coincided with the increased interest and application of science and technological innovation and a belief in progress. Paper-based writing was the dominant form of communicating knowledge.

Postmodernism emerged in the mid-twentieth century as a challenge to the dominance of modernism. It highlighted that there are many different ways of knowing and understanding the world. Reflecting new technologies, knowledge is communicated in many different formats.

In the pre-modern era, risk management was as much a matter of superstition as of rationality. Risks were generally ascribed to fate, or to some specific supernatural cause. People could try to manage risk by propitiating these supernatural forces by carrying out culturally ordained rituals. The response to risk in the pre-modern world view was thus a matter of correct ritual observance coupled with luck and divine favour. Mythological, historical and anthropological works, for example Bernstein (1996) and Frazer ([1890] 1998), give many instances of pre-modern styles of risk management. Frazer, for example, recounts a belief once common, according to him, in Tonga and other Pacific islands, that any commoner who inadvertently touched a chief or his belongings would swell up and die, unless he disinfected himself by means of a ceremony that included touching the sole of the chief's foot. The consequence was, says Frazer, that anybody suffering from an illness resulting in bodily swelling, such as scrofula, assumed that the cause was an unwitting breach of the taboo, and therefore sought a remedy by touching the chief's foot, often to the latter's annoyance. For many people, ritual behaviour and suspicion survive. For example, many believe that an appropriate response to a sneeze is to say 'bless you', that black cats can be a lucky omen and that Friday the thirteenth is a bad day to do just about anything.

In the modern era, rational thought, or science, developed, superstitions and ritual behaviour lost some of their attractions, and attempts were made to find explanations for the links between hazards and the harm they caused. Some risk was believed to be objectively measurable as a feature of the external environment, and individual and societal strategies of risk management were adopted.

Risk assessment and management strategies cannot, of course, always be objectively based. Indeed, in daily life, judgements of risk are often highly subjective: people differ, both in their estimation of the likelihood of a future event, and in their evaluation of its consequences. There are often significant differences between public and expert assessments of risk. (An example is the case of the alleged link between MMR vaccine and autism, where repeated assurances that there is no evidence of a connection have failed to fully assuage public anxiety (Better Regulation Commission, 2006).)

Both Giddens (1991) and Beck (1992) have argued that risks are actively generated by processes of a postmodern society, such as globalisation. Beck (1992) suggested that the risks prevalent in contemporary society have distinctive characteristics.

- They are qualitatively different, often stemming from environmental problems.
- They are often global in scope.
- The threats they pose to human life and wellbeing are on an unprecedented scale.
- They are open-ended in duration.
- They are again becoming incalculable, in defiance of the rational, modernist approach to risk management.
- They are relatively unsusceptible to prevention or compensation, thus rendering the classical insurance approach to risk management less effective.

Risks proliferated by globalisation – for example, climate change, terrorism, HIV-Aids, avian flu – are often only imperfectly understood. In postmodern societies, by contrast with those that are still modernising, says Beck (1992), the main political and economic issues no longer concern the distribution of 'goods', but the avoidance of 'bads'. Everyone is caught up in defensive battles against hostile influences on their daily lives.

Thinking point 5.2   What do you see as the most important 'bads' to protect children from?

In a postmodern society, not only does risk become more diverse and diffuse, but the very notion of risk as an objectively measurable phenomenon weakens. Authors such as Douglas (1992) depict risk as largely a social construct, developed to police the boundaries between Self and Other, in this way dividing acceptable and unacceptable behaviour. 'Risky' behaviour then becomes a social taboo that can be used to blame and marginalise 'Others' who constitute a threat to the integrity of the Self (a process that may well have some psychodynamic projection behind it, stigmatising and rejecting unacceptable aspects of the Self in the guise of the Other).

The selection of some contingencies, and not others, as risky in specific cultures thus raises interesting questions about the reasons for different value systems. Douglas herself considers that the notion of risk has replaced that of sin as the moral underpinning for our times. Whereas the notion of sin, however, was used to protect society against transgressions by individuals, the notion of risk has the reverse impact, that of protecting individuals against society. Douglas sees the postmodern preoccupation with risk from the individual's perspective as a reaction of the 'Self' against the depredations of the 'Other', principally in the form of global corporatism.

Lupton (1999) usefully summarises 'risk society' as a breakdown of the established early modern rules of risk attribution and causality in the face of global changes, coupled with a parallel breakdown in the effectiveness of classical risk management systems such as insurance and compensation.

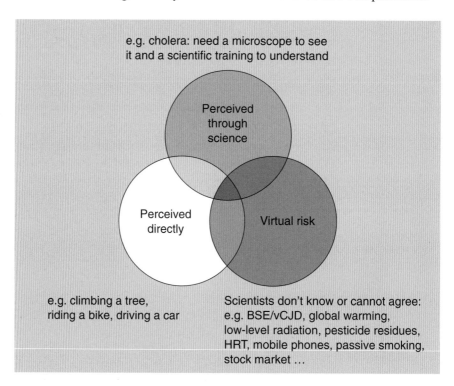

Three kinds of risk (Social Affairs Unit, webpage)

Many risks today are not apparent to the senses in everyday life, but exist only through scientific knowledge. From the individual viewpoint, this situation almost represents a return to a pre-modern state, where risk feels random and incalculable, albeit with one key difference. Whereas in pre-modern thought many risks were thought to have supernatural causes, contemporary risks are seen as the result of human agency, and therefore the responsibility of humans to manage. This perception leads to a quest for blame, but with, very often, no ready scapegoat to hand.

The point is that while the causes of risk – whether global warming, junk food or terrorism – are globalised, its management is both global and individualised. Food production and distribution are global concerns, while the purchase of food and meal preparation remain influenced by individual decisions. Security cameras and 'drones' on our streets limit individual privacy, while traffic regulations and airport-type security checks limit individual freedoms. Such security measures are initiated by the government, but managed by individuals, even if they are increasingly operated by privately owned companies. Beck (1992) regards individualisation as a process whereby people increasingly are seen, and see themselves, as continually responsible for their own situation in relation to both economic and personal life, with no social demarcations taken as given. For the individual, this process is clearly risky in itself, since both life outcomes and the means of reaching them are unpredictable; additionally, however, individualisation takes place in a globalised world increasingly subject to risk from all quarters.

1.2 Risk managing and risk assessment

Governmentality: the process by which people are categorised and managed as populations by public authorities.

Beck (1992), Giddens (1991) and Douglas (1992) analyse risk society primarily from the standpoint of the individual as a potential risk subject. A different perspective is that of the institutional risk manager. Foucault (1991) viewed risk management as a key feature of **governmentality**. Governmentality seeks to measure individuals against norms and to promote conformity to desired standards in the interests of social cohesion and maximising social and economic productivity. In meeting this aim, the individualisation of responsibility for risk management is important, since it reduces the need for more costly interventions (financially or politically) by the state. Health education campaigns are a prime example. Lupton (1999) commented that risk-avoiding behaviour becomes publicly defined as a moral enterprise linked to self-control and self-improvement, and hence a form of self-government.

Another manifestation of governmentality as risk management may be seen in attempts to identify 'at risk' individuals through increasingly sophisticated monitoring techniques. The British government's social exclusion action plan (Social Exclusion Task Force, 2007) shows the ambitions of this predictive approach to risk management:

> through early identification, support and preventative action, positive change is possible. We can tackle problems before they become fully entrenched and blight the lives of both individuals and wider society.
>
> (Social Exclusion Task Force, 2007, p. 8)

In contrast with this highly interventionist approach to a minority trapped in what the government refers to as the 'cycle of disadvantage', Lupton (1999) described as the 'new prudentialism' the increasing governmental expectation that the majority of individuals should avoid or minimise risks for themselves, with government's role confined to the provision of information and the management of markets.

Depending on one's perspective, this can be seen either as a liberation of people to make their own life choices free of state intervention, or as an abdication of responsibility that exacerbates social and economic inequality. For example, as a result of the 'new prudentialism', smoking in enclosed public places was gradually banned across the UK. Whether this was a positive move to protect the health of those working in smoking environments and to reinforce the message that smoking damages health or an infringement of individual rights with unintended consequences depends on individual attitudes and beliefs. Some argued, for example, that a smoking ban would close 'sheesha lounges' frequented by people for whom smoking is a social event, particularly in communities who prefer not to frequent bars or clubs, leaving 'nowhere for people of our age (20-something) to go in the evenings for an alcohol-free environment where you can relax with no trouble' (Loat, 2007).

Where children are concerned, the delegation of responsibility to individuals is often to parents and carers rather than to children themselves, at least while the children are young. In addition to managing their own personal risks, therefore, parents are obliged to manage risks on behalf of their children. While this responsibility has always existed, the proliferation of risks arising through the twin processes of globalisation and individualisation means that contemporary parents in the West may have more to contend with in some respects than earlier generations. Consider, for example, the increase in risks and risk management issues brought about by changes to food production, marketing and transport over the last thirty years. The balance between global, government and individual responsibilities remains contentious and disputed.

Thinking point 5.3   What do you see as potential risks associated with another area of huge change, information technology? Should these be handled primarily at an individual or at a governmental level?

Models of risk management are based on factors in the external environment and on psycho-social characteristics of the individual. Cognitive scientists such as Richards and Rowe (1999) have investigated the psychological and social factors affecting the way that different people estimate risks. They found that people tend to exaggerate the seriousness of risks when:

- risk information is clear and simple
- risks are seen as personally applicable
- risk events are rare but memorable
- risk levels cannot easily be controlled by the subject
- risk events occur in clusters
- risk consequences are immediate
- risks are the subject of media attention.

Conversely, people underestimate the seriousness of risks when:

- risk information is complex
- risk events are commonplace and familiar
- risks are accepted voluntarily
- risk exposure can be controlled by the subject
- risk events are incremental or take place over a long period
- risk consequences are delayed.

In other words, people are likely to underestimate the risks associated with activities of benefit to themselves, that they undertake voluntarily in the course of everyday life, while exaggerating the risk of remote, shocking events from which they derive no benefit and over which they have no control. For example, people may exaggerate the risk of child abduction, which is extremely rare, but shocking and high-profile when it occurs, while underestimating the risk of smoking, which is an everyday, voluntary activity whose most harmful effects lie in the future.

Socio-psychological characteristics of individuals, as well as the characteristics of risk situations, have been found to influence people's risk management strategies. Douglas and Wildavsky (1982) propose a typology of risk management styles linked to personality types based on levels of personal autonomy (the extent to which individuals feel able to make

People frequently take risks deliberately; this behaviour is not necessarily to be characterised as irrational

independent decisions about matters affecting them) and group identification (the extent to which individuals subscribe to the norms of collectives such as organisations, communities or societies).

In this model, the authors suggest that hierarchists, characterised by high group identification but low personal autonomy, seek to manage risks by adhering to official rules set by authority ('I'll be all right because I'm following instructions'). Egalitarians, also with high group identification but with high personal autonomy, prefer to seek group support in a democratic pooling of risks on a 'safety in numbers' principle ('I'll be all

Risk management styles (Adapted from Douglas and Wildavsky, 1982)

			Group identification	
			High	Low
Personal autonomy	High		Egalitarians	Individualists
	Low		Hierarchists	Fatalists

right because everybody's doing it'). Individualists, high on autonomy but low on group identification, take personal responsibility and make their own decisions about risk ('I'll be all right because I understand the situation and I can take care of it'). Fatalists, in contrast, low in both autonomy and identification, see themselves as powerless and adopt no conscious risk management strategy ('It doesn't matter what I do: what will happen, will happen').

Key points

1   Risk is a double estimate of possibility: how likely is it that something is happening or will happen and how harmful or beneficial is it likely to be?

2   Judgements of risk can be highly subjective, contextual and change over time.

3   The balance of individual, government and global responsibilities to manage risk remains a contested and important area for children and parents.

2 Why do children make us so anxious?

So far we have considered the propensity of postmodern society to generate new approaches to risk and risk management, compared with earlier historical periods. But why should *children* be on the receiving end of so much adult anxiety?

Thinking point 5.4 Do you think that adults are more anxious about children in society today than was the case during your own childhood? Why?

Furedi's well-publicised and frequently discussed work *Paranoid Parenting* (2001), for example, argued that contemporary valuations of children and childhood reflect both a lack of confidence in the values of adulthood, and a lack of satisfaction in adult activities and relationships. Sources of meaning and value in adult life, such as work, community and national allegiance, and even personal relationships between adults, have become more transient and more problematic, he suggested, while consumerist values fail to satisfy. Relationships with children can,

The anxiety levels of adults can often be increased by the actions of children

according to some commentators, be an important antidote to adult dissatisfaction. Furedi argued that some parents may over-invest in relationships with their children in order to meet their own emotional needs, rather than those of their children. This emotional over-investment links with beliefs in the inherent emotional vulnerability of children and in the uniquely significant role of parenting in child development – disregarding the importance of influences such as peers and social circumstances – to produce a state of 'hyper-parenting'. This means that expectations of what it takes to be a good parent are continually rising, parenting becomes increasingly professionalised and onerous, and anxieties about risks to children proliferate.

At the same time, Furedi (2001) considered that many parents lack confidence in their own authority and therefore fail to set appropriate boundaries between adult and child roles, out of a misplaced desire to be 'best friends' with their children. He links this phenomenon with what he sees as the increasing denigration of adult values and adult authority in popular culture, in favour of superficially rebellious (but at bottom hedonistic) manifestations of youth values (see also Bly, 1996). In this context, the question of discipline, says Furedi, is replaced by concern for the child's safety as the alibi for all restrictions:

> Regulating children's lives on the grounds of safety is accepted without question as an act of good parenting. ... Keeping children under constant adult supervision creates the illusion of retaining control without having to confront the issue of discipline. These excessive restraints on the experience of childhood are the price that children pay for the problems that grown-ups have in coming to terms with their role as parents.
>
> (Furedi, 2001, p. 138)

Thus, Furedi considered that overt concern for one's own children can be a narrow impulse, which not only is unmatched by civic concern for the welfare of children generally, but does not always distinguish between the genuine needs of the child and the emotional needs of the protective adult.

In the long run, an over-protectiveness towards children can cause more harm than it prevents (Lindon, 2003). A parental obsession with safety can lead, first, to children adopting the disabling belief that the world is an inherently dangerous place, in which they are constantly at risk, and, second, to them being prevented from acquiring useful self-protection skills, because of the restrictions placed on their scope to explore and learn about the world.

An alternative way to deal with risk is to involve children in a problem-solving approach. According to Lindon:

> The basic steps in effective problem solving are to:
>
> 1   enable a full discussion about the nature of the problem;
>
> 2   generate a range of possible solutions to the problem;
>
> 3   decide on the best solution out of those discussed;
>
> 4   put the proposed solution into action for long enough to see how it works;
>
> 5   monitor and evaluate the situation, and discuss again as necessary.
>
> (Lindon, 2003, p. 27)

This clearly takes time, but it can provide a productive way forward and can have a generally positive effect on child–adult relationships.

2.1 Children's safety and adult sexual anxiety

Walkerdine (2001) attributes a preoccupation with children's safety to, essentially, adult insecurities. Her argument draws upon a number of adult anxieties: real space versus cyberspace, children as pre-rational versus children as rational, children as innocent versus children as dangerous. These oppositions, Walkerdine maintains, find their expression above all in adult anxieties about children's exposure to popular culture, especially if it is delivered via new technologies. Walkerdine (2001) argues that children's access to real public space has become increasingly restricted as risks proliferate and former safe havens – even children's spaces such as schools – are seen as places of potential danger. At the same time, children, via the internet, are increasingly able to access cyberspace, which adults are even less able to control. There is another layer of anxiety here too: adults are aware of children as vulnerable and exposed in the virtual world, but at the same time know that this technology is already part of their lives.

Thinking point 5.5   How are gender differences played out in terms of adult anxieties?

Walkerdine (2001) argues that gendered models of childhood define certain kinds of risk behaviour as normal and others as deviant. While boys and girls may be seen by adults at different times as 'risky' and 'at risk', the content of this riskiness is gendered in ways that reflect the normative behaviour expectations held of each sex. 'Normal' boys were playful, creative, assertive, naughty: the social risks of boyhood, whether *to* boys or *from* boys, were concerned with violence. 'Normal' girls, on the other hand, were demure, hard working, self-effacing, obedient: the social risks of girlhood, whether *to* girls or *from* girls, were concerned with sexuality.

It's significant that girls who are playful, creative and assertive are still liable to attract labels such as 'tomboy', 'besom', 'bossy', and so forth, whereas serious, quiet, self-effacing behaviour in boys attracts labels such as 'wimp', 'nerd', 'boff', and the like.

While Walkerdine (2001) did not explore further the riskiness of boys in terms of violence, focusing instead on the sexualisation of girlhood, it would seem possible to construct a parallel argument about the significance of adults' psychological defence mechanisms against the ubiquity of violent impulses, in the creation and deployment of popular stereotypes about violent behaviour by boys. Here, too, there is a newspaper fascination with the stigmatised 'Other' – in this case boys, who figure in a constant stream of stories about record-breaking numbers of ASBOs (Anti-Social Behaviour Orders). Support for this viewpoint is provided by Waiton (2002), who noted the stereotyping of boys as violent in his study of local youth curfews in Scotland. Behaviour such as congregating in groups, that young people adopted defensively, for self-protection, was seen by adults as threatening and aggressive.

Key points

1   Over-protectiveness towards children may be rooted in several causes, including adult insecurities.

2   A problem-solving approach may allow children to develop self-protection skills while enhancing relationships between adults and children.

3   There are some real anxieties about children; for example, the sexualisation of girlhood and the expectation and acceptance of violence in boyhood are things to be anxious about.

3 Children, risk and the practitioner's perspective

Practitioners working in children's services are not, of course, immune from general adult anxieties about children. Indeed, it seems likely that those who work all day with children and are committed to children's wellbeing may be particularly sensitive to generalised anxieties about children and young people. Moreover, practitioners have to deal with anxieties stemming from their position of responsibility for 'other people's children' and the risk management strategies of the institutions for which they work. In section 4 we consider the effects of **secondary risk management** on organisational performance. First, however, we consider the impact of risk anxiety on individual practitioners.

Secondary risk management: the policies and practices that agencies adopt to safeguard their own reputation and stability in the event of blameworthy failure.

Lindon (2003) addressed, from a professional perspective, the counter-productivity of an excessive preoccupation with safety on the part of early years workers. Fear of blame leads to the adoption of the 'precautionary principle' whereby avoidance of risk, however slight, is always taken as a guide for action where outcomes are uncertain. Lindon considered that this mindset can divert practitioners from their primary goals, and replace a focus on children's learning and development with endless speculation about what might go wrong. Paradoxically, this behaviour actually creates additional risk for children (Lindon, 2003). Cautious children have their natural tendencies reinforced and become unable to learn by experiment, rather than being helped to overcome their inhibitions; while confident children may become reckless and unable sensibly to handle the hazards of daily life, because their environment has been so sanitised that they have no experience of dealing with risk.

Practice box 5.1

An example of the precautionary principle in operation is the advice to members of the National Association of Schoolmasters Union of Women Teachers (NASUWT) (BBC News, 2001, 2006) to boycott taking children on trips out of school, especially abroad, because of the risks of litigation in the event of accidents. The advice followed a number of well-publicised incidents where teachers or other practitioners were found legally liable for accidents to children engaged in adventurous pursuits. The NASUWT standpoint aroused widespread concern because of the clearly harmful effect on children's lives that such a policy would entail. Following speeches by the Prime Minister and the Secretary of State for Education in 2005, the DfES issued guidelines designed to reassure teachers, followed by the launch of the *Learning Outside the Classroom Manifesto* (DfES, 2006), with the aim of promoting wider support in schools for outdoor activities. It is to be hoped that this Manifesto will help to counter a climate of excessive risk aversion in schools.

Differences in practitioner perspectives on risk to children

We have seen how Douglas (1992) drew attention to the function of risk as a maintainer of boundaries between the permitted and the taboo. It is therefore to be expected that risk assessments undertaken by children's services practitioners in different societies will reflect different cultural traditions. Unfortunately, systematic comparative research on this topic is lacking. There is some evidence, however, that, as discussed in Chapter 4, traditions in Nordic countries are more favourable to risk-taking in children's play – for example, play involving fire and the use of tools – than is the case in the UK. Sandseter (no date) commented on risky play among four- and five-year-olds in preschools in Norway, defining 'risky play' as play that involves at least one of the following:

- heights
- speed
- tools
- fire
- open water
- rough and tumble
- being out of sight of adults in open areas such as woodland.

Thinking point 5.6   What might children learn from 'risky play' as defined above?

By this definition, 'risky play' was frequently observed in the Norwegian preschool studied and was justified by staff in terms of its developmental value for children. Traditions in UK preschool education seem considerably less accommodating of risky play.

3.1 Risk and context in children's lives

In subsection 1.2 we discussed Douglas and Wildavsky's (1982) four risk management styles. The behavioural paradigm for these personal strategies is risk avoidance. Whether risks are external realities or social constructs, and whatever means of risk management are available, there is an assumption that rational behaviour means risk reduction. Yet the observation that voluntary risk-taking is in fact a common form of behaviour is confirmed daily in the media and by many people's personal experience. The risk-avoidance paradigm is also challenged by a number of writers on child development and quality of life, particularly on play (see Chapter 4), who see an element of risk as an integral part of some play and as something that can benefit children.

Anthony (2001) reflected as follows on his childhood experience of adventure playgrounds compared with what he feels to be the sanitised contemporary version:

> No-one [at the playground I attended as a child] seemed unduly bothered about the casualties. It was all part of the risk, which was all part of the fun. We weren't fearless. We were attracted to fear ... Mortality is always looming. That is why it is perfectly natural for children to want to climb up, every now and then, and face it down. And who are we to stop them?
>
> (Anthony, 2001, p. 8)

Gladwin (2005) found evidence for children's adoption of hierarchical, egalitarian and individualist strategies for the management of voluntary risk-taking in a play setting. He considers that voluntary risk-taking, as well as being an expression of children's existential impulses and of their neurological need for arousal, also serves an important function in making and maintaining peer group relationships through the performance of shared bonding rituals.

Lupton (1999) discussed the notion of risk equilibrium, whereby individuals seek to maintain a personal balance between excessive uncertainty and excessive predictability. This is, in effect, to see risk-taking as a drive that, like arousal, can be satiated. Such a theory invites investigation of the

A real issue for those working with children is developing the skill, and helping children develop the skills, to consider the potential levels of risk

conditions affecting equilibrium levels of risk for different individuals. Variables such as gender, class, ethnicity, disability and personality are likely to be important, as well as the social context in which risk-taking behaviour is exhibited. Research evidence about the association between such variables and voluntary risk-taking is, however, lacking. There is some evidence that class- and ethnicity-linked social deprivation is associated with a higher incidence of accidents to children, both inside and outside the home (Child Accident Prevention Trust, 2004), but this is not evidence of differences in attitudes to risk-taking. It is sometimes argued that disabled children are over-protected by their parents and are thus less likely to be allowed to experience risk-taking, but, again, hard evidence of this link is scanty (see Hartman et al., 2000). Of these social variables, the one to have attracted significant research interest is gender.

Green (1997) found significant gender differences in children's narratives about accidents and risk-taking. Girls in her sample stressed the need to ensure safety and to avoid risk for themselves and those in their care, whereas boys rejected responsibility for others' welfare and emphasised the courage and skill of risk-taking. The study by Crawford et al. (1992) of adult recollections of childhood risk-taking gives a similar picture. Men recalled boyish misbehaviour and punishment as heroic, a way of demonstrating to peers their contempt for adult authority. Recollections of fear and danger were similarly cherished. Women, on the other hand, were more likely to feel shame, guilt and remorse for irresponsible behaviour, or to feel anger at the memory of unjust punishment. Gender differences such as these in attitudes to risk-taking fit with what is known about gender socialisation, and with commonplace views of what it means to be a girl or a boy. Lupton (1999) observed that girls are likely to feel under more constraint than boys because they have fewer socially sanctioned opportunities for risk-taking. It may be hypothesised that some characteristically female forms of deviancy and self-harm, for example around body image and sexuality, could be at least in part a response to the lack of such opportunities.

Yet surely this stereotyped picture is only half the story. The rigid gender divide in attitudes to risk-taking may already be a thing of the past. As Lupton puts it, in the context of participation in extreme sports:

> the dynamic and variegated nature of femininities and masculinities has implications for the gendered meanings of risk-taking. While risk-taking has been most closely linked to the performance of dominant masculinities, and risk-avoidance is associated with dominant femininities, there is evidence of some shifts in these meanings. Dominant notions linking certain risk-taking activities with masculinity have begun to be challenged by women seeking to perform alternative femininities through such activities.
>
> (Lupton, 1999, p. 163)

These shifts in the gendered meaning of risk-taking are highly significant, given the fact that preschool and primary education in the UK, as well as day care for preschool and school-age children, are overwhelmingly the preserve of female practitioners. Girls and boys both need the opportunity to make judgements about risks, and the attitude of care givers, as Lindon (2003) demonstrated, is crucial in encouraging or suppressing such behaviour.

Thinking point 5.7   Can you think of examples that challenge the gendered responses identified above? What might you do to challenge such gender stereotypes with regard to risk-taking?

Studies confirm the importance of children having the freedom to regulate their personal perceptions of risk (Ward and Bayley, 2007). There are four reasons why this is important. The first is practical: children need to practise risk-management skills in order to cope with the everyday adversities of life. The second reason is neurological: children, like adults, need to maintain a certain level of arousal to function efficiently, and risk-taking is part of this process. The third is existential: children may need to confront their own mortality and comparative insignificance if they are not to suffer psychological harm. The fourth reason is socio-emotional: risk-taking seems to be an important element in making and maintaining social relationships for children.

Key points

1   The 'precautionary principle' can divert settings from their primary focus. This principle can also be unequally applied – to girls, for example.

2   Risk-taking is an important part of some play.

3   There are significant gender differences in children's experiences of risk-taking.

4 Adult anxiety and children's lives

Several authors have drawn attention to the positive connotations of risk-taking; Cohen and Taylor (1992) saw risk-taking as an essential ingredient of the 'escape attempts' which people make against dull, everyday routines, and Lyng (1990) has advanced a similar concept, 'edgework', which is characterised by skilled performance of dangerous activities, especially around cultural boundaries between order and disorder, and by strong group bonding among those who engage in such behaviour. Lupton (1998) argued that over-regulation of individual behaviour – whether implemented by external sanctions or by internalised norms of self-control – is a source of stress, which can be alleviated through the excitement produced by risk-taking. She described deliberate risk-taking not only as an essential ingredient of self-actualisation, but as an expression of part of risk's Janus-like status *vis-à-vis* modernity. In one sense, risk is an embodiment of modernity's need for constant change; in another sense, risk-taking is a resistance to the institutional controls of modern life.

Adults are faced with a dilemma. On the one hand, children need opportunities to become competent risk managers and only real life practice can give them such opportunities. On the other hand, risk-averse adult society seems dedicated to the pursuit of an unattainable ideal of total risk management, while new risks and anxieties proliferate as a result of global, social, technological and environmental change. How can children, parents, carers and practitioners attempt to address this dilemma? Child-initiated

Risk is an essential element of some activities

play, and being allowed out without an adult, perhaps better than any other areas of children's lives exemplify the impact of a disabling climate of fear and anxiety, through the combination of individualised responsibility for risk management with an environment in which poorly understood, ill-defined or even imaginary risks proliferate.

This dilemma is played out not only in the daily lives of families, but also between the covers of self-help books and parenting manuals. Palmer's alarmingly titled *Toxic Childhood* (2006), a work that functions as both a campaigning tool and a parental self-help guide, seems dedicated simultaneously to raising anxiety in some spheres, while decrying in other contexts the harmful effects on children's development of excessive anxiety. Palmer blames 'parenting experts' for contributing to what she calls 'toxic childhood syndrome' by de-skilling parents and leading them to distrust their own instincts. However, she herself is guilty of portraying contemporary parenting as uniquely challenging, while stressing that good parenting is crucial to combat adverse external influences on children. As an attempt to lessen parental anxiety, this approach seems a little misguided, which is all the more unfortunate because Palmer actually provides many practical and level-headed suggestions for ways in which parents and practitioners can combat on behalf of children the 'toxic' influences that she describes. These include junk food; restrictions on children's outdoor play; disordered sleep patterns; the decline in interactive verbal communication between young children and their caregivers; family instability and excessive parental working hours; inconsistent and ineffective parenting; the variable quality of paid-for childcare; rigid school curricula; commercial marketing influences on children's aspirations and self-image; and the effects of individualised access to all-pervasive electronic media.

It is not the intention of this chapter to critique this list of 'toxic' influences, but rather to observe that the impact of analyses such as this must surely be to raise anxiety levels. This raising of anxiety may be a necessary prelude to taking action to address the problems. In relation to one key area – restrictions on children's play – Palmer identifies anxiety itself as one of the chief problems to be overcome:

> Anxiety is insidious. It amplifies rational fears and stimulates irrational ones. There seem so many things to worry about now – health issues, all sorts of possible accidents, crime and violence, paedophiles and other people with evil intent ... But when the gathering paranoia begins to threaten children's emotional, social and intellectual development, we have to confront the problem.
>
> (Palmer, 2006, p. 51)

Palmer contrasts physically active, real-world social play, especially outdoors, with the sedentary, solitary, virtual-reality play typified by computer games, and notes that the 'pull' factors towards the latter – the seduction of ever more sophisticated technology – are matched by 'push' factors discouraging outdoor play. The beneficial effects of free play outdoors for children's physical, emotional, social and cognitive wellbeing and development are well documented (see, for example, National Playing Fields Association, 2000). Children strongly prefer playing out to sedentary play indoors, and yet are unable to play out as much as they would like, and parental fears are keeping children indoors more in the UK than in other parts of Europe (see Chapter 4).

On the publication of the Good Childhood Inquiry (Children's Society, 2007), the *Guardian* reported that:

> According to a poll commissioned as part of its [the Good Childhood Inquiry's] investigations into childhood today, the researchers found that almost half of adults questioned – 43% – thought 14 was the earliest age at which children should be allowed to go out unsupervised. Other evidence from government sources revealed that 67% of 8- to 10-year-olds had never been to a shop or to the park on their own, together with 24% of all 11- to 15-year-olds. A further third of 8- to 10-year-olds had never played outside without an adult being present.

> Unwarranted restrictions, the inquiry team said, were blighting kids' lives. Parents were getting it wrong, big-time. But parents are in a quandary: we're not locking our children indoors because we're uncaring or stupid. It's much more complicated than that. There are a whole host of reasons for our anxiety; but could anything persuade us to let our children have their freedom back? What do parents say would give the green light to the kind of experience my daughters can only dream of, but which I took for granted every single day of my childhood from the age of starting primary school?

> (Moorhead, 2007, webpage)

According to Moorhead, what parents said was:

    reduce the speed limits on residential roads;

    persuade the media to report child abduction responsibly;

    put authority figures in the places our kids want to play;

    foster a deeper sense of community responsibility;

    join forces with other parents – there's safety in numbers.

Playing out, children have the chance to learn at first hand about the physical and social worlds, to develop coordination and control, and to grow in independence (see Chapter 4). Palmer (2006) argues that virtual-reality adventures on screen are no substitute for real-life, everyday adventures, however humdrum, in preparing children for real-life risk assessment. Lack of practice in this crucial skill can lead to children becoming either reckless or excessively timid. Such a large proportion of children's encounters with peers take place under the supervision of watchful adults that children may lack opportunities, without adult interference, to stand up for themselves, negotiate, compromise, make and break friendships, and resolve conflicts. Perhaps levels of bullying, at a record height according to Childline (2004), may be partly a result of over-supervision, leading to the labelling of children as aggressors or victims and an inability to deal with conflict without adult support.

Better safe than sorry?

Every so often, reports surface in the media about restrictions on children's play, imposed seemingly out of misplaced concerns about safety.

'An East Sussex school has banned the use of egg boxes as a craft material out of fear of salmonella infection', *Financial Times*, 18 June 2005.

'The Tory Shadow Minister for Children, Tim Loughton, volunteered to be one of Santa's elves at the grotto of an animal welfare charity of which he is president, yet he could not because he did not have a CRB check', *Hansard*, 28 June 2006.

'A decision by a referee to stop parents taking pictures of their children at an under-16s football match has led to an FA enquiry. The ref had misinterpreted the FA's child protection guidelines', BBC News, 2 January 2007.

'Pupils at a school in Lincolnshire have been banned from playing tag and other contact games in the playground because their teachers say it's too rough', CBBC Newsround, 19 February 2007.

'A school in Buckinghamshire clamped down on lunchtime kickabouts in case passers-by were hit by a football', *Sunday Telegraph*, 21 February 2007.

The good news is, of course, that these examples are reported in this way because it is recognised that they are bizarre.

Concern about risks *to* children frequently co-exists with concern about risks *from* children. This certainly applies to restrictions on children's outdoor play. Children are prevented from playing out because of the perceived risks they present to adults as much as because of the risks children themselves may face. The ubiquity of 'No ball games' signs in housing estates across the country is perhaps the commonest example of this phenomenon. Bans by police on skateboarding, however, have attracted more media attention, especially when they are contested by young people (West Country Independent Media Centre, 2006). It sometimes appears that such bans have more to do with preserving public spaces from pollution by children and teenagers than with any objective safety considerations.

How much do we encourage children to play outdoors?

Moreover, when children do manage to get out to play without adult interference, if they choose to go to an equipped playground they may find little there to interest them. Ball (2002) has documented playground managers' increasing preoccupation with liability in the event of accidents. Together with the introduction of more restrictive trade standards for the manufacture of playground equipment, this risk anxiety on the part of playground managers has often resulted in safer but less exciting playgrounds that fail to attract children.

> We have made playgrounds so monumentally boring that any self-respecting child will go somewhere else to play – somewhere more interesting and usually more dangerous ...
>
> (Heseltine quoted in Ball, 2007, p. 72)

This failure can paradoxically result in children choosing to play in more dangerous places, in order to achieve the level of arousal they need (McKendrick et al., 2000). The National Children's Bureau's Play Safety Forum is so concerned by the trend in 'dumbing down' playgrounds that they have issued a position statement, 'Managing risk in play provision', which argues strongly for the balancing of safety considerations with play value, and especially with the recognition of children's need to take risks (Play Safety Forum, 2004).

4.1 How children and parents negotiate risk

So, how do children and young people themselves, and their families, describe the way in which they navigate the landscape of a risk society? Scott et al. (1998) carried out a study on the impact of risk and parental risk anxiety on the everyday worlds of children. The researchers found that children and parents alike identified 'stranger danger', illegal drugs and traffic as the three main risks to children. By contrast, health issues and accidents in the home – among the commonest of actual risks to children – were not mentioned as being risky. Children under twelve, however, also saw teenagers as a threat. Most parents saw the world as a more dangerous place than it had been when they themselves were children. Children, however, generally had confidence in their parents' strategies to protect them from harm, and saw home as a safe haven. Parents were caught in the dilemma discussed earlier, of wanting to allow their children some independence while still ensuring their safety. Most parents managed this by imposing a set of ground rules, often in negotiation with their children, which paid more attention to the skills and abilities of individual children than to their chronological age. Mobile phones may help here, as parents may gain confidence to allow children to go out alone, or with friends, if telephone contact is possible.

Children in the Scott et al. (1998) study appeared to have a good understanding and to be good managers of risk in their everyday environment. The study reinforced the common observation that children feel safer on their home turf. It also found that 'stranger danger' messages were often confusing for children, since they did not fully understand either the nature of the dangers against which they were being warned, or how to identify the 'strangers' who might be a threat. That 'stranger danger' is such a big worry when the objective risk is so tiny clearly demonstrates the distortions of popular risk perceptions (discussed in section 1). It also demonstrates the influence of the media, which invariably treats the very rare cases of assaults on children by strangers – as opposed to the much more common assaults by family members – as headline news.

Disturbingly, some children appeared to be frightened of any adult they did not know. If this is a trend, it has disturbing implications for relations between adults and children and community cohesion.

Practice box 5.2

Children appear to hold realistic attitudes to risk in cases where excessive safety-consciousness has led to the banning of customary activities. In the case of the Lincolnshire ban on playing tag in school playgrounds, for example, the overwhelming majority of children who joined the discussion on the CBBC Newsround chat room (2007) were strongly opposed to the ban, and explicitly accepted the need to take risks and learn from them:

I think banning tag is a stupid idea. I know children get knocked over but they'll also fall over out of school so it's all part of growing up.

Head teachers are getting way too serious about health and safety nowadays, they need to just relax and let children hurt themselves so they can learn from their mistakes.

4.2 The 'risk management of everything'

We have considered in this chapter some of the ways in which adult anxieties and risk aversion affect children's wellbeing in one crucial aspect of their lives, their freedom to play. The rest of the chapter considers risk management from the perspective of service providers. Reference was made in section 1 to Foucault's (1991) concept of 'governmentality', his name for the methods by which public authorities seek to categorise and manage populations. An important governmental tool in promoting conformity to desired standards of behaviour is the individualisation of responsibility for risk management. It makes people feel there is no 'big brother' or 'nanny state', even if there is. It is also a way for public authorities to limit their risk exposure in a political climate where such authorities are increasingly expected, as Power (2004) put it, to 'risk manage everything'.

Power's (2004) work examined the impact on government of 'risk society' – the proliferation of novel, global risks coupled with an increasing trend to individualised responsibility for risk management, and a consequent rise in individual risk aversion. Power considered that political pressure on public authorities is resulting in an unwillingness to exercise professional judgement and a culture of institutional defensiveness, which together create their own risks. In particular, Power argues that institutions become preoccupied with formal risk management procedures that create rigidity and actually reduce their ability to perceive and deal with novel risks.

Power further argues that events such as the BSE (bovine spongiform encephalopathy) crisis have led to a political climate where public authorities are obliged to adopt the precautionary principle, whereby those proposing innovations face the burden of proof to demonstrate their safety.

This principle fails to acknowledge the opportunity costs of failing to innovate. An alternative principle would be to adopt a cost–benefit approach to risk acceptance or avoidance. Current controversies over GM (genetically modified) food provide another example of conflict between the two approaches, with some groups promoting the benefits of innovation against the defensive stance of opponents. Risk management can become as much to do with managing secondary, reputational risks to institutions as with managing the primary risks from which they are supposed to protect the public.

The increasing involvement of the public and stakeholders in risk management processes, Power (2004) maintains, comes in the wake of some high-profile failures. This shift in outlook has come about primarily because of the changing politics of risk management, the greater demand for transparency and external accountability, and the quest for public trust. The reassurance created by such systems, however, may be more apparent than real. As Power puts it:

> Risk management and certifications of the effectiveness of internal control systems may do little to enhance public trust in the senior management of organisations. While practitioners are well aware of the limitations of these systems, 'better' control systems continue to be regarded as politically acceptable solutions to crisis, even where it is known that such systems would not have prevented the crisis in question.
>
> (Power, 2004, p. 28)

The trend for ever more elaborate forms of regulation and risk management seems likely to continue, even while it fails to assuage the anxieties that drive it. Indeed, it is possible to discern here a vicious circle, where increased regulation serves only to increase anxiety by identifying new sources of risk, leading to further regulation and a repetition of the cycle, with dysfunctional results. Some professionals who previously absorbed risks on behalf of others now seek to offload their own risk by taking refuge in a defensive proceduralism that reduces the value of their expert judgements (Power, 2004). This is not helpful when pressing and unpredictable problems cannot be solved without the application of new thinking. The result may be a pile-up of useless information, filed to provide evidence of procedure rather than a basis for decision-making. Fear of blame can also lead practitioners to avoid responsibility in other ways. The example has already been cited of teachers refusing to lead school trips because of fear of litigation if anything goes wrong. Similarly, doctors have been criticised as practising techniques of 'defensive medicine', which may reduce immediate risks to the practitioner but fail to achieve optimum results for patients.

Power (2004) sees the trend to secondary, reputational risk management as having profound implications for democracy, because it casts stakeholders (the public) as a threat to the legitimacy of public authorities and institutionalises a breakdown of trust between government and governed, fostering accusations of spin-doctoring, cover-ups and manipulation. In its place he calls for a new 'politics of uncertainty', premised on the acceptance that failures happen in complex environments even with the best oversight possible, and that innovation is essential to development.

Within this politics of uncertainty, the authority of experts must be reconciled with legitimate demands for transparency and respect for lay views. Power considered that a more intelligent risk management strategy would include the following elements:

- refusal to allow internal control systems to override essential organisational aims and management judgement

- acceptance of a greater degree of uncertainty and a willingness to experiment

- ability to envisage alternative futures, rather than setting up elaborate control systems around a narrow range of futures

- retention, subject to periodic challenge, of control systems that work well

- understanding of the cultural basis of risk selection

- realisation that not all public panics are justified

- understanding of how public trust in organisations is sustained or eroded

- acceptance of the possibility of failure in innovation

- questioning of the assumption that all risk is manageable.

While organisations may well pay lip service to these ideals, however, it is not so clear that there are volunteers ready and waiting to expose themselves to further reputational risk by pioneering a new and more relaxed approach.

Risk management strategies remain a key part of children's services. The inquiry report (Bichard, 2004) into the murders of Holly Wells and Jessica Chapman at Soham found evidence of failures on the part of the police, social services and education services. These failures essentially concerned the processing and transmission of information within and between agencies, which meant that the murderer was not identified as a risk to children before appointment to his position of trust. The Bichard recommendations accordingly focus on police IT systems, codes of practice on information management, the processing of alleged offences, and procedures for the vetting of people working with children.

The headline recommendation called for the creation of a centralised registration scheme to determine whether an individual constitutes a risk in relation to work with children and vulnerable adults. The compulsory scope of the new barring scheme is wider than that of the existing Criminal Records Bureau (CRB) system, and it will also be open on a voluntary basis to additional categories of workers, including domestic carers and self-employed teachers. The aim of the scheme is clearly to reduce the risks of harm to children, by preventing people with a record of violent or sexual offences from gaining easy access to children through their employment.

The case for the prosecution is essentially that vetting – a prime example of an internal control system – is more about secondary, reputational risk management by organisations wanting to protect themselves than it is about genuine protection of children. Children ultimately will be the losers if a bureaucratic system designed to protect them actually makes friendly relations between children and adults more difficult. The controversy over vetting thus illustrates the dilemma associated with attempts to manage risk in children's service, illustrating Power's warning about the counter-productivity of responding to risk management failures by stepping up bureaucratic internal controls, while neglecting the unintended consequences of such controls, the broader social context in which risks arise, and the possibility of alternatives.

Key points

1   Adults are faced with a dilemma: on the one hand, children need opportunities to become competent risk managers; on the other, adults have the responsibility to keep them safe.

2   While the beneficial effects of free play outdoors for children are well documented, adult anxieties continue to curtail freedom to play; this may affect children's ability to judge and manage risk.

3   Within public institutions and service providers, the management of risks can become as important as fulfilling their primary functions.

Conclusion

Whether as parents or carers, as children's services practitioners and policy makers or simply as citizens, adults have to take some responsibility for children, while at the same time giving children enough space to take responsibility for themselves. This is one of the dilemmas at the heart of all relationships between adults and children. Children need protection from risks of many kinds, yet in protecting them from the risks we choose to highlight, paradoxically we may expose them to others of which we choose to remain only dimly aware. Children really can sometimes be too safe for their own good.

Risk society theory indicates that our society will constantly proliferate new risks, and make some of us increasingly risk-aware and fearful, but risk cannot be measured by experts, and sources of information need to be judged. The origins and appropriate responses to conflicting risks are real issues for parents and practitioners. Risks, both real and imaginary, can be amplified through the media.

We may know that this is not how things ought to be, and indeed the picture overall is not nearly so gloomy. There are many real risks to children, against which adults should be on their guard. But we also know that children need to judge risks to develop life skills, for their emotional health, and for their social development. Furthermore, an excessive preoccupation with safety means that opportunities for physical exercise and fitness are likely to be curtailed. There is evidence that, in the right circumstances, children can become competent risk managers. Of course, adults will need to assess risks that lie outside children's experience, and another challenge for adults might be in finding sources of sound evidence. A respect for children's competence, and for their rights to participate in the decisions that shape their lives, should help adults to worry when they need to but not when they don't and to make decisions about risk that are in children's long-term interests.

References

Adams, J. (1996) *Risk*, London, University College London Press.

Anthony, A. (2001) 'Why safety is a dangerous obsession', *Guardian*, 27 June.

Ball, D. (2007) 'Risk and the demise of children's play' in Thorn, B., Sales, R. and Pearce, J.J. *Growing Up With Risk*, Bristol, Policy Press.

BBC News (2006) *Schools urged to run more trips*, available online at <http://news.bbc.co.uk/1/hi/education/6188944.stm>, accessed 24 July 2007.

BBC News (2006) *Schools urged to run more trips*, available online at <http://news.bbc.co.uk/1/hi/education/6188944.stm>, accessed 24 July 2007.

Beck, U. (1992) *Risk Society: Towards a New Modernity*, London, Sage Publications.

Bernstein, P. (1996) *Against the Gods: The Remarkable Story of Risk*, New York, Wiley.

Better Regulation Commission (BRC) (2006) *Risk, Responsibility, Regulation: Whose Risk is it Anyway?*, London, BRC.

Bichard, M. (2004) *The Bichard Inquiry Report*, London, HMSO.

Bly, R. (1996) *The Sibling Society*, New York, Addison-Wesley.

CBBC Newsround (2007) *Should playground games be banned?*, available online at <http://news.bbc.co.uk/cbbcnews/hi/newsid_6350000/newsid_6356200/6356263.stm>, accessed 26 July 2007.

Child Accident Prevention Trust (CAPT) (2004) *Children and Accidents Factsheet*, London, CAPT.

Childline (2004) *Bullying – biggest ever rise in calls to Childline*, available online at <http://www.childline.org.uk/bullying-biggesteverriseincalls.asp>, accessed 23 August 2007.

Children's Society (2007) *About the Good Childhood Inquiry*, available online at <http://www.childrenssociety.org.uk/what+we+do/The+good+childhood+inquiry/about>, accessed 26 July 2007.

Cohen, S. and Taylor, L. (1992) *Escape Attempts: The Theory and Practice of Resistance to Everyday Life* (2nd edn), London, Routledge and Kegan Paul.

Crawford, J., Kippax, S., Onyx, J., Gault, U. and Benton, P. (1992) *Emotion and Gender: Constructing Meaning from Memory*, London, Sage Publications.

Department for Education and Skills (DfES) (2006) *Learning Outside the Classroom Manifesto*, available online at <http://publications.teachernet.gov.uk/default.aspx?PageFunction=productdetails&PageMode=publications&ProductId=DFES-04232-2006&>, accessed 26 July 2007.

Douglas, M. (1992) *Risk and Blame: Essays in Cultural Theory*, London, Routledge and Kegan Paul.

Douglas, M. and Wildavsky, A. (1982) *Risk and Culture: An Essay on the Selection of Technological and Environmental Dangers*, Berkeley, University of California Press.

Foucault, M. (1991) 'Governmentality' in Burchell, G., Gordon, C. and Miller, P. (eds) *The Foucault Effect: Studies in Governmentality*, Hemel Hempstead, Harvester Wheatsheaf.

Frazer, J. ([1890] 1998) *The Golden Bough: A Study in Magic and Religion* (World's Classic edn), Oxford, Oxford University Press.

Furedi, F. (2001) *Paranoid Parenting: Abandon Your Anxieties and be a Good Parent*, London, Penguin.

Giddens, A. (1991) *Modernity and Self-identity*, Cambridge, Polity Press.

Gladwin, M. (2005) 'Participants' Perceptions of Risk in Play in Middle Childhood' (unpublished MA thesis), Leeds, Leeds Metropolitan University.

Green, J. (1997) 'Risk and the construction of social identity: children's talk about accidents', *Sociology of Health and Illness*, vol. 19, no. 4, pp. 457–479.

Hartman, A., DePoy, E., Francis, C. and Gilmer, D. (2000) 'Adolescents with special health care needs in transition: three life histories', *Social Work in Health Care*, vol. 31, no. 4, pp. 43–57.

Lindon, J. (2003) *Too Safe for Their Own Good? Helping Children Learn About Risk and Lifeskills*, London, National Early Years Network.

Loat, S. (2007) *Sheesha Chic*, available online at <http://www.bbc.co.uk/birmingham/content/articles/2005/06/15/sheesha_chic_feature.shtml>, accessed 24 July 2007.

Lupton, D. (1998) *The Emotional Self: A Socio-cultural Exploration*, London, Sage Publications.

Lupton, D. (1999) *Risk*, London, Routledge and Kegan Paul.

Lyng, S. (1990) 'Edgework: a social psychological analysis of voluntary risk taking', *American Journal of Sociology*, vol. 95, no. 4, pp. 851–886.

McKendrick, J., Fielder, A. and Bradford, M. (2000) 'The dangers of safe play', *Children 5–16 Research Briefing*, December, no. 22.

Moorhead, J. (2007) 'Let's set them free', *Guardian*, 9 June, available online at <http://www.guardian.co.uk/family/story/0,,2097858,00.html#article_continue>, accessed 6 July 2007.

National Playing Fields Association (NPFA) (2000) *Best Play: What Play Provision Should do for Children*, London, NPFA.

Palmer, S. (2006) *Toxic Childhood: How the Modern World Is Damaging Our Children and What We Can Do About It*, London, Orion Books.

Play Safety Forum (2004) *Managing Risk in Play Provision: A Position Statement*, London, National Children's Bureau.

Power, M. (2004) *The Risk Management of Everything: Rethinking the Politics of Uncertainty*, London, Demos.

Richards, D. and Rowe, W. (1999) 'Decision-making with heterogeneous sources of information', *Risk Analysis*, vol. 19, no. 1, pp. 69–81.

Sandseter, E. (no date) *Risky play among four- and five year old children in pre-school*, available online at <http://www.cecde.ie/english/pdf/Vision%20into%20Practice/Ellen%20Beate%20Sandseter.pdf>, accessed 26 July 2007.

Scott, S., Jackson, S. and Backett-Milburn, K. (1998) 'Swings and roundabouts: risk anxiety and the everyday worlds of children', *Sociology*, vol. 32, no. 4, pp. 689–705.

Social Affairs Unit (no date) *Three kinds of risk*, available online at <http://socialaffairsunit. org. uk/blog/archives/john%20adams%20-%20risk%20types.jpg>, accessed 23 August 2007.

Social Exclusion Task Force (2007) *Reaching Out: An Action Plan on Social Exclusion*, London, Cabinet Office, available online at <http://www.cabinetoffice.gov.uk/upload/assets/www.cabinetoffice.gov.uk/social_exclusion_task_force/reaching_out_full.pdf>, accessed 26 July 2007.

Waiton, S. (2002) *Scared of the Kids?*, Sheffield, Sheffield University Press.

Walkerdine, V. (2001) 'Safety and danger' in Hultqvist, K. and Dahlberg, G. (eds) *Governing the Child in the New Millennium*, London, Routledge Falmer.

Ward, J. and Bayley, M. (2007) 'Young people's perception of "risk"' in Thom, B., Sales, R. and Pearce, J. (eds) *Growing Up With Risk*, London, Policy Press.

West Country Independent Media Centre (2006) *Swindon freedom to skate protest*, available online at <http://www.indymedia.org.uk/en/regions/westcountry/2006/03/335629.html>, accessed 26 July 2007.

Chapter 6

Staying safe

James Blewett and Pam Foley

Introduction

This chapter looks at the meaning of 'staying safe' to the lives of children in contemporary British society and the implications this has for practitioners in children's services. 'Safety', 'needs', 'vulnerability', 'safeguarding' and 'risk' are, like so many concepts associated with working with families, products of their time and of particular views of children and family life. This chapter explores some of the values that underpin contemporary attitudes, and, consequently, policies and practices toward safeguarding children and child welfare. Where Chapter 5 looked at the related concepts of risk and anxiety, this chapter looks specifically at the concept of 'staying safe'. It explores the language of investigation and assessment in connection with the safety and welfare of children, and, rather than the details of different roles and procedures in different parts of the UK, examines the broader issues and principles of practitioners' roles. Staying safe is, we suggest, a broad concept that needs to cover various dimensions of children's lives and signifies breadth of responsibility across children's services. It is an also approach within which it is vital to develop in children the skills that can help them to keep themselves safe.

Core questions

- What do we mean by children 'staying safe'?
- How can we challenge the assumptions and values that prevent some children from being protected from harm?
- How can parents and carers be supported to help keep children safe?
- How can practitioners make considered judgements about how to act to keep children safe?
- To what extent can children be empowered to keep themselves safe?

1 Protective environments: policy and practice

A protective environment for children has many components, but the key to building such an environment is that it is recognised as a collective responsibility, with an agreement that all members of a society can contribute to keeping children safe. This is the approach taken by the international children's organisation the United Nations Children's Fund (UNICEF) in its *Childhood Under Threat* report (2004).

The protective environment

Capacity of families and communities: All those who interact with children – parents, teachers, and religious leaders alike – should observe protective child-rearing practices and have the knowledge, skills, motivation and support to recognize and respond to exploitation and abuse.

Government commitment and capacity: Governments should provide budgetary support for child protection, adopt appropriate welfare policies to protect children's rights, and ratify with few or no reservations international conventions concerning children's rights and protection.

Legislation and enforcement: Governments should implement laws to protect children from abuse, exploitation and violence, vigorously and consistently prosecute perpetrators of crimes against children, and avoid criminalizing child victims.

Attitudes and customs: Governments should challenge attitudes, prejudices and beliefs that facilitate or lead to abuses. They should commit to preserving the dignity of children and engage the public to accept their responsibility to protect them.

Open discussion including civil society and media: Societies should openly confront exploitation, abuse and violence through the media and civil society groups.

Children's life skills, knowledge and participation: Societies should ensure that children know their rights – and are encouraged and empowered to express them – as well as given the vital information and skills they need to protect themselves from abuse and exploitation.

Essential services: Services for victims of abuse should be available to meet their needs in confidence and with dignity, and basic social services should be available to all children without discrimination.

Monitoring, reporting and oversight: There should be monitoring, transparent reporting and oversight of abuses and exploitation.

(UNICEF, 2004, p. 6)

In this chapter we focus on some of the dimensions embedded in this overview; others are addressed in Chapters 3 and 7. Here, we focus on the attitudes and capacities of successive governments and how government agencies and the public respond to their responsibilities to protect children. We also look at building on the capacities of families and communities to keep children safe, and at developing children's life skills, knowledge and participation in connection with staying safe.

1.1 From child protection to staying safe

The state's responsibility for the protection of children has raised important questions for social policy over the last forty years. Debates around the safety of children have been central to the broader child welfare agenda, producing a range of issues for those working with children in statutory and voluntary agencies, including 'protection', 'risk', 'harm', 'vulnerability', 'safeguarding' and 'need'. Different government agencies and the practitioners who work for them perceive very differently their responsibilities to ensure children and young people are safe and feel safe.

Practice box 6.1

At a multi-agency training session organised to support the Common Assessment Framework (DfES, 2006a), a group of practitioners in one locality were asked to think about how they helped children to 'stay safe'. A teacher stated that for her staying safe meant stopping a child from being bullied. A police officer replied that she saw it differently and that for her it was to stop children being the victims of crime. A social worker who joined in the discussion felt that staying safe is about 'child protection and stopping children being abused or mistreated'. A specialist nurse who worked with care leavers added that she also saw it differently; in her setting staying safe related to young people's sexual health.

Ward suggested that two underlying questions have persisted throughout the series of debates that have arisen around how children can be protected and how they can be helped to stay safe (Ward and Rose, 2002). First, what responsibility does the state have toward people, particularly those who are more vulnerable? And, second, where there are concerns about the welfare of a child, to what extent should state intervention be advisory, directive or coercive? In relation to these questions, Fox Harding (1997) identified the following four political and philosophical positions that have been present to greater and lesser degrees in debates about child welfare.

1   Laissez faire *and patriarchy:* supports only minimal state intervention in the private life of the family. The state should be wherever possible 'rolled back' and seen as almost inherently intrusive. Intervention should take place only where there are very clear concerns regarding child safety. Fox Harding linked this to patriarchy, as this libertarian position on the state is often accompanied by a normative and somewhat idealised view of traditional family life in the nuclear family.

2   *State paternalism and child protection:* supports extensive state intervention. The state is perceived as essentially benign and its role is to 'rescue' children from inadequate parental care. The negative effects of state intervention, such as poor outcomes for Looked After children, tend to be minimised and structural factors that contribute to inadequate, even damaging, care overlooked.

3   *The modern defence of the birth family and parents' rights:* also supports extensive state intervention, but believes that such intervention should be primarily supportive, with an emphasis on early intervention and preventative measures. Coercive intervention should be at much higher thresholds than those who supported the previous position, and where children are taken into state care, links with birth families should be preserved.

4   *Children's rights and child liberation:* considers children to be autonomous citizens with full civil rights, like adults. The notion of parental rights and control by the state is treated with scepticism. The emphasis is on the child's perspective, their wishes and feelings.

Thinking point 6.1   What are the strengths and weaknesses of each of these four positions? Which do you find yourself in most agreement with? Can you see them reflected in a children's service you work for or have contact with?

These positions can reflect how a particular government understands a particular society's values toward children at any given point. Child and family policies reflect often ambiguous notions about the family; it can be seen as a sanctuary from the pressures of the outside world, but also the arena in which those pressures and other dimensions of human failings are acted out. A series of pieces of legislation throughout the twentieth century, that had begun with the first piece of child protection legislation, the 'children's charter' in 1889, enabled the state to mediate and intervene in relations between parents and children. After the Second World War, protection of children outside the birth family also came under the control of legislation with the Children Act 1948. This followed the death of Dennis O'Neill in 1945 at the hands of his foster parents. The inquiry that followed Dennis's death put the emphasis on the need for family support rather than on the fact that families could be 'murderous environments' (Hendrick, 2003).

Child abuse was 'rediscovered' in terms of public debate in the 1960s with the publicity around the 'battered baby syndrome'. This debate was given further impetus by the public inquiry that followed the killing of Maria Colwell by her stepfather in 1973, which highlighted a serious lack of coordination among services concerned with child protection and child welfare. Moreover, the public inquiry into Maria Colwell's death marked another watershed as child protection came under far greater public scrutiny once the UK media started its long-term involvement with the issue.

During the 1980s and 1990s governments largely reflected the *laissez faire* approach, with politicians wary of intrusive interventions of social workers in families. However, local authorities were likely to reflect the state paternalism model, with increasing numbers of children involved with the child protection system (Parton, 2006). This, it could be argued, reflected the increasingly defensive nature of local authorities' practice in the light of reductions in resources and continuing criticisms of local practice. As Chapter 5 discussed, a concern with the management of risk was also part of a wider trend developing across the public services that in part reflected the rising awareness of the dangers of litigation. It also reflected a desire to create certainty where in reality there is as a high degree of complexity (Webb, 2001).

The Maria Colwell inquiry was one of a series of inquiries that dominated public and professional discourses around child protection over the next thirty years. There was repeated scrutiny of practitioners, mainly social workers, as the media and the public sought to feel that its governments and their agencies were capable of protecting all children. By the 1980s, the Cleveland Inquiry introduced a new element when social workers who had taken a large number of children erroneously into care because of suspected sexual abuse were castigated as over-zealous professionals showing little 'common sense' or respect for the private lives of families (Corby, 1998). Allegations of abuse among families in the Orkneys in the early 1990s again raised issues of competency and a hostile examination of the actions of the social workers, leading to yet more vacillating levels of confidence in social work and social workers. This perception of a 'damned if you do and damned if you don't' double bind for practitioners has continued to bedevil discussion around child protection.

A clear steer for practitioners was provided by a piece of legislation widely seen as progressive: the Children Act 1989 in England and Wales (and, later, with some differences, in Northern Ireland). It stressed the role of the state in supporting families, gave every child the right to protection from abuse and introduced the welfare checklist, but with the central tenet that children are best looked after within their families. The Children (Scotland) Act 1995 ensured that the child's welfare was the primary concern and included a commitment to listening to children's views. Legislation to screen those working with children was passed in 1999 in England and Wales and in 2003 in Scotland, and in 2004 another Children Act brought further measures to safeguard children, as well as establishing a children's commissioner in England (other parts of the UK already had children's commissioners). (For more on child welfare legislation see Chapter 7.)

The UN Convention on the Rights of the Child (UNCRC) enshrines a broad range of rights and principles that have also influenced developments in safeguarding children and child welfare in the UK. For example:

Article 19

Governments should ensure that children are properly cared for, and protect them from violence, abuse and neglect by their parents or anyone else who looks after them.

(United Nations, 1989)

The Convention makes clear through the other articles that the right to protection is located within a wider framework of children's rights that covers civil, political, economic and religious freedoms, all of which can contribute toward a child's feelings of safety and security.

The debates about the effectiveness of child protection systems were brought into sharp focus by the publication of an influential cohort of research studies, many commissioned by the Department of Health (DH). They produced evidence that far too many children were being caught up in the child protection system, which some families experienced as punitive and intrusive while remaining profoundly ineffective and unhelpful (DH, 1995). Black and minority ethnic children were found to fare particularly badly, being under-represented within preventative services and over-represented on child protection registers. Disabled children, likewise, were found to be both under-protected but subject to intrusive and often repetitive assessment processes.

Slowly, there were some improvements associated with seeing child abuse and neglect in context, in relation to identifiable aspects of the wider environment, and this led to an emphasis on the integration of safeguarding children into mainstream children's services. This involved training in safeguarding children for all statutory and voluntary workers, providing helplines, protection for whistleblowers, and would need empowerment work with children and clearer procedures for when abuse is suspected (DfES, 2006b). But in the early years of the new century more child deaths and more child abuse gave rise to more major public inquiries, which again highlighted failures of practitioners, services and systems to adequately protect children.

The Waterhouse Inquiry (DH, 2000) reported systematic abuse, a climate of violence and a culture of secrecy that had existed for more than two decades in residential homes in Wales. The report of the Child Protection Audit and Review (Scottish Executive, 2002) found evidence of children experiencing very serious levels of hurt and harm, living in intolerable circumstances and remaining at risk of significant harm even though known to agencies for a considerable time. Lord Laming's (2003) inquiry into the death of Victoria Climbié raised questions in relation to poor social work practice, and that of others including the police and healthcare workers, the breakdown of supervisory relationships, the culpability of senior management, the importance of listening to children, the impact of racism and a lack of a holistic assessments. The Laming Report (2003) also recognised that children in need of protection could rarely be differentiated from those with a broader range of needs. Indeed, there was a substantial body of evidence to support the position that if services are provided early enough they can prevent the situation deteriorating to the point where children suffer significant harm (Statham and Biehal, 2005).

Public inquiries were not by any means the only arena in which concerns were raised. Two joint inspectors' safeguarding reports, for example, to which the chief inspectors of all services relevant to safeguarding children contributed (DH, 2002, 2005), raised similar concerns. These were:

- poor interagency coordination when there were concerns about the welfare of a child
- a lack of ownership among childcare professionals in respect of issues of safeguarding and that it tended to be regarded as the preserve of social workers
- there appeared to be very high thresholds for social work services; they could be engaged only in cases of acute need
- poor mechanisms for the sharing of information about children for whom there were concerns.

Public inquiries in the future, like those in the past, are likely to range over individual, family and system failures. The history of child protection and child welfare, and the systems that are produced in response to them, has been strongly marked by individual cases of extreme child abuse. It can be argued that this has led to a child protection system that has found it hard to adopt an ecological perspective. Such a perspective is based on the idea that children's lives can be understood only from a holistic perspective that

Childline is a freephone helpline for children with problems including abuse

takes account of the wider systems of which a child is a part, and that emphasises the influence of social, economic and community circumstances in which child abuse and neglect occur (Jack, 2001). The dominating influence of individual cases has perhaps lead to a preoccupation with the investigation and surveillance of certain child deaths, rather than concentration on the vast majority of cases in which, while their lives are not at risk, children's health and development are at risk of significant harm (Jack, 2001).

High profile public inquiries, from that into the death of Maria Colwell in 1973 to that of Victoria Climbié thirty years later, seemed only to reiterate the same sad failures of people and systems. However, as Parton (2006) has pointed out, reports into child abuse can also reflect wider social changes. In the years between these two inquiries the growth in global mobility had had a particular impact on the nature of the demands on social services departments and on the cohesion and stability of local communities (Parton, 2006). And in distinct contrast to the Maria Colwell case, major issues arose about Victoria Climbié's national and family identity, leading to repeated difficulties, with appalling consequences, with respect to whether, and to whom within children's services, she was known. The search for the 'lessons to learn' will continue but changes to children's services are likely to remain closely focused on how well agencies work together and how well practitioners work together within their regulatory frameworks. There remain attitudes, prejudices and beliefs that facilitate abuse, and further commitment is needed in order to engage the public fully with accepting co-responsibility to protect children (UNICEF, 2004).

1.2 Significant harm

Embedded in procedures to protect and safeguard children, the threshold of 'significant harm' is a trigger for action, whether that is in respect of abuse happening or being likely to happen. This concept was part of a concerted attempt to try to re-focus assessments and interventions onto the child (Adcock and White, 1998). Practitioners can sometimes become over-focused on the behaviour of adults rather than on the impact that the behaviour is having on a child for whom they are responsible. This can lead professionals to reach conclusions about safeguarding a child on the basis of parental culpability, which may or may not reflect the consequences on the child's wellbeing. Parental drug misuse, for example, may well have detrimental and damaging consequences for a child. However, drug misuse can also be relatively stable or occasional, and there may be protective factors such as the presence of another, drug-free carer in the home. Decisions about the likelihood of significant harm would have to take these factors into account, rather than just a parent's illegal use of drugs. In reviewing social work files where there were concerns raised about parental substance misuse, Forrester and Harwin (2006) found that often practitioners were quick to respond to concerns about illegal drug use, but tolerated chaotic alcohol use far longer, despite in some cases the clearly negative impact on a child.

Domestic violence is one area of children's experience that has come under increasing attention (Hester et al., 2000). In the past, the focus tended to be on valid but limited acknowledgement of assault or threats to a child's safety that were witnessed. However, it has become clear that there has been a high level of under-reporting of domestic violence in cases where there have been other concerns about children's welfare, and that it is an extremely common feature of children's lives (Hester et al., 2000).

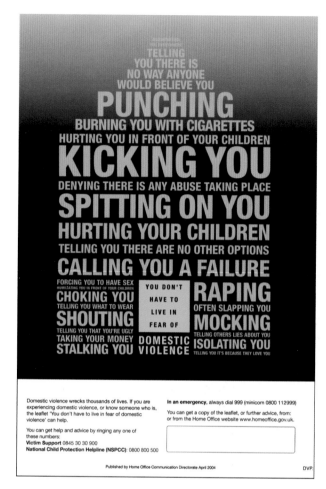

The level of violence in families is the focus of repeated campaigns

Domestic violence wrecks thousands of lives. If you are experiencing domestic violence, or know someone who is, the leaflet 'You don't have to live in fear of domestic violence' can help.

You can get help and advice by ringing any one of these numbers:
Victim Support 0845 30 30 900
National Child Protection Helpline (NSPCC): 0800 800 500

In an emergency, always dial 999 (minicom 0800 112999)

You can get a copy of the leaflet, or further advice, from: or from the Home Office website www.homeoffice.gov.uk.

Published by Home Office Communication Directorate April 2004   DVP.

McGee (2000) undertook research with children and their mothers who had witnessed and experienced violence. The picture she paints, using their words, is of an extremely frightening and dangerous world in which some of the fundamental relationships of trust are violated and undermined:

> Most people if they get drunk they like laugh and be funny and joke but he didn't. He would like beat Mummy up. And he keeps on smacking me and [my brother] round the head. Mummy tells him not to because she says, you'll give them brain damage, that can happen, and he kept on doing it. He didn't listen to Mummy.
>
> (Child quoted in McGee, 2000, p. 52)

What is striking about the mothers' accounts is that many believed that they were protecting their children from the abuse and keeping them safe, and it was only after the mothers left that they realised the true extent to which their children had been involved and affected by the violence. As one mother commented:

> 'She said "I could hear you Mum, I could hear you crying, I could hear you screaming. I actually went once or twice into the hallway and saw him beating you on the stairs." Because we had an open plan staircase and I didn't even know she'd seen it. She even told my ex-husband. She said "I saw what you did to my mum"'

> (McGee, 2000, p. 95)

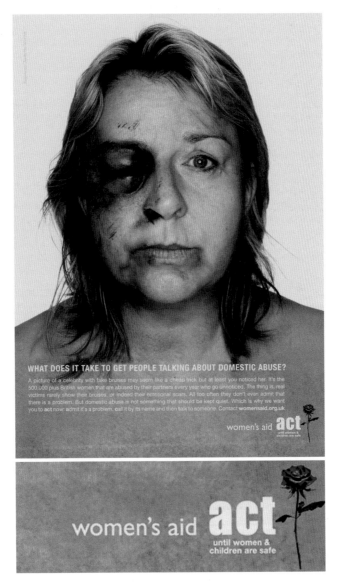

Women in the media can help raise the issue of domestic violence

It remains common for violence to be hidden within families and some practitioners may still feel uncomfortable about raising concerns, as though even raising the issue is a violation of family privacy.

Practice is still evolving in this area, but Humphreys and Stanley (2006) argue that some traditional interventions, particularly with regard to expecting the women to leave the perpetrators to keep children safe, may themselves be fraught with danger. They highlighted findings from research that showed that women and their children are in the most danger at the point where they separate from the man. Practitioners need to make sure that women and children taking such a course of action have robust arrangements in place for ensuring their safety, provide full support, and ensure that child contact is very carefully considered.

Assessments of significant harm, therefore, need to be based on contextual judgements about the impact on the individual child in question. To constitute 'significant harm', behaviour must be 'attributable to the care given or likely to be given' by a 'reasonable' parent. A Black child, for example, may be living in a racist neighbourhood and the impact of that racism, in the form of verbal and physical abuse, may be extremely harmful. Even though, in a sense, this may constitute significant harm, clearly the parents cannot be blamed and expecting them to always protect their children would serve only to compound the injustice and harassment they were facing. This problem could be most reasonably and productively approached using an ecological model, as adopted in the *Framework for the Assessment of Children in Need* (DH et al., 2000), focused on improving children's wellbeing through recognising the impact of a wide range of agencies and on the wider environment in which families live. Here, both the child and the family need to be living in a society which openly confronts racism through the media and agencies such as the police, and through practitioners who will ensure that a child and family know their rights and how to protect themselves from abuse and exploitation (UNICEF, 2004).

The Assessment Framework (DH et al., 2000) recognised the complex interrelationships of the three domains of the ecological approach: the child's developmental needs; the family and environmental factors; and the parental capacity (DH et al., 2000). So, in terms of significant harm, practitioners could consider whether harm to a child was the result of care attributable to the parent or was the result of wider factors. The guidance also introduced the concept of 'parenting capacity' into policy, significant because it required thinking about the potential an individual parent had to care for a child. This challenged the concept of 'good enough parenting' that had been highly influential in childcare practice since Winnicott (1964) had proposed the idea forty years earlier.

Good enough parenting is an attractive model because it recognises that all parents are to some degree sub-optimal and it appears to be realistic and based on strengths. Its weakness, however, is that it appears to promote the idea that there is an abstract, absolute minimal level of parenting skill needed to successfully care for a child. The true picture is rather more complex. Hackett points out that what is needed is an assessment that takes account of the parenting capacity needed to meet the needs of a *particular* child (Calder and Hackett, 2003). So, for example, a child who is adopted or fostered could possibly require a higher level of parenting skills. Assessments of families based simply on the principles of good enough parenting would have no way of making sense of this kind of real complexity in the lives of children and families.

Concepts such as good enough parenting and attachment behaviour (DH et al., 2000; Seden et al., 2001) remain widely used ways of understanding the impact on children of living with stress and uncertainty and of making sense of longer-term issues of emotional and social development, including how people themselves go on to parent. There can, however, be a danger of attachment theory being used in an over-simplistic diagnostic manner (Thompson, 2002), and there have been criticisms of what has been perceived as a tendency towards bio-determinism. Attachment theory has also been criticised as being heavily reliant on a Eurocentric, normative view of the family and reflecting outdated gender stereotypes.

Debate among those who promote attachment theory as a helpful framework has refined many of Bowlby's (1988) original ideas. Aldgate et al. (2006) drew on the work of attachment theorists such as Howes (1999) to argue that, if attachment theory is to be applied to the wide range of often complex family systems that professionals encounter in diverse and dynamic social environments, a more useful way of conceptualising children's worlds is as a 'network of attachments'. They believe that this addresses some of the criticisms of attachment theory.

1.3 Safeguarding children

New Labour governments from 1997 did not introduce sharp changes in policies for safeguarding children. Rather, an evolutionary process continued. However, the attempt to focus children's services away from responding exclusively to child protection and towards a holistic assessment of children's needs now took place within the wider modernisation agenda in the public sector. Furthermore, it became clear that the government had some major concerns about child welfare and the political will to make changes and spend money.

First, a key priority was the identification of children 'at risk', which had been synonymous with the safeguarding of a narrow group of children identified as being at risk of significant harm. Children were now judged to be at risk against a much broader range of indices, such as school exclusion, teenage pregnancy, child mental health problems and child poverty.

Second, the significant cross-departmental interest in child welfare was clearly acknowledged. In contrast to previous administrations, the Labour governments saw child welfare as central to its social justice agenda and took action to directly address the levels of child poverty in the UK and the large number of children and families who were defined as socially excluded. (Section 2 discusses the impact of this action.) This was not simply about concern for poor children. Rather, Labour believed that if the UK economy was to be successful, rates of exclusion had to be minimised because being socially excluded meant being excluded economically as both consumer and producer. Sure Start, a hallmark of New Labour social policy, emerged from the Treasury as a measure to tackle social exclusion through early intervention in children's health and social care, parental guidance and support and community involvement.

A third priority was more integration, believed to be capable of achieving better outcomes for children; policy makers proposed that services for children and families needed to be more 'joined up' (DfES, 2003). As far back as 1998 there had been a clear admission that there was a 'silo based workforce' in children services with, in particular, education, health and social care services often working in parallel with the same families but in an uncoordinated manner (DH, 1998). Central governments set out to establish a more cohesive workforce whose practice was based on a core of common knowledge and skills, including 'safeguarding and promoting the welfare of the child' (DfES, 2005a). Safeguarding children increasingly involved integrated services, and work in multi-disciplinary teams, sometimes co-located.

To facilitate the process of joined-up working, extensive new policies and guidance were issued on setting up multi-agency services. In England this has taken the forms of a common assessment framework, a common core of skills and knowledge, information sharing, lead professional working, workforce reform and integrated working (DfES, 2007), and moves towards integrated children's workforces have begun across the UK. Similar policy directions, focused on safer homes and communities, comprehensive education and learning opportunities, family and parenting monitoring and support, better systems for vetting and barring those who seek to work with children and the development of safeguarding children policies across all departments of governments, can be found in other parts of the UK (Children and Young People's Unit, 2006; Scottish Executive, 2002; Welsh Assembly Government, 2007).

While the major driver for these reforms has been the desire to improve general outcomes for children, concerns about the levels of child abuse and neglect and about the specific arrangements for safeguarding children most at risk have been a major contributor. The DfES (2006b) identifies four types of abuse: physical abuse, sexual abuse, neglect, and emotional abuse.

Child Protection Register: England					
Category of abuse	2002	2003	2004	2005	2006
Neglect	10,100	10,600	11,000	11,400	11,800
Physical abuse	4,200	4,300	4,100	3,900	3,600
Sexual abuse	2,800	2,700	2,500	2,400	2,300
Emotional abuse	4,500	5,000	5,100	5,200	6,000
Mixed/not recommended by 'Working Together'	4,100	4,000	3,600	3,000	2,700
Total of all abuse categories	25,700	26,600	26,300	25,900	26,400

(NSPCC Inform, 2006, webpage)

Physical abuse includes 'hitting, shaking, throwing, poisoning, burning or scalding, drowning, suffocating or otherwise causing physical harm to a child'. Sexual abuse involves forcing or enticing a child to take part in sexual activities, including prostitution, whether or not the child is aware of what is happening. Neglect is the 'persistent failure to meet a child's basic physical and/or psychological needs' and emotional abuse 'is the persistent emotional maltreatment of a child ... it may involve conveying to a child that they are worthless or unloved, inadequate or only valued insofar as they meet the needs of another person.'

(DfES, 2006b, p. 38)

In a review of the research of children's experiences of living with parental substance misuse, Kroll (2004) presented a series of children's voices which are both stark and disturbing:

Mum is fond of drink ... gets grumpy and shouts a lot which makes dad angry. I think they might get separated and I don't think they want me.

(Gemma, aged thirteen)

(Childline, 1997, quoted in Kroll, 2004, p. 134)

Dear Mommy,

Don't worry. I went out to play. I let you sleep ... Harry will be in the yard and I will be at Joanne's or Mary Anne's. Harry wore a sweatshirt ... and ... play jacket with just the hood on his ears. I wore my red pants with my red and white hat with hood.

(Linda, aged eight)

(Brooks and Rice, 1997, quoted in Kroll, 2004, p. 136)

> She has no control and falls over all the time. She pees on the settee and me and my brother have to clean up after her. She fits, too.
>
> (Debbie, aged thirteen)
>
> (Childline, 1997, quoted in Kroll, 2004, p. 136)

As Chapter 5 showed, adult anxieties about children can be pervasive and take many different forms: some are about immediate risks, others are about very remote possibilities, while some enter intensive phases, such as that caused by the growth of child pornography on the internet. Practitioners are subject to these adult anxieties about children and childhood, as well as having to deal with the concerns that are particular to their role and responsibilities with regard to children's wellbeing.

Each practitioner needs to ensure that they:

- have access to up-to-date and explicit guidance concerning safeguarding children; government guidance is readily accessible for each part of the UK

- know the policy for safeguarding children of the setting in which they work

- are aware of who to discuss their concerns with

- create an environment where children are able to tell someone about their concerns

- receive adequate training concerning safeguarding children, either within the setting or elsewhere, ideally with practitioners from other agencies.

Judgements about the welfare of a child are rarely straightforward. Because of the chronic nature of parental neglect and emotional abuse, for example, it is not always possible to see the impact on children. Relationships that are low in warmth and high in criticism can be profoundly damaging but difficult to identify. O'Hagan (1995) argued that emotional abuse or maltreatment is far too broad as a typology of abuse and that emotional neglect, for example, should be differentiated from more contrived forms of psychological abuse such as humiliation or sadistic behaviour. Research into children's experiences of living in environments where their needs are neglected go well beyond the absence of routine or basic care.

The reform of children's services that got underway across the UK in the early 2000s should have major implications for the effective safeguarding of children and the network of children's services that is involved. An emphasis on prevention has led to a far broader remit for the state and its agencies with regard to early invention, multi-agency working, integrated assessment and the sharing of information. Practitioners in health, welfare, education and criminal justice agencies will be working with a different threshold for information sharing, rather than for intervention, being required to share information if they have 'any cause for concern'.

> This was a lower threshold than 'significant harm or the likelihood of significant harm' or a 'child in need'. ... The changes were ambitious and the government was not exaggerating when it claimed that the Children Bill was 'the most far-reaching reform of children's services for 30 years'.
>
> (Parton, 2006, p. 163)

Surprisingly little has been written on thresholds (Tunstill et al., 2005), but they are important because they not only define causes of concern on the part of professionals, but also serve as the access point to services. With regard to the emphasis on information sharing, it is important to note that children, when consulted, are anxious about confidentiality and who has what information about them (Morgan, 2006).

As we saw in the Child Protection Register statistics for England, the most common areas of significant harm to children are neglect and emotional abuse. While these are likely to have a long-term negative impact on outcomes for children, the difficulty with both emotional abuse and neglect is that they sit on a continuum on which it is hard to draw the line between what is acceptable and unacceptable. There is often a complex relationship between child poverty and neglect, and discriminating between the two can call for fine judgements. Both emotional abuse and neglect rarely relate to a single event, but are part of a process that develops over time, sometimes many years. Emotional abuse can be about the complex dynamics of a relationship that does not lend itself to processes of assessment. The absence of a specific incident or crisis can mean that this behaviour can go unrecognised and unchecked for many years. Neglect, in particular, is associated with a range of parental situations, among the most common being parental learning disability, mental health problems and substance misuse. The use of chronology and the recognition of patterns of parenting and care are crucial if decisive action is to be taken for children to stay safe in these kinds of circumstances.

The aim of government guidance is to reinforce the notion that keeping children safe is the responsibility of *all* those working with children and their families and not the exclusive territory of social workers. *Every Child Matters* argued that:

> barriers to implementing effective child protection procedures will be addressed through:
>
> - clear practice standards across services, setting out what should be done in relation to child protection;
> - shared responsibility across all agencies for protecting children through new statutory duties;

- someone in charge locally with statutory responsibility for child protection and co-ordinating the work of social services, police, housing, education and other key services;
- an inspection system that assesses how well agencies work together to create an effective system of protection;
- workforce reform to ensure all people working with children are trained in child protection.

(DfES, 2003, p. 64)

Murphy (2004) and Frost (2005) are among many who have demonstrated that there are considerable barriers to overcome, especially with regard to the different professional cultures that exist across agencies and shape working practices, language, approaches and procedures, including the power dynamics of inclusion and decision making. When there are concerns about a child's welfare, these differences can become heightened. In the worst cases, practice can become defensive as agencies and practitioners 'cover their backs' at the expense of collaborative working with either each other or, often, with children and families. Hierarchies can prevent practitioners challenging others perceived to have more power and status. The Social Care Institute for Excellence argued that agencies need to become 'learning organisations' in which mistakes can be used to improve practice (SCIE, 2005), although this can be easier to sustain in the abstract then in the pressurised environments in which practitioners work.

In practice, making decisions about the safety of a child will remain complex and will require sensitive and clearly thought out processes of professional analysis and judgement. The challenges of creating integrated services should not be underestimated, and it will take some time before it can be seen how multi-agency working can mitigate against poverty, abuse, social exclusion and discrimination. The blurring of boundaries may not in itself be all good news either:

> There is blurring of the boundaries between different categories of children, institutions and professionals, such that the division between the public and the private becomes increasingly porous and fluid. The state increasingly broadens its responsibilities and thereby 'penetrates' and 'absorbs' institutions which were seen as beyond its purview, particularly the family and community, so that the boundaries and lines of accountability of civil society are redrawn. ...

> At the core of these changes ... agents and agencies ... have become engaged in the tasks of governing childhood ... which generates potentially new tensions and instabilities.

(Parton, 2006, p. 169)

Despite all the complexities, some believe that certain features are identifiable among those agencies associated with better outcomes for children and families. These include professionals who are non-judgemental in their dealings with families; involving families in the decision-making process; clear policies and procedures concerning confidentiality, information sharing and joint interventions; and a holistic approach to family difficulties (Cleaver, 2006). Practitioners can listen to children, include children and families, and achieve the appropriate balance between participation and protection. When practitioners get this balance right, the results can be profound.

> It's not rocket science! Kids just want to be wanted because when you are in care you feel like no-one wants you. You just want people to listen, understand and be there on a regular basis so you know that you've always got something to hang on to. It's not too much to ask.
>
> (Child quoted in Morgan, 2006, p. 28)

Key points

1   The key to building a protective environment is that it is recognised as a collective responsibility, with all members of a society contributing to keeping children safe.

2   A focus on individual cases of extreme child abuse has made it hard for child protection systems to adopt an ecological, holistic perspective that emphasises the influence of social, economic and community circumstances.

3   Intervening to protect children requires judgement, supported by training and research, and an understanding of the complex interrelationships between the child's developmental needs, the family and environmental factors and the parental capacity.

4   There has been a significant move towards 'joined-up' working, with integrated services and multi-disciplinary teams, all of whom have had training in helping children stay safe.

2 Adverse environments

People have different views and experiences of where's safe and what's safe in children's lives, and these views will be reflected in the advice and support given to children in their families and communities and in places in which they are cared for and educated. Schools, for example, can be portrayed as havens or horrors by parents. Schools can, indeed, be places of safety, security and continuity in difficult circumstances, but they can also feel profoundly unsafe.

As well as threatening the physical safety of some children, bullying can be more subtle, with distressing psychological and emotional effects. As Oliver and Candappa (2003) point out, particular groups of children – those from poor backgrounds, with disabilities, from minority ethnic groups and those living away from home, or with a combination of these factors – are more likely to be, or to feel, unsafe.

There is an extensive body of literature on the impact on children's wellbeing of living in adverse environments. There are strong associations between not being safe and not feeling safe for a child with parents who

There is an increasing willingness to address homophobic bullying in schools (DfES, 2004)

have problems such as mental illness, drug and alcohol misuse or domestic violence. The parent may lead a very disorganised life, struggle to provide basic care, have difficulty controlling their emotions or be insensitive, unresponsive, angry or critical of their children (Cleaver, 2006). Siblings and close relatives who are able to provide positive relationships and support are important when parents are experiencing difficulties, but parental substance misuse, poor mental health or domestic violence can also disrupt or destroy support from outside the family (Cleaver, 2006). It is important, however, to look at children 'staying safe' beyond simply acts of commission or omission carried out by their parents.

Thinking point 6.2   What do families and communities need to enable them to contribute to children staying safe?

An adverse environment may consist of a series of factors inside and outside families that need to be targeted in order for children to stay safe. There are still high levels of child poverty and inequalities in the UK, despite a decade of economic and social measures that have sought to reduce poverty and social exclusion generally (Office of the Deputy Prime Minister, 2004). Child poverty remains worse in the UK than in most other European countries and the hardship poor children experience now, when they are unable to enjoy the basic living standards or participate fully in society like their peers, will also mean further disadvantage as they become adults (Hirsch, 2006). Indeed, despite a host of anti-poverty measures, there is still evidence of growing inequality in the UK (Jack and Gill, 2003; HM Treasury, 2007) and a reduction in social mobility (Blanden et al., 2005). When assessing the impact of poverty, it is all too easy to focus primarily on material deprivation. However, in their influential study Ghate and Hazel (2002) drew attention to those more profound and complex dimensions of poverty. They highlighted how parenting in poor environments was about coping in deprived, decaying neighbourhoods within networks in which there were multiple stressors. In this context, parenting in conditions of poverty was characterised by a lack of choice and the cumulative and corrosive impact of life-limiting opportunities. This account of poverty is echoed by parents themselves, who report that any assessment and support must incorporate a full and sophisticated understanding of the complex relationships between the factors that shape their lives (ATD Fourth World, 2006).

An important dimension of living in poor neighbourhoods is the presence and fear of crime. Batmanghelidjh (2006) graphically illustrated the brutalising impact on young people of living in environments of high crime, environments portrayed in the local media and perceived by some sections of the community as dangerous. However, she also emphasised that, despite circumstances, many young people are resilient and creative. When considering the impact of places on people, a careful balance needs to be struck between not colluding with the demonisation of certain places, particularly when they may be stereotyped because of large working class or minority ethnic populations, while not minimising the real day-to-day pressures on some children and young people's lives. Ghate and Hazel (2002) found that, overall, the most difficult aspect from the perspectives of the parents they interviewed was the ongoing and relatively low-level signs of deprivation such as graffiti, dog fowling and vandalism. However, they also found that the daily movements of a significant number of children were curtailed by fear of crime.

While children's fear of crime and victimisation is related to living in poorer neighbourhoods, it is important to recognise that children's safety and levels of fear can be compromised in many, if not all, neighbourhoods. Deakin (2006) reinforced this point when reporting on the findings of the *Children and Young People's Safety Survey,* a survey of the different forms of victimisation that 2420 young people aged nine to sixteen experienced across a range of different rural and urban localities. The survey found that:

- eighty per cent had at some point experienced harassment which they found frightening, defined as a range of threatening non-contact behaviours that included being stared at and being followed

- fifty-five per cent reported being physically assaulted in some way

- there were, perhaps unsurprisingly, marked gender differences with boys being more vulnerable to physical assault and theft and girls to sexual harassment

- there was a correlation with age; although theft was associated with adolescence, other forms of victimisation rose from the age of nine, peaking at twelve and thirteen

- most forms of victimisation involved children of approximately similar ages or children who were slightly older

- most problems occurred in either the street or local parks, although a substantial minority of incidents took place within schools

- there were higher levels of harassment in more deprived neighbourhoods, but it was by no means exclusive to these areas.

What this study did not consider was victimisation within the family home, where, as we saw in section 1, children experience some of the greatest threats to their safety and wellbeing. But it is important to keep in mind that children are not passive recipients of adult interventions in their lives. Theories around childhood resilience (Newman, 2004) and research into areas such as domestic violence and substance abuse (Kroll, 2004; McGee, 2000) demonstrate that children devise all sorts of strategies and measures for keeping themselves safe, even in the most adverse circumstances. Sometimes these will bring a different set of problems, such as the child who becomes the main carer for an adult who is struggling with their own difficulties.

As Chapter 2 discussed, resilience can be supported and built on, and whenever possible children should be empowered to keep themselves safe, whether this be on the street, in the playground, at school or at home.

Roger Morgan (2006), Children's Rights Commissioner, surveyed the views of children looked after by local authorities. He found that strangers, including paedophiles, were perceived as the biggest danger, followed by the impact of drugs, but children also complained of frequent bullying, gangs and vandalism in the neighbourhood within which they lived. These high levels of fear and anxiety were compounded by their perception that they often did not feel they had anyone to express these fears to: 'if I had a social worker I would prefer a choice of two people, I would talk to them about everyday things, something I'm really worried about' one child said (Morgan, 2006, p. 10).

Refugee children face particular challenges, with a contradiction existing between punitive immigration and asylum legislation and childcare legislation that stresses the paramouncy of the welfare of the child. Many of these children and young people have fled to the UK from areas of serious conflict and, as such, have often been traumatised, leaving them feeling profoundly 'unsafe' (Kohli, 2006; Okitikpi and Aymer, 2003). Moreover, Cemlyn and Briskman (2003) found that it was refugee children and young people who frequently faced living in poverty, particularly when they were with residing with their parents who had severe limitations placed on their access to public funds. The impact on young refugees of both trauma and discrimination is still a relatively under-researched area.

The experience of disabled children and young people has been much more widely explored (DH, 1995; Marchant and Jones, 2003; HM Treasury and DfES, 2007). Depressingly, despite the insights these studies provide, the outcomes for this group are often poor. Research over the past twenty years has consistently shown disabled children to be both under-protected from harm and more vulnerable to abuse, while somewhat ironically facing far more scrutiny of their lives by parents, carers and practitioners. This is all too often a process in which they are given only very limited choice and their aspirations and independence are rarely realised. Services are at best patchy, and many disabled children still live in relative isolation and poverty (Audit Commission, 2003).

Key points

1 Some children face multiple and interrelated sources of possible harm, including those relating to parental capacity, discrimination and deprivation.

2 Children from poor backgrounds, with disabilities, from minority ethnic groups and those who are refugees or Looked After children are more likely to be, and to feel, unsafe.

3 Staying safe, feeling safe

Perhaps the most important question not asked frequently enough is whether and how much the adult world is able to assist children to *feel* safe. Perhaps adults are more focused on whether they *appear* safe, according to adult definitions (Parton, 2006).

Thinking point 6.3   Who is responsible for children staying safe? Who is responsible for children being able to feel safe? Is there a difference?

If children aren't safe and don't feel safe, this causes some profound feelings of disquiet, confusion, even guilt among adults. It undermines any residual beliefs adults might have that all children are and feel protected, and that a protected and safe childhood can exist separated from the political and social contexts of children's lives (Foley, 2008). And yet, it is important that practitioners can and should believe they can contribute to children being and feeling safe. Not all children are at risk or vulnerable, but all will be or will feel unsafe at some time. Children's exposure to risk and their feelings of safety are influenced by practice and context.

Deakin (2006) suggests that there is a complex and sometimes paradoxical relationship between a child's objective *position* of relative safety and their subjective perception of *feeling* safe. Children living in relatively stable situations can, for a number of psycho-social reasons, feel highly anxious about their lives, while other children can be living in profoundly unsafe circumstances and yet feel quite safe. This may be because of protective factors that promote their resilience, or it may sometimes be because the way they see the world diminishes their estimation of possible, and possibly very real, dangers.

Anxieties and risks are common features of children's lives (see Chapter 5), as a young researcher discovered when researching bullying and how safe children thought their school was.

> Results suggested participants felt less safe in times and places when out of school places e.g. getting home and at the bus stop. Results also suggested participants felt less safe in places and at times of the day in which teachers were less likely to be present e.g. lunch time and between lessons. Common reasons of unsafe feelings were reported and general themes that emerged included bullying in and out of school and fear of attack from strangers to and from school.
>
> (O'Reilly, 2006, webpage)

Deakin (2006) also looked at children's anxieties, fears and perceptions of danger.

Children's and young people's fears

Children's and young people's fears	Expressed fears			
	Yes	%	No	%
Being pulled into a car	1229	59	677	33
Being followed	1210	58	696	34
Attack by a stranger	1155	56	751	36
Doing badly at school and in examinations	1333	55	655	27
Home being broken into	1036	50	870	42
Being shot	964	46	942	45
Having something stolen	862	42	1045	50
Gangs of teenagers	989	41	999	41
Being offered drugs	850	41	1056	51
Being watched	844	41	1062	51

Children's and young people's fears (Deakin, 2006, p. 384)

This accords with findings from surveys of adults' perceptions of crime, that the perceived and actual threats do not always correlate. Children's fears of being abducted or followed were greater than the fear of a much more everyday situation a child is likely to face. Even the extreme, and thankfully very rare, incidence of being the victim of a shooting still registered highly in the scale of fears. Perhaps reflecting how issues are dealt with by the media, fears and anxieties don't correlate with actual statistical risks. Nonetheless, fears are part of children's lives and part of what services and practitioners need to recognise as part of children's lives.

3.1 Children's participation in staying safe

Thinking point 6.4   What life skills, knowledge and levels of participation do children need in order to stay safe?

Several approaches could potentially empower children, as individuals and as groups, to keep themselves safe. Taking issues such as bullying seriously, for example, with adults and children tackling it together, has been a positive development and examples of this approach are evident in many children's services.

Rose (in Aldgate et al., 2006) argued that there are no simple solutions to pervasive problems around staying safe, but that any actions, such as instigating anti-bullying strategies, should be devised with the active participation and therefore ownership of children and young people themselves. Campaigns that have the participatory and child-centred philosophy promoted by Rose have been positively evaluated by both children and teachers.

Practice box 6.2

When children were asked by the Children's Rights Director's Team what would help to keep them safe from dangers, they listed the following:

1   Stay with an adult – this was suggested by one in five children (20%)

2   Stay with your family – suggested by one in eight children (12%)

3   Stay away from the dangers – suggested by one in eight children (12%)

4   Don't play with dangerous things – suggested by one in ten children (10%)

5   Don't talk to strangers – suggested by just under one in ten children (9%)

6   Listen to what adults tell you – suggested by nearly one in ten children (8%)

7   Lock away dangerous things – suggested by just over one in twenty children (7%)

8   Stay close to people you know – suggested by one in twenty (5%)

9   Know road safety and your Green Cross Code – this was suggested by one in twenty children (5%)

(Morgan, 2005, p. 13)

Bullying, something experienced for generations, can blight people's lives. Some believe that the bullying they experienced has affected their self-esteem, ability to make friends, and success in education and in work and social relationships:

'I am bitter, but also feel great regret. I would have been capable of so much more had not my school years been so frightening. If I had enjoyed school I might have "bloomed" into a more confident person. It makes me wish that I hadn't been born, as I have now wasted my life being too scared and nervous to try to succeed.' (woman, aged thirty-four).

'Yes I am bitter and angry, but also annoyed that nothing was done about the bullying. Teachers have a chance to put it right and I look back partly with bitterness towards them, as well as the bullies.' (man, aged twenty-four).

'The bullying has left me with an inability to cope with change or stress, severe depression and agoraphobia. I am afraid of anything new and most people think I am recluse and they are probably right. I only trust myself.' (woman, aged sixty-eight).

'I am hypersensitive and raw to slights. I am constantly on the look out for criticism and have the mentality of a perpetual victim. It is as if I am still waiting for those bullies to come around the corner and get me. I tell myself that it is ridiculous ...' (man, aged sixty-eight).

(Kidscape, 1999, pp. 7, 8)

Practice box 6.3

Primary aged children offered the following tips on how to deal with bullying:

top 10 tips from children

1 Teachers should involve parents.
If someone's being bullied they should tell the teacher and the teacher should ring the parents up and say "Your child has been bullied" and the parents can sort it out.
Male 9

2 It helps if bullies don't get a reaction from you.
They'll stop bullying you if they feel like you're not taking any of it in.
Male 10

3 Teachers could try and make bullies understand how it feels.
Bullying's not nice. It makes people feel a bit upset and sad and a bit like crying. If someone was being bullied it would make them concentrate on the bullying and not do very well at school. If someone was being bullied and it's at school like, tell the teacher and ask the teacher if they can try and like stop them. The teacher should speak to the bullies and just like say "don't bully people 'cause how would you like it if they were bullying you?"
Male 10

4 Friends can be a real help.
When my friend was being bullied, this person was being nasty to her and calling her names and that. And I asked her stop it and then they wouldn't, so I ran and told the teacher, they just sorted it out and now they're friends.
Female 8

5 Supervise at key times.
The teachers should keep an eye on people. They get bullied more in the afternoon because there's a longer playtime in the afternoon.
Male 9

6 Find out what's behind the bullying.
Some bullies are just unhappy so you need to talk to them and get them to be friends.
From a group discussion, primary ages.

7 Support groups in the playground.
If they still bully in the playground the teacher should ask people to be kind to the person they are doing it to. I would get people to be friends with her.
From a group discussion, primary ages.

8 Lunchtime clubs can reduce playground problems.
In my school we have lunchtime clubs for anyone who's being bullied where you can play and make things. The teachers choose if you can go to the club. You have to speak to them about why you want to go. My cousin was bullied a lot at school and she goes. They get stickers, furry pens, play bingo and get prizes.
From a group discussion, primary ages.

9 Split playgrounds
In my school they try and stop bullying by having two playgrounds. They have one playground on the roof for the year 3 class, and another big one at the bottom for years 4, 5 and 6.
From a group discussion, primary ages.

10 Clear sanctions
They also have this thing where you get a yellow card warning and a red card if you hit someone. This means that you have to sit on the bench for the rest of playtime. I got a yellow card the other day and they called my Mum. Sometimes if you get a red card you can't be sports captain anymore, you get time out slips.
From a group discussion, primary ages.

(Aynsley-Green, 2006, p. 10)

As well as tackling issues such as bullying, children can be supported to understand anxieties and what they mean to them and to the adults they know. They can also be actively supported to find their own ways to think about and deal with the risks, anxieties and dangers many of them experience and some of them experience frequently.

Practice box 6.4

The National Charity Kidscape was founded in 1984 by Dr Michelle Elliott and works to prevent the abuse and exploitation of children and any kind of bullying – emotional, physical, racial, homophobic, and so on. Kidscape encourages self-reliance and works to provide individuals and communities with practical skills and the resources necessary to prevent harm.

(Kidscape, 2005, webpage)

While some adults may be inclined to see children's views as too subjective, naïve or simplistic, they may change these preconceptions when they actually ask children who then come up with a range of ideas and solutions that make sense to them. There are models of policy and practice that work for children. In connection with domestic violence for example, including providing educational programmes in schools, work with children

simple street sense!

DO:
- Keep your valuables **out of sight** (e.g. mobile, discman or mp3 player).
- Tell an adult or teacher if you **feel threatened** – you won't look stupid.
- **Trust your instincts.** If it feels wrong, it probably is wrong.
- Make a fuss or yell or even break a window – anything to bring help. Don't be embarrassed: **your safety is too important.**
- If there are houses nearby, you could either **pretend to ring the bell** or really ring it if you are frightened. Just going up to a house might put an attacker off.

DON'T
- Hitchhike, **walk home alone** through isolated places, take lifts from strangers.
- Go up to a car to give someone directions – **it could be a trick.**
- Fight to keep possessions if you are going to be hurt – **just throw them and run.** Possessions can be replaced, you can't.
- Blame yourself if something happens – **it is the fault of whoever hurt or attacked you.**

Kidscape (2005) simple street sense Dos and Don'ts leaflet

in refuges and direct work with groups of children who are experiencing, or have experienced, violence at home can work. This kind of work should be grounded in a full awareness of what domestic violence means for women and children (Mullender et al., 2003). Children can share information about what they understand, what they have experienced and what to do.

Respect for children's participation in their own protection does not mean an abdication of adults' responsibility to create safe environments and effective mechanisms to challenge abuses that arise.

> The lesson to be learned is that effective protection of children can only be achieved by listening to and taking them seriously. The conventional view of protection has been as a one-way process, with adults as agents and children as recipients. What is now needed is a more sophisticated approach, in which it is understood as a dynamic process, in which adults take responsibility for keeping children safe by listening to and respecting their perspectives, while empowering them to contribute towards their own protection.
>
> (Lansdown, 2006, p. 149)

Commission for Social Care Inspection (CSCI) research with children in care showed they were able to give clear views about what they wanted and how they wanted to be treated. It also illustrated the dynamic processes at work between adults and children, including in relation to their safety:

- *how they want to be treated:* 'Treat us individually, not as children as a whole; treat our private worries confidentially – they're not for chatting and joking'

- *about the choices they want to make:* 'Children have a right to privacy; check for risks – but balance fun (and other things) and risks; if you are placing us somewhere, give us a real choice of placement'

- *about personal safety:* 'We have a right not to be bullied – and when dealing with bullying, please ask the bullied child and get it right so you don't make things worse; understand where to draw the line; beware untrained staff using restraint; get police checks done properly to protect us after what happened at Soham'

- *about consultation:* 'listen to quiet children; even troublemakers have a point to make and need to be protected'.

> (CSCI, 2007, p. 4)

Some of these issues can be brought into particularly sharp focus when adults attempt to take action on children's behalf to safeguard their welfare. Bell's (2002) research with children who were the subject of child protection processes concluded that adult perspectives dominate child protection inquiries. Insofar as adults have a responsibility to keep children safe, this is entirely appropriate. However, Bell argued that this dominance was often at the *expense* of children's voices, which could all too easily be silenced. Despite government guidance that professionals should see, observe, engage and talk to children (DH et al., 2000), partnership practice was for the most part limited. There were positive examples of good practice:

> most of the children and young people reported that their social worker had 'explained why they were coming – it meant a great deal' and were clear about the reasons for the visit – 'getting my family sorted out', 'tried to stop my mum walking out on us'.
>
> (Bell, 2002, p. 4)

However, all too often children were extremely anxious about the process, in some instances with good reason:

> 'I didn't want her [the social worker] to see my dad. I knew he'd go mental – but she told him anyway. It was twice as bad'. [Another] respondent felt responsible for what then happened, and that they had done something wrong: 'I was naughty – fighting at school, fighting Mum, breaking windows ...'. Their greatest fear was of removal from home: 'I thought we might be taken away ... I still worry about that'.
>
> (Bell, 2002, p. 4)

Involving children in staying safe is complex and at times raises real ethical dilemmas about what they have a right to know, what choices they actually have, what they can decide upon, and what they have a right to be protected from. As the quotes from Bell illustrate, however, it is all too easy to have a default setting that excludes children, or, even worse, colludes with clumsy professional interventions in which practitioners do not think through the implications of their actions and inadvertently make a child more vulnerable. As Parton (2006) points out, this means it cannot stop at listening to and working with children and this presents a significant challenge yet to be met:

> it is not simply that the voices of children and young people have to be heard but that they have to be given more control about what happens to them once they have raised their voice. This is a major challenge. ... It takes considerable maturity to give the primary control to children and young people themselves so that they can report what they want, where and when, and how 'their concerns' should be addressed, so that they feel they have a large degree of control about what happens to them.
>
> (Parton, 2006, p. 186)

Key points

1   Fear and anxiety are features of some children's lives.

2   It is important that children *feel* safe. Children who live in relative safety can feel very fearful and, conversely, children who live in comparative danger can feel safe.

3   If children live with insecurity and do not feel safe, this is not only a breach of their human rights but can have a significant impact on their wellbeing in both the short and long term.

Conclusion

Governments, and their agencies, have the capacity to persistently challenge attitudes and beliefs that facilitate abuse and to put into place robust systems to monitor, report and oversee those with responsibility to safeguard children. Practitioners who work with children can be challenged to expand their skills and think much more holistically about a protective environment for children. The strength of this ambitious agenda is that it attempts to break down division between practitioners and groups of practitioners and to deliver proactive services that reflect the 'joined up' nature of children's lives. This can contribute to keeping children safe and children feeling safe only if it means involving wider services than those traditionally associated with safeguarding children and involves giving children the vital information and skills they need to stay safe.

References

Adcock, M. and White, R. (eds) (1998) *Significant Harm*, Croydon, Significant Publications.

Aldgate, J., Jones, D., Rose, W. and Jeffery, C. (eds) (2006) *The Developing World of the Child*, London, Jessica Kingsley.

ATD Fourth World (2006) *What We Say Should Change Our Lives*, London, ATD Fourth World.

Audit Commission (2003) *Services for Disabled Children*, London, The Stationery Office.

Aynsley-Green, A. (2006) *Journeys: Primary Age Children Talk About Bullying*, London, Office of the Children's Commissioner.

Batmanghelidjh, C. (2006) *Shattered Lives*, London, Jessica Kingsley.

Bell, M. (2002) 'Promoting children's rights through the use of relationship', *Child & Family Social Work*, vol. 7, no. 1, pp. 1–11.

Blanden, J., Gregg, P. and Machin, S. (2005) *Intergenerational mobility in Europe and North America*, available online at <http://cep.lse.ac.uk/about/news/IntergenerationalMobility.pdf>, accessed 2 August 2007.

Bowlby, J. (1988) *A Secure Base: Clinical Applications of Attachment Theory*, London, Tavistock/Routledge.

Brooks, C. and Rice, K. (1997) *Families in Recovery: Coming Full Circle*, Baltimore, Paul H. Brookes Publishing.

Calder, M. and Hackett, S. (eds) (2003) *Assessment in Child Care: Using and Developing Frameworks for Practice*, Lyme Regis, Russell House.

Cemlyn, S. and Briskman, L. (2003) 'Asylum, children's rights and social work', *Child & Family Social Work*, vol. 8, no. 3, pp. 163–178.

ChildLine (1997) *Beyond the Limit: Children Who Live With Parental Alcohol Misuse*, London, ChildLine.

Children and Young People's Unit (2006) *Our children and young people – our pledge: a ten year strategy for children and young people in Northern Ireland 2006–2016*, available online at <http://www.allchildrenni.gov.uk/tenyearstrategychildren1.pdf>, accessed 22 August 2007.

Cleaver, H. (2006) 'The influence of parenting and other family relationships' in Aldgate, J., Jones, D., Rose, W. and Jeffery, C. (eds) *The Developing World of the Child*, London. Jessica Kingsley.

Commission for Social Care Inspection (CSCI) (2007) *Children's services: CSCI findings 2004–07*, available online at <http://www.csci.org.uk/PDF/childrens_services_csci_findings.pdf>, accessed 2 August 2007.

Corby, B. (1998) *Child Abuse: Toward a Knowledge Base*, Maidenhead, Open University Press.

Deakin, J. (2006) 'Dangerous people, dangerous places: the nature and location of young people's victimisation and fear', *Children & Society*, vol. 20, pp. 376–390.

Department for Education and Skills (DfES) (2003) *Every Child Matters*, London, DfES.

Department for Education and Skills (DfES) (2004) *Stand up for us: challenging homophobia in schools*, available online at <http://publications.teachernet.gov.uk/eOrderingDownload/SUFU%20Final.pdf>, accessed 24 August 2007.

Department for Education and Skills (DfES) (2005a) *A common core of skills and knowledge for the children's workforce*, available online at <http://publications. teachernet.gov.uk/eOrderingDownload/DfES11892005.pdf>, accessed 2 August 2007.

Department for Education and Skills (DfES) (2005b) *Common Assessment Framework for Children and Young People*, London, The Stationery Office.

Department for Education and Skills (DfES) (2006a) *Information Sharing and the Common Assessment Framework*, available online at <http://www.everychildmatters.gov.uk>, accessed 25 June 2007.

Department for Education and Skills (DfES) (2006b) *What to do if You are Worried a Child is Being Abused*, London, DfES.

Department for Education and Skills (DfES) (2007) *Every Child Matters: Change for Children*, available online at <http://www.everychildmatters.gov.uk>, accessed 25 June 2007.

Department of Health (DH) (1995) *Child Protection: Messages from Research*, London, HMSO.

Department of Health (DH) (1998) *Modernising Health and Social Services: White Paper*, London, The Stationery Office.

Department of Health (DH) (2000) *Lost in care: report of the tribunal of inquiry into the abuse of children in care in the former county council areas of Gwynedd and Clwyd since 1974 (The Waterhouse Inquiry)*, available online at <http://www.dh.gov.uk/en/ Publicationsandstatistics/Publications/PublicationsPolicyAndGuidance/DH_4003097>, accessed 21 August 2007.

Department of Health (DH) (2002) *Safeguarding children: a Joint Chief Inspector's report on arrangements to safeguard children*, available online at <http://www.dh.gov.uk/en/ Publicationsandstatistics/Publications/PublicationsPolicyandGuidance/DH_4103427>, accessed 21 August 2007.

Department of Health (DH) (2005) *Making safeguarding everybody's business: a post Bichard vetting scheme*, available online at <http://www.dh.gov.uk/en/Consultations/ closedconsultations/DH_4114901>, accessed 21 August 2007.

Department of Health, Department for Education and Employment, Home Office (DH, DfEE, HO) (2000) *Framework for the Assessment of Children in Need and their Families*, London, The Stationery Office.

Foley, P. (2008) 'Listening across generations' in Foley, P. and Leverett, S. (eds) *Connecting With Children: Developing Working Relationships*, Bristol/Policy Press, Milton Keynes/Open University.

Forrester, D. and Harwin, J. (2006) 'Parental substances misuse and child care social work: findings from the first stage of a study of 100 families', *Child & Family Social Work*, vol. 11, no. 4, pp. 325–335.

Fox Harding, L. (1997) *Perspectives in Child Care Policy*, London, Longman.

Frost, N. (2005) *Professionalism, Partnership and Joined-up Thinking: A Research Review of Front-line Working with Children and Families*, Dartington, Research in Practice.

Ghate, D. and Hazel, N. (2002) *Parenting in Poor Environments: Stress, Support and Coping*, London, Jessica Kingsley.

Hendrick, H. (2003) *Child Welfare: Historical Dimensions, Contemporary Debate*, Bristol, The Policy Press.

Hester, M., Pearson, C. and Harwin, N. (2000) *Making an Impact: Children and Domestic Violence: A Reader*, London, Jessica Kingsley.

Hirsch, D. (2006) *What will it take to end child poverty?*, available online at <http://www.jrf.org.uk/bookshop/eBooks/9781859355008.pdf>, accessed 22 August 2007.

HM Treasury and Department for Education and Skills (DfES) (2007) *Aiming High for Disabled Children: Better Support for Families*, London, The Stationery Office.

Howes, C. (1999) 'Attachment relationships in the context of multiple carers' in Cassidy, J. and Shraver, P.R. (eds) *Handbook of Attachment: Theory, Research and Clinical Applications*, London, The Guilford Press.

Humphreys, C. and Stanley, N. (2006) *Domestic Violence and Child Protection: Directions for Good Practice*, London, Jessica Kingsley.

Jack, G. (2001) 'An ecological perspective on child abuse' in Foley, P., Roche, J. and Tucker, S. (eds) *Children in Society: Contemporary Theory, Policy and Practice*, Basingstoke, Palgrave.

Jack, G. and Gill, O. (2003) *The Missing Side of the Triangle: Assessing the Importance of Family and Environmental Factors in the Lives of Children*, Ilford, Barnardo's.

Kidscape (1999) *Kidscape survey: long-term effects of bullying*, available online at <http://www.kidscape.org.uk/assets/downloads/kslongtermeffects.pdf>, accessed 2 August 2007.

Kidscape (2005) *Street Sense: Protect Yourself*, available online at <http://www.kidscape.org.uk/assets/downloads/ksStreetSense.pdf>, accessed 24 August 2007.

Kohli, R. (2006) 'The comfort of strangers: social work practice with unaccompanied asylum-seeking children and young people in the UK', *Child & Family Social Work*, vol. 11, no. 1, pp. 1–10.

Kroll, B. (2004) 'Living with an elephant: growing up with parental substance misuse', *Child & Family Social Work*, vol. 9, no. 2, pp. 129–40.

Laming, Lord (2003) *The Victoria Climbié Inquiry: Report of an Inquiry by Lord Laming*, London, The Stationery Office.

Lansdown, G. (2006) 'International developments in children's participation: lessons and challenges' in Tisdall, E.K.M., Davis, J.M., Prout, A. and Hill, M. (eds) *Children, Young People and Social Inclusion: Participation for What?*, Bristol, The Policy Press.

Marchant, R. and Jones, M. (2003) *Getting it Right: Involving Disabled Children in Assessment, Planning and Review Processes*, Brighton, Triangle.

McGee, C. (2000) *Childhood Experiences of Domestic Violence*, London, Jessica Kingsley.

Morgan, R. (2005) *Younger Children's Views On 'Every Child Matters'*, London, Commission for Social Care Inspection.

Morgan, R. (2006) *About Social Workers: A Children's Views Report*, London, Commission for Social Care Inspection.

Mullender, A., Hague, G., Farvah Imam, U., Kelly, L., Malos, E. and Regan, L. (2003) '"Could have helped but they didn't": the formal and informal support systems experienced by children living with domestic violence' in Hallett, C. and Prout, A. (eds) *Hearing the Voices of Children: Social Policy for a New Century*, London, Routledge Falmer.

Murphy, M. (2004) *Developing Collaborative Relationships in Interagency Child Protection Work*, Lyme Regis, Russell House Publishing.

Newman, T. (2004) *What Works in Building Resilience?*, Ilford, Barnardo's Policy and Research Unit.

NSPCC Inform (2006) *Child protection register statistics: England 2002–2006*, available online at <http://www.nspcc.org.uk/Inform/resourcesforprofessionals/Statistics/ChildProtectionRegisterStatistics/england_wdf49858.pdf>, accessed 30 July 2007.

Office of the Deputy Prime Minister (2004) *Indices of Deprivation: Population Denominators*, London, The Stationery Office.

O'Hagan, K.P. (1995) 'Emotional and psychological abuse: problems of definition', *Child Abuse & Neglect*, vol. 19, no. 4, pp. 449–461.

Okitikpi, T. and Aymer, C. (2003) 'Social work with African refugee children and their families', *Child & Family Social Work*, vol. 8, no. 3, pp. 213–222.

Oliver, C. and Candappa, M. (2003) *Tackling Bullying: Listening to the Views of Children and Young People*, Nottingham, DfES Publications.

O'Reilly, R. (2006) *How safe is your school day? Investigating year 8 pupils' perception of safe places and times*, available online at <http://childrens-research-centre.open.ac.uk/ research/How%20safe%20is%20your%20school%20day.doc>, accessed 3 August 2007.

Parton, N. (2006) *Safeguarding Childhood: Early Intervention and Surveillance in a Late Modern Society*, Basingstoke, Palgrave Macmillan.

Scottish Executive (2002) *'It's everyone's job to make sure I'm alright': Report of the Child Protection Audit and Review*, available online at <http://www.scotland.gov.uk/ Resource/Doc/47007/0023992.pdf>, accessed 6 August 2007.

Seden, J., Sinclair, R., Robbins, D. and Pont, C. (2001) *Studies Informing the Framework for the Assessment of Children in Need and Their Families*, London, The Stationery Office.

Social Care Institute for Excellence (SCIE) (2005) *Managing risk and minimising mistakes in services to children and families*, available online at <http://www.scie.org.uk/ publications/reports/report06.pdf>, accessed 21 August 2007.

Statham, J. and Biehal, N. (2005) *Research and Practice Briefings Number 11: Supporting Families*, London, DfES.

Thompson, N. (2002) *Building the Future*, Lyme Regis, Russell House Publishing.

Tunstill, J., Meadows, P., Allnock, D., Akhurst, S., Chrysanthou, J., Garbers, C., Morley, A. and Van de Velde, T. (2005) *Implementing Sure Start Local Programmes: An In-Depth Study*, London, DfES.

UNICEF (2004) *Childhood Under Threat: The State of the World's Children 2005*, New York, UNICEF.

United Nations (1989) *United Nations Convention on the Rights of the Child (UNCRC)*, Geneva, United Nations.

Ward, H. and Rose, W. (2002) *Approaches to Needs Assessment in Children's Services*, London, Jessica Kingsley.

Webb, S.A. (2001) 'Considerations on the validity of evidence-based practice in social work', *British Journal of Social Work*, vol. 31, no. 1, pp. 57–79.

Welsh Assembly Government (2007) *Children First*, available online at <http:// www.childrenfirst.wales.gov.uk/content/about.htm>, accessed 24 August 2007.

Winnicott, D. (1964) *The Child and the Family and the Outside World*, London, Penguin.

Chapter 7

Children, families and the law

Michael Isles

Introduction

Support for children and families is closely linked with the political and legal systems of the countries in which the support is being sought or offered. Whether a particular support or service is being provided by a statutory service provider (such as a local authority), a voluntary sector organisation (such as a registered charity) or a private company, it will clearly always be offered within a social and political context, but it will have a legal context too. Virtually all services offered to families exist within a regulatory framework and many will also work within an inspection framework. Funding will usually be accompanied by conditions adhering the parties to the terms of the agreement, all existing 'non-subject-specific' law such as criminal law, human rights law and the laws of tort and of contract will also apply to specialist service provision, and the motivations and political directions of government will profoundly affect the focus of the support or service at issue.

The formation and implementation of law is in itself an intensely political process, as politicians make law, political executives (that is, governments and governmental bodies) implement it and those to whom the law is directed are required to adhere to it. Laws lead to policies which lead to practices that need to support children as having separate and distinct interests from those of adults, that support families and safeguard children, and that support human rights across the generations. This, then, is the focus of this chapter. Essentially, we will be exploring the legal and policy framework that directs and enables the broad range of supports and services available to children and families. Having an understanding of these issues is essential to all who work with children and families, as even the most empathic and effective interpersonal work will be limited without some knowledge of the basis on which external or additional services are provided, what they are, and where to go to get them.

The nature of the systems operating in the various parts of the UK means that law and policy – from which services and supports derive – is changing constantly. New government policies and targets are set, new legislation is implemented and existing legislation updated and amended, the effects of devolution are considerable and increasing, and the interpretation of law through the courts impacts on the application of legislation. Some practitioners need an in-depth knowledge of the law, but everyone engaged in the children's workforce will benefit from knowledge of relevant legislation. While it is not suggested that this chapter will equip you with a full understanding of the complexities of law and social policy in this area, it intends to help you to ask the questions and look in the right places, in order to achieve better outcomes for children.

Core questions

- What is the legal basis underpinning the provision of support and services for children and families?
- How does the state become involved in overseeing/monitoring children, parents and parenting, and what are the primary sources of relevant law, guidance and regulation?
- What are 'rights' in the context of work with children and families? Who has them, what is their purpose and do they promote children's wellbeing?

1 Support and services for children and families: the legal framework

Consider how, at this current time and in your particular circumstances, you are actually using the law on a continuing basis; it may not appear immediately obvious, but law is in fact part and parcel of everyday life for all of us. If you classify law by its function – for the purposes of punishment, deterrence, compensation, regulation and protection – it actually extends (either actively or passively) to all aspects of our lives. Some brief examples follow, but these are not of course exhaustive; the average law library is full of literally thousands of examples where law is involved with the everyday and the extraordinary, in private as well as public life. Families, even as the concept flexes and evolves, are a legal as well as political and social concept. Marriage, for example, is legal as well as religious, and is therefore governed by various legal rules. The same applies to civil partnerships, and co-habiting couples can sometimes use the law to provide themselves with contractual protections (that is, joint mortgages, wills, and so on). The absence of comprehensive legal coverage and protections for co-habiting heterosexual couples is also an issue.

The private home, as another example, is affected by building regulations, and your mode of occupation – whether you're an outright owner, mortgagee or tenant – will be subject to regulatory law. What you can actually do

A civil partnership: the law constantly changes in response to wider social change

with your property is not entirely a private decision – the planning authority may well have its own views. A huge number of laws also apply to the physical environment and affect the buildings and roads we all use.

The law in relation to issues such as housing, healthcare, safeguarding children, education and social and emotional wellbeing plays a crucial role in determining what assessments and/or interventions may be required on the part of relevant agencies. In 'real life', situations are complex and cross agency and professional boundaries, involving as they often do health, social care, law, education, safeguarding children and child welfare. Thus, as the circumstances in which children and families live are exceedingly diverse, so too must be the range of assessments, supports, resources and services available to meet these circumstances.

Thinking point 7.1   Why do all practitioners need to have knowledge of the legal frameworks of work with children and families?

Those working in the children's workforce can benefit from looking in more breadth and in more depth at the law and policy that underpins and shapes practice, who is entitled to what and in what circumstances, and the role of the state in intervening in family lives where certain specified criteria are met. A working knowledge of relevant legislation and national and local policy and guidance is viewed as essential for children and families practitioners. This group of practitioners is very wide and involves people working in statutory and voluntary agencies, including child and family health practitioners, early years workers and educationalists, social workers, teachers and teaching assistants, play workers, Children and Family Court Advisory and Support Service (CAFCASS, or CAFCASS Cymru in Wales) workers, family support workers, and many more.

There will be a variety of reasons for practitioners to become familiar with the legal framework that affects their role and their practice, including:

- to know which actions are mandatory duties on the part of practitioners, and which are discretionary powers

- to possess a more complete understanding of their role and responsibilities

- to advocate on behalf of children and families, ensuring their rights are upheld

- to access supports and resources for children and families by applying legal and policy criteria

- to communicate concerns and issues precisely and effectively within the context of the law and policy

- to write reports and give evidence (in court or at quasi-judicial hearings) in relation to a case in which they have been involved

- to advise service users accurately and to know when to refer them to specialist legal advisers

- to work efficiently when required with legal advisers.

What, therefore, are the sorts of areas covered by the law on support and services for children and families? Perhaps the first things that come to mind are the services for children and families, including child welfare services. There will be particular aspects of health and education, such as the provision of education for children with special educational needs, particular requirements or additional learning supports (Scotland), or family-centred health services, the provision of preschool care for children or school admission and school exclusion procedures. Family law and mediation in times of family breakdown could also be included.

These suggestions are by no means exhaustive, and you might wish to consider some others that apply to specific practitioners. Whatever your specific role, it is increasingly clear that practice within and according to the law is a pre-requisite – even those who should know the law sometimes don't – and failure to do so will attract criticism:

> In 1998, the Social Service Inspectors at the Department of Health published a report called *Someone Else's Children* (DH, 1998). This set out the results of a large-scale inspection of local authorities in England and Wales. It gave a dreadful picture of how the law was actually put into practice. It described 'a catalogue of concerns about how important decisions are made and the arrangements to ensure that children are safe' ... Failure to understand and act within the legal framework let these children down. The law may say that the interests of the child are important, or, where a court is concerned, 'paramount' (Children Act 1989, s.1). It is the practitioner who carries this into effect.
>
> (Brayne and Carr, 2005, p. 9)

The response to Lord Laming's report into the death of Victoria Climbié in England in 2000 (Laming, 2003) noted that while the legislative framework for safeguarding children set out in the Children Act 1989 was basically sound (and this was before the changes implemented in the Children Act 2004, designed to further strengthen it), there were serious weaknesses in the way in which it was interpreted, resourced and implemented.

In an ideal world, children would promptly receive or have access to whatever is necessary for their wellbeing. We evidently don't live in an ideal world, and we therefore have a number of problems to consider: who defines what is 'necessary', who has priority in the reality of a very resource-hungry climate, and who bears legal responsibility in ensuring, at the very least, that minimum standards are met (not to mention the question of who defines those minimum standards)? We must also remember that children also have distinct and separate interests from those of adults.

This is where the law, national, regional and local policy and those charged with their implementation play a part. We will shortly explore the statutory legal framework that underpins assessments, interventions and services for children and families in the UK. However, even given a fairly comprehensive package of services available to families in certain circumstances, there are debates about the 'broad-brush' approach to both the definitions of the services themselves, and the families they are intended for.

> The concept of support for families is problematic ... in its lack of precision as a goal underlying government policy. However, the concept of the family itself is completely taken for granted in policy-making where it appears as a single, static and homogenous unit, which can be targeted unproblematically by services. A number of commentators have drawn attention to the limitations in such policy representations of the family, showing this portrayal to be inconsistent with current sociological representations of diversity, multiple memberships and fluid, lived realities.
>
> (Warin, 2007, pp. 94–95)

Thinking point 7.2   What does Warin mean by the concept of family support being imprecise as a governmental policy goal? How do you think the concept of the family might be more considered and less taken for granted, as Warin suggests is the case currently?

The politics of intervention and support for families is discussed in Chapters 3 and 6 of this book and in *Changing children's services: working and learning together*, Book 3 of this series (Foley and Rixon, 2008), but family law has its own history and traditions. In the past it was primarily associated with regulating relationships within families and providing some guidance when relationships between parents broke down. Because of a societal acknowledgement, enforced in law, of children as being vulnerable and requiring 'protections', family law has created enforceable obligations on the part of all those involved in their care, whether as parents and carers or formally as teachers, doctors, early years workers, social workers, child minders or nursery nurses, for example.

The law, shaped as it is by societal change and political direction, is fine-tuned almost continually through new legislation and case law. It will never reflect the views of everybody, nor can it always keep up with the pace of change in rapidly developing areas of life such as social care or education. Added to this, jurisdictional differences within the four UK countries and administrations together with the authority and influence of various international bodies and conventions – the European Union (EU), the European Convention on Human Rights (ECHR), the United Nations

Some families regularly move between different parts of the UK and will be affected by different jurisdictions

Convention on the Rights of the Child (UNCRC; United Nations, 1989) – make for a complex legal system, with the inevitable possibility of parts of it becoming outdated or subject to variations in interpretation and implementation.

A practical example of this is the contentious issue of 'reasonable chastisement' – a defence available to parents who strike their children, since 1933, although rooted in historical perceptions and treatment of children going back much further. Although the UK is part of the European Union, this is a topic for individual nation states to legislate on (at least to a certain degree), and other countries such as Italy and Germany have effectively prohibited the physical punishment of children. The UK parliament has not, although its use has been restricted in England, Wales and Northern Ireland where, since 2006, it is an offence to hit a child if it causes mental harm or leaves a mark on the skin. This follows a European Court of Human Rights (ECHR) ruling against the UK in 1998 (A v UK (Human Rights – Punishment of Child) (1998) 27 EHRR 97), and the subsequent implementation of the Children Act 2004, section 58. In Scotland, under section 51 of the Criminal Justice (Scotland) Act 2003, the offence is not confined to causing harm or leaving marks; it also concerns the implement used and the type of punishment, and the Scottish Executive strongly endorses non-physical punishment. So, different jurisdictions view the issue of parental chastisement to children in different ways, provide for different legislation and consequently apply different sanctions and remedies – yet the punishments done to children and the children themselves are the same, regardless of administrative or legal jurisdiction.

1.1 Law-making

Essentially, law is produced by two main processes: first the passing of legislation in the Houses of Parliament in London or the Scottish Parliament in Edinburgh, also known as statute law; second the judgements made by the senior courts, also known as case law. European law also plays an important role, although it falls outside the scope of this chapter. Case law in particular goes back many hundreds of years, and in some areas of law, cases from the eighteenth and nineteenth centuries are still followed. These cases combined form the 'backbone' of what is called the 'common law', and continue to form an important backdrop to legal instruments such as contracts, wills and deeds. The role of judges in interpreting the law to the facts of a particular case remains a cornerstone of our system of law, and applies equally to judgements involving criminal law, land law, family law or any other practice area. The diagrams that follow show the court systems in England and Wales and in Scotland.

We noted above the way in which an important ECHR case concerning the smacking of children – A v UK (1998) – directly contributed to a significant change in statute law. Note, though, that case law actually developed the original premise that children could be physically chastised. While statute law in an area such as children and families is often subject to debate, consultation and some degree of planning through parliamentary and governmental systems, case law is by its nature built up over a period of time, reflecting the way in which the statutes apply to 'real life' situations, or cases.

An example of a case relevant to children and families practitioners that still has significance today is the 'Gillick' decision made by the House of Lords in 1986 (cited as 'Gillick v West Norfolk and Wisbech Area Health Authority and another [1986] 1 AC 112', where Gillick is the claimant, the Area Health Authority is the respondent, 1986 is the year of the hearing and AC 112 is the type of law report and its page number). The case centred on the question of whether a young person under the age of sixteen years could consent to medical treatment, specifically contraceptive treatment, or whether parental consent must be required, as was put forward by Mrs Gillick as an interpretation of section 8 of the Family Law Act and section 131 of the Mental Health Act 1983. Following appeals against rulings made by the lower courts, the House of Lords ruled that young people under the age of sixteen, if they are of sufficient maturity, are able to give effective consent to medical examination and treatment. As the existing law as stated above had been unclear about the issue, the House of Lords was able to clarify the matter, applying it to the facts of the case, and set it as a precedent, that is, binding on all the lower courts. You can see from the diagram that follows how the basic court system in England and Wales is set up, and that the House of Lords is at the top (subject only to judgements made by the European courts, including the European Court of Human Rights).

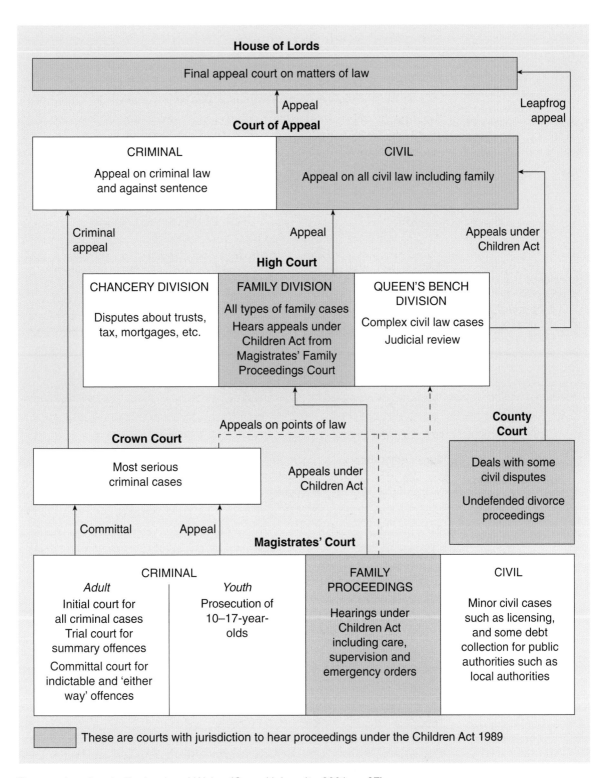

The court system in England and Wales (Open University, 2001, p. 37)

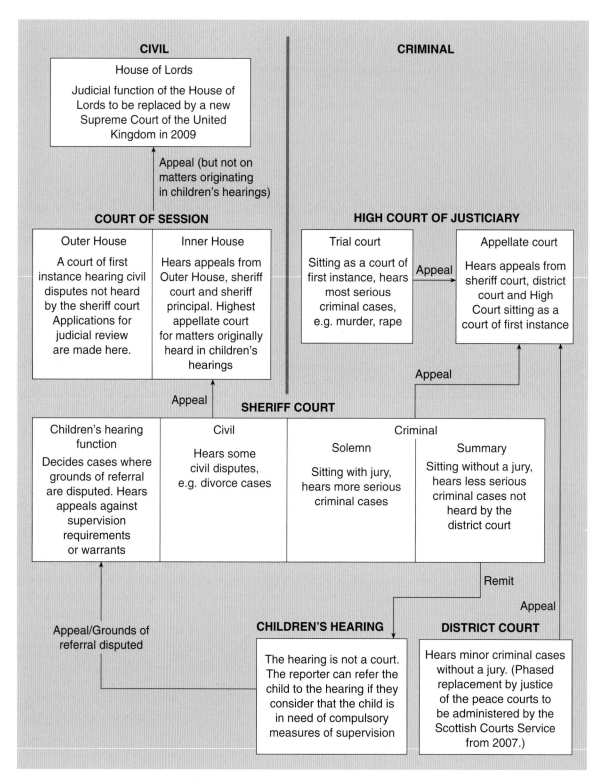

The court system in Scotland (Open University, 2007a, p. 56)

Although the Gillick judgement is now quite old, it still has legal authority and will be followed by lower courts where the facts of the case are similar. Thus, the case-law system has the ability to apply often very broad-brush statute law to the facts of each specific case, tailoring judgements to fit different circumstances within the law.

Thinking point 7.3   Are there any disadvantages to judges interpreting the law to the facts of each case? What might an alternative be?

You may be forgiven for thinking, from reading the previous paragraphs, that case law forms the basis of law in the UK. In fact, primary legislation, the law made by the Westminster Parliament for the whole of the UK and the jurisdictions of Wales and England, the Edinburgh Parliament for Scotland, and – at the time of writing – Acts of the Northern Ireland Assembly at Stormont, always has primacy (that is, superiority) over case law, and is the pre-eminent process of law-making. Law derived from the parliamentary process is known as legislation. Terms such as Acts of Parliament or statutes are also used to identify specific pieces of legislation. The role of parliament is to make, amend and repeal law, while the judges' role is to interpret it. Therefore, while the Gillick judgement remains legally valid at the time this chapter is being written, it could be rendered obsolete if, for example, it directly conflicted with a statutory provision passed by parliament. Given its standing and legal authority, however, this is fairly unlikely!

The 'Crown in Parliament' – the law-making process – comprises the Houses of Commons and Lords in the Westminster Parliament, or the whole Parliament in the case of Scotland, and the Queen in her role as Head of State. Many pamphlets and chapters of books have been written about this process, but, in summary, this is how it works. A Bill will be laid before the relevant house or parliament – perhaps, as with the Children Acts 1989 and 2004 and the Adoption and Children (Scotland) Act 2007, following a period of consultation – and after debates, periods of scrutiny and possible amendment, the Bill as passed will go forward to the Queen for Royal Assent. Royal Assent is nowadays a constitutional formality, but still an important technical characteristic of law-making in the UK. This 'act' of parliament results in the Bill becoming an Act of Parliament, or an Act of the Scottish Parliament, which forms a part of the title for pieces of legislation such as the Children Acts 1989 and 2004, Adoption and Children Act 2002 or Criminal Justice (Scotland) Act 2003. New pieces of legislation are being added all the time as the governments of the day seek to legislate on their manifesto and policy commitments.

Occasionally, an individual member of a legislative body can bring a Bill for consideration to the parliament (a Private Member's Bill), or an amendment to a Bill, but these are fairly unusual and often still need the support of the government to make it on to the statute books. In 2004, for example, proposing an amendment to the Children Bill then going through parliament (the amendment was defeated), David Hinchcliffe MP, the Chair of the Commons Health Select Committee, opened the debate thus:

> 'New clause 12 deals with the physical chastisement of children. I accept that this is a highly contentious matter for some, and that it generates strong feelings among a significant number of people. I also accept that it is not any easy matter for any Government to address, as some people will accuse them of establishing a so-called nanny state and of interfering in the private domain of the family. I am therefore very grateful to the ministerial team responsible for the Bill for their willingness to listen, over a long period of time, to the concerns and arguments of those of us who believe that children should have equal protection in law from assault.'
>
> (TheyWorkForYou, 2004)

Table 7.1 lists some of the pieces of legislation that are most important to the children and families practitioner from the last twenty years in each of the jurisdictions of the UK, together with important constitutional legislation governing devolution, and brief summaries of some of their focuses. The list cannot be exhaustive, but provides examples of the scope and movement of legislation.

Table 7.1 United Kingdom legislation important to children and families practitioners	
Children Act 1989	Consolidating legislation, plus new concepts – welfare of child, children in need, etc.; major UK legislation for public and private law (including Scotland until 1995).
Children (Scotland) Act 1995	Major piece of legislation for public and private law in Scotland, including welfare of child, parental responsibility, child protection, etc.
Education Act 1996	Arrangements for statutory education of children, types of schools, etc.
Family Law Act 1996	Private law concerning marriage, family breakdown, domestic violence provisions, etc.
Crime and Disorder Act 1998	'Restorative justice', introduction of Anti-Social Behaviour Orders, etc.
Scotland Act 1998	Establishment of and arrangements for a Scottish Parliament.
Human Rights Act 1998	UK-wide legislation enabling the provisions of the European Convention on Human Rights to be heard and dealt with by the UK court systems.

Government of Wales Act 1998	Establishment of and arrangements for a National Assembly for Wales.
Northern Ireland Act 1998	Establishment of and arrangements for a National Assembly for Northern Ireland.
Protection of Children Act 1999	Identification and listing of people deemed unsuitable to work with children.
Youth Justice and Criminal Evidence Act 1999	Special measures enabling evidence given by children to be in private, video evidence, etc.
Family Law Act (Northern Ireland) 2001	Acquisition of parental responsibility by fathers in Northern Ireland.
Children's Commissioner for Wales Act 2001	Establishment of a Children's Commissioner for Wales.
Education (Disability Strategies and Pupils' Educational Records) (Scotland) Act 2002	Improving access to education for pupils with disabilities.
Special Educational Needs and Disability Act 2001	Education in mainstream schools of children with special educational needs.
Adoption and Children Act 2002	Major legislation completely reforming adoption law in England and Wales.
Commissioner for Children and Young People (Northern Ireland) Order 2003	Establishment of a Children and Young Person's Commissioner for Northern Ireland.
Commissioner for Children and Young People (Scotland) Act 2003	Establishment of a Children's Commissioner for Scotland.
Children Act 2004	Establishment of a Children's Commissioner for England, plus key legislation about safeguarding children partnerships for England and Wales.
Education Act 2005	Powers and duties of school inspectors in England and Wales, plus accountability of individual schools.
Childcare Act 2006	Places responsibility for childcare provision with local authorities, charging them to raise quality, improve delivery and achieve better results.
Family Law (Scotland) Act 2006	Rules regulating divorce, parental responsibilities and rights (PRRs) for fathers, protection against domestic abuse, etc.
Adoption and Children (Scotland) Act 2007	Major legislation completely reforming adoption law in Scotland.
Northern Ireland (St Andrews Agreement) Act 2007	Restoration of the Northern Ireland Assembly on 8 May 2007.

Children's services frequently need to work within changing legal frameworks; a fostering and adoption team

All recent legislation is now published on the internet, and available to download or read online free of charge. This is a remarkable resource, but be warned; the statutes themselves can be difficult to understand, as they use a very specific legal form of English, and they should not be viewed as an absolute authority, as amendments and interpretations may well have taken place since an Act was passed.

Although the Westminster Parliament still retains the primary legislating role for both England and Wales, devolution has significantly altered the way in which legislation is implemented in Wales, with the Welsh Assembly Government given responsibility for budgetary decisions on a wide range of areas including health, education, local government and social services. Additionally, the National Assembly for Wales (that is, the democratically elected body) can make what is known as 'delegated legislation' on areas devolved to it (including those mentioned above), when powers are given to it to do so by an Act of Parliament. The Scottish Parliament deals with all devolved matters; most important in this context are education, the justice system, social work and health. The National Assembly for Northern Ireland can pass primary legislation on subjects made available to it by the UK Parliament. This has led to different priorities, emphases, processes and procedures, and institutions, reflecting the different approaches of the different countries to finding solutions to problems. For example, Practice box 7.1 describes the children's hearing system in Scotland.

A children's hearing is a legal tribunal arranged to consider and make decisions on the cases of children and young people who are having problems in their lives and who may need legal steps to be taken to help them. Children's hearings are held in private and only those people who have a legal right to be there or are allowed to be there by the chairman will be present. A children's hearing is made up of three panel members.

A hearing is usually held in the child's or young person's home area. The layout of the room is relatively informal with the participants usually sitting round a table. Normally, the child or young person must attend and always has the right to attend all stages of his or her own hearing. The hearing may decide that the child does not have to attend certain parts of the hearing or even the whole hearing if, for example, matters might come up that would cause the child significant distress.

It is important that the relevant persons (for example, the parents) should be present at the hearing so that they can take part in the discussion and help the hearing to reach a decision. Their attendance is compulsory by law, and failure to appear may result in prosecution and a fine. The child or young person and the relevant persons may take a representative to help them at the hearing, and each may choose a separate representative. However, this does not mean that they do not have to attend themselves. In certain cases the hearing may appoint a publicly funded legal representative.

The parents or other relevant persons and their representatives can be excluded from any part of the hearing so that the panel members can get the views of the child or young person, or if the child may be distressed by their presence. However, the chairman must afterwards explain the substance of what has taken place in their absence. Although the proceedings are private, a person from the press is allowed to attend the hearing, but may be asked to leave the room if the hearing decides it is necessary in order to get the views of the child, or if the child may be distressed by their presence. The press is not allowed to disclose the identity of the child. Other observers may attend a hearing, but nobody is admitted unless they have a legitimate concern with the case or with the hearings system and have the agreement of the chairman of the hearing, the child and the child's family. The hearing is therefore a small gathering able to proceed in a relatively informal way and to give the child and parents the confidence and privacy to take a full part in the discussion about what needs to be done for the child.

The hearing has to decide on the measures of supervision that are in the best interests of the child or young person. It receives a report on the child and his or her social background from a social worker in the local authority, and where appropriate from the child's school. Medical, psychological and psychiatric reports may also be requested. Parents, and in general the child if she or he is over 12, are provided with copies of the reports at the same time as the panel members. The hearing discusses the circumstances of the child fully with the parents, the child or young person and any representatives, the social worker and the teacher, if present. As the hearing is concerned with the wider picture and the long-term wellbeing of the child, the measures that it decides on will be based on the welfare of the child. They may not appear to relate directly to the reasons that were the immediate cause of the child's appearance at the hearing. For example, the hearing may decide that a child or young person who is not receiving adequate parental care should not be removed from the home, because suitable support is available within their home area. Alternatively, a child who has committed a relatively minor offence may be placed away from home for a time if it appears that the home background is a major cause of the child's difficulties and the hearing considers that removal from home would be in his or her best interests.

(Open University, 2007b, pp. 79–80)

In summary: for any assessments, support or services that have a statutory basis, together with all statutory agencies that are involved in service delivery, legislation must be passed in parliament, brought into force and implemented by central government departments and/or the devolved executives. As you will see by looking through an Act of Parliament, legislation can be difficult to interpret, extremely broad in scope, and generally not aimed at individual practitioners. Increasingly, therefore, Acts of Parliament are accompanied by regulations (setting out, sometimes more clearly and precisely, arrangements for the implementation and enforcement of the legislation), orders, codes of practice and guidance. These will often link more clearly and directly with practice on the ground, so to speak, and are perhaps the most important for the practitioner to be aware of.

1.2 Regulation and guidance

The Children Act 1989 was a groundbreaking and innovative piece of legislation when it was implemented during the 1990s, seeking to consolidate an array of previous legislation. It made the welfare of the child paramount and introduced new concepts, such as parental responsibility. It is also enormous, with 108 sections arranged over twelve parts, each of which deals with a different subject. For example, Part I is introductory and deals with general principles to the Act, Part II addresses 'private law' orders made with respect to children in family proceedings, Part III deals with the 'public law' of local authority support for children and families, and so on.

Section 53 of the Children Act 2004 amends sections 17 and 47 of the Children Act 1989 to give 'children in need' and children involved in child protection inquiries the legal right to have their views given due consideration. Other parts of particular relevance to those working with children to the Children Act 2004 are:

- A legislative requirement for better integrated planning, commissioning and delivery of children's services, with the provision of clear legal accountability. These requirements apply in both England and Wales, but allowance is made for implementation in Wales to follow the different contexts that exist for children's services there.

- The establishment in England of statutory local safeguarding children boards (LSCBs) to replace the existing non-statutory area child protection committees (ACPCs).

- The strengthening of the existing notification arrangements in England and Wales for private fostering, with a reserve power (that is, one that can be implemented if necessary without any further legislation) to introduce a registration scheme if this is not effective.

- The creation of a new duty in England and Wales for local authorities to promote the educational achievement of Looked After children.

- A new duty on local authorities in England and Wales to ascertain a child's wishes and give due consideration to them, before determining what (if any) services are to be provided under section 17 of the Children Act 1989.

- The removal of the power to make a care order at a lower threshold than would be usual under the Children Act 1989 as a sanction for not complying with a Child Safety Order imposed under section 11 of the Crime and Disorder Act 1998.

- A restriction of the grounds on which the battery of a child may be justified as reasonable punishment.

Legislation itself is reviewed in light of experience, and – as in this case – new legislation is sometimes required to give effect to changes needed in the original law.

The commentary in subsection 1.1 on reading and interpreting primary legislation certainly applies to the Children Act 1989, and – with the intention of giving clear and specific guidance to those involved with implementing the Act – the government also released nine substantial volumes, plus an index, of guidance and regulations, each addressing a particular focus of the Act itself. For example, volume 1 deals with court orders, volume 2 with family support, volume 3 with family placements, and so on. Each is written with a view to practical implementation, but being regulations they do still carry the full force of law. This, then, is one of the primary purposes of regulations (a form of what is known as 'delegated legislation').

> A vast body of law is produced this way [by use of regulations and orders], and often serves to provide the detail to an associated Act of Parliament. The lack of parliamentary scrutiny means that delegated legislation can be introduced fairly quickly. Regulations often deal primarily with processes and procedures ... but can also deal with substantive issues.
>
> (Brammer, 2007, p. 40)

As well as regulations, there are different types and forms of guidance available, from a variety of sources. These will vary greatly in terms of their legal status, and the practitioner should always confirm the source of the guidance to make sure it can be relied upon, and also whether it has legal standing. As a general rule, guidance, when issued by a reputable source such as a regulatory body or government department, should always be followed unless there is a very good reason indeed for not doing so.

Practice box 7.2

Many practitioners will be working within codes of practice. The General Social Care Council's (GSCC) Code of Practice for Social Care Workers, for example, is:

> a list of statements that describe the standards of professional conduct and practice required of social care workers as they go about their daily work ... The intention is to confirm the standards required in social care and ensure that workers know what standards of conduct employers, colleagues, service users, carers and the public expect of them ...

Social care workers must:

- Protect the rights and promote the interests of service users and carers;
- Strive to establish and maintain the trust and confidence of service users and carers;
- Promote the independence of service users while protecting them as far as possible from danger or harm;
- Respect the rights of service users whilst seeking to ensure that their behaviour does not harm themselves or other people;
- Uphold public trust and confidence in social care services; and
- Be accountable for the quality of their work and take responsibility for maintaining and improving their knowledge and skills.

> (General Social Care Council, 2002, webpage)

Thinking point 7.4   With all the requirements set out in Acts of Parliament, regulations, codes of practice, directions and guidance, is there room for creative practice? Indeed, can the two (that is, rules and creativity) work together in children and families practice?

1.3 Policies for children and families

We now move to the final category of 'rules' of one sort or another that affect the way services are provided to children and families. Perhaps to call a policy a rule is a little misleading, as in fact policies exist to set out courses of action: organisational strategic plans, if you will. However, when the organisation setting out and publishing a policy is an employer, or professional body, or the government, and when complying with a policy means more resources or a failure to adhere to the policy results in a sanction, it can certainly feel more like a rule than a plan.

Policies, therefore, do indeed set out courses of action and plans for current and future behaviour (for example, an anti-bullying policy, special needs policy, health and safety policies, and so on), but unlike a discussion paper, the formal adoption of a policy will usually mean that there is an expectation it is followed. Major policies are subjected to considerable consultation processes as they proceed through their various stages and practitioners as individuals and as groups are able to comment and contribute to their development.

Again, as you would expect, policies can have slightly different statuses, as there are certain policies that are legally required, perhaps by a regulatory body. Health and safety policies and equal opportunities policies both fit into this category; the policy is there to enable the organisation (in this case, usually an employer) to fit the regulatory requirement to their characteristics and specifics. Thus, a policy can mention particular job roles, reporting procedures and departments, which no national regulation could hope to do. In fact, organisations can develop policies for absolutely any area they choose, for example a school's anti-bullying policy.

The operation of the policy will, however, always be subject to law, in that a policy may never enable something that would in fact be unlawful. However, a policy can 'fill in the gaps' where law is non-existent. An example of this is where many employers' equal opportunities policies go beyond what is required in law, stipulating that employees would not be discriminated against on grounds of age or sexual orientation. While these are both now legal requirements, they are both very recent. Arguably, some employers led the way with good policy practice, before parliament legislated as a result of a European directive.

Thinking point 7.5   Can you think of any other areas where policies directly shape a service for children and families? Would you say that they are an example of innovative thinking, likely to get the best outcomes for children?

An example is the national service framework (NSF) in England and Wales. NSFs are sometimes referred to as though they were primary law; actually they are national governmental policy – a strategic plan, usually with aims and measurable objectives. In this way, an NSF can be very specific in a way that primary legislation could not be, and can be adjusted on an ongoing basis in order to take account of new developments. The Department of Health (DH) says this about its programme of NSFs in England:

> National service frameworks (NSFs) are long term strategies for improving specific areas of care. They set measurable goals within set time frames.
>
> NSFs:
>
> - set national standards and identify key interventions for a defined service or care group
> - put in place strategies to support implementation
> - establish ways to ensure progress within an agreed time scale
> - form one of a range of measures to raise quality and decrease variations in service, introduced in The New NHS and A First Class Service. The NHS Plan re-emphasised the role of NSFs as drivers in delivering the Modernisation Agenda.
>
> Each NSF is developed with the assistance of an external reference group (ERG), which brings together health professionals, service users and carers, health service managers, partner agencies, and other advocates. ERGs adopt an inclusive process to engage the full range of views. The Department of Health supports the ERGs and manages the overall process.
>
> (DH, 2007, webpage)

Clearly, it is intended that NSFs are followed by agencies affected by them, and to this end adherence relies on a combination of the fact that the NSF is government policy, together with the belief that the plan is in the interests of the service-user group and associated professionals and carers. This certainly does seem to be the case; the National Service Frameworks for England and Wales would seem to be generally well regarded and seen as positive developments rather than bureaucratic or interfering. An article in the *British Medical Journal* on the NSF for children notes:

Children have been invisible in the NHS. Until now they have been regarded as an addendum to adult services. In the NHS Plan children were largely ignored ... Recent reforms have focused on adult services, with targets set by government to achieve them. One can argue that, as patients, pregnant women and children benefited from these reforms in terms of quantitative measures such as waiting times. However, the care of children requires a clearer vision in the more difficult qualitative areas. The national service framework emphasises that the majority of service needs for children are in the community and can only be provided by the NHS in partnership with education and social services as envisaged in *Every Child Matters* and the Children's Bill [now the Children Act 2004].

(Lachman and Vickers, 2004, p. 693)

This NSF, as with others in the series, is arranged into 'standards', which represent achievable quality measures the government has set as targets. There are eleven standards in the children's NSF, and these are listed in Practice box 7.3 with a brief explanation of each, taken from the government's executive summary. Note the broad range of standards representing various dimensions of the lives of children and their parents.

Practice box 7.3

Standard 1: Promoting Health and Well-being, Identifying Needs and Intervening Early

The health and well-being of all children and young people is promoted and delivered through a co-ordinated programme of action, including prevention and early intervention wherever possible, to ensure long term gain, led by the NHS in partnership with local authorities.

Standard 2: Supporting Parenting

Parents or carers are enabled to receive the information, services and support which will help them to care for their children and equip them with the skills they need to ensure that their children have optimum life chances and are healthy and safe.

Standard 3: Child, Young Person and Family-Centred Services

Children and young people and families receive high quality services, which are co-ordinated around their individual and family needs and take account of their views.

Standard 4: Growing Up into Adulthood

All young people have access to age-appropriate services, which are responsive to their specific needs as they grow into adulthood.

Standard 5: Safeguarding and Promoting the Welfare of Children and Young People

All agencies work to prevent children suffering harm and to promote their welfare, provide them with the services they require to address their identified needs and safeguard children who are being or who are likely to be harmed.

Standard 6: Children and Young People who are Ill

All children and young people who are ill, or thought to be ill, or injured will have timely access to appropriate advice and to effective services which address their health, social, educational and emotional needs throughout the period of their illness.

Standard 7: Children and Young People in Hospital

Children and young people receive high quality, evidence-based hospital care, developed through clinical governance and delivered in appropriate settings.

Standard 8: Disabled Children and Young People and Those with Complex Health Needs

Children and young people who are disabled or who have complex health needs receive co-ordinated, high quality child and family-centred services which are based on assessed needs, which promote social inclusion and, where possible, which enable them and their families to live ordinary lives.

Standard 9: The Mental Health and Psychological Well-being of Children and Young People

All children and young people, from birth to their eighteenth birthday, who have mental health problems and disorders have access to timely, integrated, high quality multidisciplinary mental health services to ensure effective assessment, treatment and support, for them, and their families.

Standard 10: Medicines for Children and Young People

Children, young people, their parents or carers, and health care professionals in all settings make decisions about medicines based on sound information about risk and benefit. They have access to safe and effective medicines that are prescribed on the basis of the best available evidence.

Standard 11: Maternity Services

Women have easy access to supportive, high quality maternity services, designed around their individual needs and those of their babies.

(DH and DfES, 2004, webpage)

As the standards set out in any NSF or equivalent from any of the various jurisdictions are not law, they are not in themselves directly enforceable in the courts. However, the fact that standards are government policy based on consultation and lessons learned from past errors could be an issue. There may be funding implications dependent on achieving (or failing to achieve) particular standards. Negative publicity or low ratings by auditors could also be an issue. Direct legal enforcement is therefore not the only mechanism to ensure compliance with policy objectives; legal action, as you may know from your professional or personal lives, is really to be regarded as a 'last resort' only, as the costs – both emotional and monetary, and in terms of time and commitment – are inevitably high.

Having looked at the legal systems and structures at work in the UK, we now move on to look at the issues of rights and responsibilities.

Key points

1   There are many reasons why children and families practitioners need to have a working knowledge of the law, the development of policy, regulation, and frameworks for practice since they underpin ordinary and extraordinary work with children and families.

2   The law is shaped by social and political change, is frequently fine-tuned by new legislation and case law, and plays a crucial part in the relationship between the state and children and families.

3   Devolution is contributing to the rapid evolution of law, guidance and regulation in relation to children and family practice.

2 Children, families and rights

The following was written by a group of children and young people reflecting on what the UNCRC meant to them; a different group, in a different time and place, may have come up with a different list of rights.

All of us are annoyed at the fact that we were never told about our rights before and we believe they are broken on a regular basis. We all decided we wanted to do more to inform young people like us of what our rights are, but first we decided to find out how aware the other young people of Derry actually were about their rights. What we found was disappointing.

After completing a number of interviews across the city we were shocked to find out that three out of ten children didn't know anything about what rights they had or had never even heard of the UN Convention on the Rights of the Child. Why is this so?

We need ways to enforce these rights and make sure that every child knows them because we believe children will feel better about themselves and treat one another better.

Instead of perhaps boring you with the full list we, as a group, decided to compile a list of our ten top favourite rights, if you like, because after all children have a right to know them! If you want to find out more check out the website www.unicef.org.

As a child or young person:

1   You have the right to live (pretty straightforward but important!).

2   You have the right to choose your own religion.

3   You have the right to an education.

4   You have the right to be with your parents if it is best for you.

5   You have the right to be protected from abuse and neglect.

6   You have the right to express the views you have and your views to be listened to in anything that affects you (teachers take notice).

7   You have the right to a decent standard of living.

8   You have the right to choose your friends and hang out with them.

9   You have the right to be protected from all forms of cruelty, exploitation and torture.

10   The government must uphold your rights.

(Headliners, 2004, webpage)

What do we mean when we talk about 'rights'? Most of us can remember quite easily instances when we have said – or heard others say – that so-and-so has a right to something; this is my right; I'm entitled to this. It is perhaps a truism to say that our expectations of the availability of rights can be at odds with the reality of the daunting complexities of establishing and pursuing an individual right or entitlement. In other words, even though there may be a claim to a right, and denial of the right feels unfair, the reality of having the right established and/or enforced in law can be another matter entirely. This is not to say that rights are not, or should not be, recognised in law. Life in the UK is probably more rights-based now than at any time in history. Rather, it is to say that legally recognised and practically enforceable rights and entitlements are perhaps still not as prolific as we sometimes believe.

The Human Rights Act (HRA) 1998 has incorporated the provisions of the European Convention on Human Rights (ECHR) into UK law, with the result that the principles enshrined in the articles of the ECHR are directly applicable within the UK. These principles include respect for family privacy (Article 8) and an insistence on procedural fairness in the resolution of disputes (Article 6). Further, Article 14 aims at ensuring that the rights contained within the ECHR are secured without discrimination on any ground.

Although referring to human rights, rather than rights to a resource or service (note, though, that the two can easily interweave; provision of a support might enable a family to continue as a family, for example), Burns Weston's commentary illustrates the wide array of opinions, ideas, debates and questions on the whole subject of rights and entitlements.

> To say that there is widespread acceptance of the principle of human rights on the domestic and international planes is not to say that there is complete agreement about the nature of such rights or their substantive scope – which is to say, their definition. Some of the most basic questions have yet to receive conclusive answers. Whether human rights are to be viewed as divine, moral or legal entitlements; whether they are to be validated by intuition, custom, social contract theory, principles of distributive justice, or as prerequisites for happiness; whether they are to be understood as

irrevocable or partially revocable; whether they are to be broad or limited in number and content – these and kindred issues are matters of ongoing debate and likely will remain so long as there exist contending approaches to public order and scarcity among resources.

(Burns Weston quoted in Steiner and Alston, 2000, p. 326)

Thinking point 7.6   What would you see as rights in the context of working with children and families? Can you give some examples of rights for children and say why you believe they are 'rights'?

Rights for children are possibly the closest there is to a set of 'universal' rights, on which there is widespread agreement on the theories and fundamentals (if not on the details and the practicalities) in most of the world's nations. As long ago as 1924 the Assembly of the League of Nations (the predecessor to the United Nations, albeit in very different form) stated in the Geneva Declaration on the Rights of the Child that 'mankind' owes to the child the best it has to give. Eighty-three years on, with the United Nations General Assembly proclaiming its own Declaration on the Rights of the Child in 1959, and establishing a Convention on the Rights of the Child (UNCRC) in 1989 (United Nations, 1989), which has attracted almost universal ratification, this belief clearly still holds true. The essential theme underlying these and other declarations and ratifications is that children need special protection and priority care. The rights of the UNCRC are frequently grouped as the 'three Ps': protection, provision and participation in decisions affecting the individual and collective lives of children.

> Human rights are not just for children in distant countries; they are for children here in this country too – the children we live with, that go to school at the bottom of the road, that share our neighbourhoods, and the children that cause trouble and hurt people. If the Convention on the Rights of the Child had a strap line it would be 'respect for children'.
>
> (Children's Rights Alliance for England, 2005, p. 12)

As international conventions and declarations, these agreements are not directly enforceable in the UK courts (as opposed to the ECHR, which is directly enforceable through the Human Rights Act 1998), although they remain important as indicators of the international strength of feeling and consensus on children in any given society. The UNCRC has also embodied important provisions and principles of national legislation, such as the Children Act 1989 and the Children (Scotland) Act 2005, which are, of course, directly enforceable in courts in the UK.

Children are recognized as having particular needs, distinct from those of adults. Inherently vulnerable, children depend on others for their well-being in a manner not matched by any other group which has been accorded protection (refugees, women, migrant workers, prisoners). The very survival of an infant is dependent on external nutritional provision.

(Smith and Van den Anker, 2005, p. 42)

The rights held by or on behalf of children (by, for example, their parents or the state) enshrined in the UNCRC are intended to include all perspectives on rights in the life of a child. Thus, civil, political, economic, social and cultural rights are all included, with a stipulation calling upon governments to ensure that the rights are available to all children within their jurisdiction 'without discrimination of any kind'.

There are fifty-four articles in the Convention, forty of which directly ascribe rights to children. Table 7.2 outlines some of the key provisions, and illustrates the Convention's breadth and importance.

The UK Children's Commissioners are now a focus of children's rights work (Northern Ireland Children's Commissioner for Children and Young People, 2005, webpage)

Table 7.2 Key provisions of the Convention on the Rights of the Child	
Article 1	Everyone under the age of 18 has all the rights in this Convention.
Article 2	The Convention applies to everyone whatever their race, religion, abilities, whatever they think or say, no matter what type of family they come from.
Article 3	All organisations concerned with children should work towards what is best for them.
Article 6	Children have the right to life. Governments should ensure that children survive and develop healthily.
Article 11	Governments should take steps to stop children being taken out of their own country illegally.
Article 12	Children have the right to say what they think should happen when adults are making decisions that affect them, and to have their opinions taken into account.
Article 24	Children have the right to good quality health care and to clean water, nutritious food and a clean environment so that they can stay healthy. Rich countries should help poorer countries achieve this.
Article 27	Children have a right to a standard of living that is good enough to meet their physical and mental needs. The government should help families who cannot afford to provide this.
Article 28	Children have a right to an education. Discipline in schools should respect children's human dignity. Primary education should be free. Wealthy countries should help poorer countries achieve this.
Article 34	The government should protect children from sexual abuse.
Article 39	If a child has been neglected or abused, s/he should receive special help to restore self-respect.
Article 41	If the laws of a particular country protect children better than the articles of the Convention, then those laws should stay.

(United Nations, 1989)

Thinking point 7.7   What use are these 'rights' if they are unenforceable?

The Children Act 1989 and the Children (Scotland) Act 1995 remain the primary legislation for the rights and entitlements of children in the UK. Although not directly modelled on the UNCRC, you will note as you read the following extract from the accompanying guidance and regulations to the Children Act 1989 (which, you will remember, carries the full force of law) that there are clear similarities between the two. The rights of the family are also enshrined, in context to and associated with the rights of the child. Thus, the family is recognised and given legal protections (see also Article 8 of the Human Rights Act 1998), but the emphasis of these protections is that the central underpinning ethos of the Act, so far as any legal proceedings or legal remedy is concerned, is the welfare of the child [s.1 (1) CA 1989].

> The Act's philosophy [is] that the best place for the child to be brought up is usually in the [child's] own family, and the [child] in need can be helped most effectively if the local authority, working in partnership with the parents, provides a range and level of services appropriate to the [child's] needs. To this end the parents and [the child] (... where [the child] is of sufficient understanding) need to be given the opportunity to make their wishes and feelings known and to participate in decision-making.
>
> (HMSO, 1991)

The UNCRC has also proved a powerful tool with which to argue for change. It can be used to support international comparisons of children's wellbeing in order to influence change (UNICEF, 2007). Individual countries can use it to carry out detailed analysis of the various aspects of childhood and look at children's lives in different contexts. In Wales, for example, a report, using the lens of children's rights, examined participation, corporal punishment, child protection, child poverty, health inequalities, education and citizenship, asylum seeker children, disabled children, Looked After children, sexual exploitation and juvenile justice, as well as measures to implement the UNCRC in Wales (Save the Children, 2006).

While the UNCRC is embodied within the roles of the four children's commissioners, the responsibilities of the commissioners vary across the four countries of the UK.

Rights can be a powerful tool with which to urge change. (Source: From the front cover of Croke, R. and Crowley, A. (2006) *Righting the wrongs: The reality of children's rights in Wales*, with kind permission from the artist Bradley Woods and the Save the Children Fund www.savethechildren.org.uk/wales)

Legislation to set up Children's Commissioners in the UK was enacted and produced four Commissioners by 2006.

Table 7.3   The powers and independence of the UK commissioners

Commissioner Independence	Wales	Northern Ireland	Scotland	England
Secretary of State can direct Commissioner to carry out an inquiry	NO	NO	NO	YES
Commissioner must consult Secretary of State before holding an independent inquiry	NO	NO	NO	YES
Commissioner's annual report goes directly to Parliament/Assembly	YES	YES	YES	NO
Legislation ties Commissioner to government policy	NO	NO	NO	YES

We have touched on some of the complexities of what we mean by 'rights' and looked at rights of the child that are enshrined in law. But how can we define 'rights'? There are very many different definitions of a right, including sub-classifications of rights such as absolute or conditional, legal, moral or ethical, and such definitions have been discussed and debated over a long period of time. We can, for the purposes of this chapter, work on the proposition that a 'right' in law is something to which there is an entitlement, which can be claimed, and to which specified others owe the claimant a duty either to provide the right or not to interfere with its use – sometimes referred to as a claim-right. As John Chipman Gray wrote in 1921, 'Right is correlative to duty; where there is no duty, there can be no right' (Chipman Gray, 1921).

Put this way, children's rights become more tangible and subject to enunciation by reference to the corresponding duty. A child's right to protection, for example, invokes duties to ensure that the child is protected from harm. These duties involve us all, as denial of the right is sanctionable in law (that is, in the criminal law). Added to this, the law requires the state (that is, the local authority social services department), by duty, to make inquiries if it has reason to believe a child might be at risk of significant harm, to decide whether they should take any action to safeguard or promote the child's welfare (Children Act 1989, s.47 (1)). Finally, the European Convention on Human Rights also has bearing, through its

associated court in Strasbourg, as it has been found that a failure of a local authority to protect children is a breach of Article 3, the prohibition on torture and inhuman or degrading treatment (Z v UK [2001] 2 FLR 603; E and Others v UK (4 December 2002)). Note, also, that even though these cases went to Strasbourg, the Human Rights Act 1998 means that similar cases can be dealt with in the UK courts.

Thinking point 7.8   Consider a 'right' you believe that a child and/or family hold, perhaps to a support or a service. Is it a claim-right, as defined above? Are there any rights you believe may be moral or ethical, but perhaps not legally enforceable?

The reality of life for children, families and, indeed, all of us, throughout the UK, is that 'rights' are not contained within one body of work; nor are they able to be approached from one angle. Rights are a collection of powers, duties, responsibilities, and interpretations of circumstances. They are governed by what people, agencies and authorities believe a right to mean. In short, there is no true universality to what the word means in theory or in practice.

Key points

1   The United Nations Convention on the Rights of the Child can be an effective tool to challenge and stimulate change in children's services and practices.

2   Despite the rights discourse being widely used in many settings, there are many different definitions of rights.

3   It can be useful to think of the rights of a child in relation to the corresponding duties of others.

Conclusion

The services available to children and families that promote children's wellbeing are contingent upon a range of factors. Provision in law or policy must exist with any form of funded or regulated service or support. Law, particularly if it is new legislation, is open to challenge through the courts; policy decisions of service providers are also usually open to judicial supervision, and, ultimately, the actions of those providing the support or service are subject to review or appeal. Albeit they are necessary in a democratic society where there exists a 'rule of law', all of these challenges have the potential to complicate the process of providing a support or a service to a child or a family. To this must be added the very real difficulty of reaching those who, by the very nature of the way in which we structure our society and provide services, are excluded – or feel excluded – from the process.

The quality of the skills and attitudes of those providing support and services cannot be overstated. Although a detailed discussion on this subject has been beyond the remit of this chapter, the professional training and interpersonal skills of those attempting to work in a productive, meaningful and empowering way with children and families is clearly absolutely crucial to effective service delivery. However, knowledge of the legal and policy framework in which services operate, its strengths and areas for development, is equally important as a pre-requisite of effective and equitable practice with children and families.

References

Brammer, A. (2007) *Social Work Law* (2nd edn), Harlow, Pearson Education.

Brayne, H. and Carr, H. (2005) *Law for Social Workers* (9th edn), Oxford, Oxford University Press.

Children's Rights Alliance for England (2005) *State of children's rights in England: annual review of UK government action on 2002 concluding observations of the UNCRC*, available online at <http://www.crae.org.uk/cms/dmdocuments/State%20of%20childrens%20rights%202005.pdf>, accessed 7 August 2007.

Chipman Gray, J. (1921) 'The nature and sources of law' in Garner, B.A. (ed.) (2004) *Black's Law Dictionary* (8th edn), Minnesota, Thomson West.

Department of Health (DH) (1998) *Someone else's children: inspections of planning and decision making for children looked after and the safety of children looked after*, available online at <http://www.dh.gov.uk/en/Publicationsandstatistics/Publications/PublicationsPolicyAndGuidance/DH_4007847>, accessed 27 August 2007.

Department of Health (DH) (2007) *National service frameworks (NSFs)*, available online at <http://www.dh.gov.uk/en/policyandguidance/healthandsocialcaretopics/dh_4070951>, accessed 7 August 2007.

Department of Health (DH) and Department for Education and Skills (DfES) (2004) *National service framework for children, young people and maternity services: executive summary*, available online at <http://www.dh.gov.uk/en/Publicationsandstatistics/Publications/PublicationsPolicyAndGuidance/DH_4089100>, accessed 27 August 2007.

Foley, P. and Rixon, A. (eds) (2008) *Changing Children's Services: Working and Learning Together*, Milton Keynes, The Open University/Bristol, The Policy Press.

General Social Care Council (GSCC) (2002) *Code of Practice for social care workers*, available online at <http://www.gscc.org.uk/NR/rdonlyres/8E693C62-9B17-48E1-A806-3F6F280354FD/0/Codes_of_Practice.doc>, accessed 7 August 2007.

Headliners (2004) *Young people wronged over rights*, available online at <http://www.headliners.org/storylibrary/stories/2004/youngpeoplewrongedoverrights.htm?id=5684917129472700323728>, accessed 7 August 2007.

HMSO (1991) *The Children Act 1989: Guidance and Regulations Volume: Family Support, Day Care and Educational Provision for Young Children*, London, HMSO.

Lachman, P. and Vickers, D. (2004) 'The national service framework for children', *British Medical Journal*, vol. 329, pp. 693–694.

Laming, Lord (2003) *The Victoria Climbié Inquiry: Report of an Inquiry by Lord Laming*, London, The Stationery Office.

Northern Ireland Commissioner for Children and Young People (NICCY) (2005) *Welcome to NICCY's website!*, available online at <http://www.niccy.org>, accessed 25 January 2008.

Open University (2001) K269, *Social Care, Social Work and the Law (England and Wales)*, Milton Keynes, The Open University.

Open University (2007a) K207, Block 1, *The Law and Social Work: An Introduction*, Milton Keynes, The Open University.

Open University (2007b) K207, Block 2, *Children and Families*, Milton Keynes, The Open University.

Save the Children (2006) *Righting the wrongs: the reality of children's rights in Wales*, available online at <http://www.childreninwales.org.uk/policy/news/5296.html>, accessed 22 August 2007.

Smith, R.K.M. and Van den Anker, C. (2005) *The Essentials of Human Rights*, London, Hodder Arnold.

Steiner, H.J. and Alston, P. (2000) *International Human Rights in Context: Law, Politics and Morals* (2nd edn), Oxford, Oxford University Press.

TheyWorkForYou (2004) *House of Commons debates Tuesday, 2 November 2004*, available online at <http://www.theyworkforyou.com/debates/?id=2004-11-02.238.2>, accessed 6 August 2007.

UNICEF (2007) *Child Poverty in Perspective: An Overview of Child Well-being in Rich Countries*, Innocenti Report Card 7, Florence, UNICEF Innocenti Research Centre.

United Nations (1989) *United Nations Convention on the Rights of the Child (UNCRC)*, Geneva, United Nations.

Warin, J. (2007) 'Joined up services for young children and their families: papering over the cracks or re-constructing the foundations', *Children & Society*, vol. 21, pp. 87–97.

Acknowledgements

Grateful acknowledgement is made to the following sources:

Text

Page 57: Department for Education and Skills (2001) *Promoting Children's Mental Health within Early Years and School Settings*, DfEE Publications. Crown copyright material is reproduced under Class Licence Number C01W0000065 with the permission of the Controller of HMSO and the Queen's Printer for Scotland; Page 204: Office of the Children's Commissioner (2006) *Journeys - Primary Age Children Talking About Bullying*; Page 205: Simple Street Sense (2005) Kidscape. Copyright © Kidscape; Page 238: Lynch, N. (2004) www.headliners.org/storylibrary/stories/2004/youngpeoplewrongedovoerrights.htm, Headliners.

Tables

Page 78: UNICEF (2007), *Child Poverty in Perspective: An Overview of Child Wellbeing in Rich Countries*, Innocenti Report Card 7, UNICEF Innocenti Research Centre, Florence. © The United Nations Children's Fund, 2007; Pages 134–136: Hadler-Olsen, S. and Springate, D. (2003) 'Children's Free Time Activities: An exploratory study of English and Norwegian children's out of school activities', Hall, N. and Springate, D. (eds) *ETEN 13: The Proceedings of the 13th Annual Conference of the European Teacher Education Network*, 2003, European Teacher Education Network, the University of Greenwich and the University of Groningen; Page 191: Department for Education and Skills (2006) *Statistics of Education: referrals, assessments and children and young people on child protection registers: year ending 31 March 2006*, London, The Stationery Office. Crown copyright material is reproduced under Class Licence Number C01W0000065 with the permission of the Controller of HMSO and the Queen's Printer for Scotland.

Illustrations

Page 12 (left and right): educationphotos.co.uk/walmsley; Page 15: www. JohnBirdsall.co.uk; Page 19 (left and middle): www.JohnBirdsall.co.uk; Page 19 (right): © Nick Hanna/Alamy; Page 25: © Stephen Simpson/Getty Images; Page 26: © David Gowans/Alamy; Page 28: www. JohnBirdsall.co.uk; Page 31: © Ian Shaw/Alamy; Page 33: www. JohnBirdsall.co.uk; Page 45: © Alex Segre/Alamy; Page 48: © f1 online/Alamy; Page 49: © Greg Gerla/Alamy; Page 50 (left): © PHOTOTAKE

Index